Ghosts of Samarra

U.S. Army Strykers at War in Iraq

Tobias Vogt

© 2023 Tobias Vogt von Heselholt

All rights reserved

1st Edition

No part of this book may be reproduced or transmitted in any form or by any means, electronic, or mechanical, including photocopying, recording, or by any information storage, and retrieval system without written permission from both the copyright owner and publisher of this book.

U.S. Department of the Army security review February 1, 2023.

Cover photo courtesy of Combat Camera.

Published by Heselholt Group, LLC

6585 Hwy 431 S, Suite E-234

Hampton Cove AL 35763

Dedicated to

Sergeant Jacob Herring

Corporal Demetrius Rice

Private First Class Jesse Martinez

and

the other soldiers of the battalion and brigade that were killed on subsequent deployments

Acknowledgments

I'd like to thank my wife Annelie. She endured long deployments and moved our home more times than I care to count while we were in the army. Thank you, my dear.

Thanks as well to Hillary Back and Daniel Wabinga. Hillary and Daniel were fabulous research assistants that've gone on to successful careers of their own.

I'd also like to thank my good friends and brothers in arms, Sean Sparks and Ricardo Rivera, for their help on the backend of this project. Their edits, notes, administrative diligence, and encouragement helped make the book a reality.

My sincerest appreciation also goes to the soldiers you'll read about in the following pages. Thank you all for your participation, service, and sacrifice.

Finally, thanks to the soldiers of 5-20th Infantry Battalion, and the 3rd Arrowhead Brigade Combat Team. They are the very best of what America represents.

Contents

I. The Road to War 1
II. 5-20 Infantry in Iraq 21
III. In Their Own Words 61
    Timothy Bennett 62
    Matthew Dabkowski 84
    Eric Evans 185
    Shawn Fleming 194
    Christopher Galka 210
    Matthew Goodine 234
    Sean Sparks 256
    Laurence "Sonny" Wabinga 290
Annexes 325
    Annex A: Photos 326
    Annex B: 5-20th Killed and Wounded* 359
    Annex C: Task Organization 363
Acronyms 364
Selected Bibliography 372

Preface

In the United States military, histories, lineages, and honors are kept by the unit's command sergeant major and recorded by the Institute of Heraldry. The 5th Battalion, 20th Infantry draws its lineage from the American Civil War period. Originally formed as Company E, 2nd Battalion, 11th Infantry Regiment in 1861, it was later designated Company E, 20th Infantry in 1866. Known as "Sykes' Regulars," the 5th battalion, named after its Civil War Regimental Commander "Tardy" George Sykes, served in numerous divisions, countries, and wars until September 16, 2001, when it was reassigned to the 3rd Brigade, 2nd Infantry Division. For their first deployment since Vietnam, the 5th Battalion, 20th Infantry was awarded the Meritorious Unit Commendation, the Global War on Terrorism campaign streamer, and two Iraq campaign streamers for the Transition of Iraq and Iraqi Governance.

Sean Sparks

I. The Road to War

Modern-day Iraq includes most of the area between the "two rivers," the Tigris and the Euphrates. The older word used for this area was Mesopotamia, meaning the land between the (two) waters. Mesopotamia was the birthplace of Abraham, who formed the lineages of the three great monotheistic religions. Famous places mentioned in the Bible and the Quran within its borders are The Garden of Eden, Ur, Nahor, Ninevah, Assyria, and Babylon.

Circa 570 CE, the Prophet Muhammed (peace and blessings be upon him) was born in Mecca. At the age of 40, Muhammed experienced an epiphany while meditating in a cave. The Archangel Gabriel revealed Allah's new prophesies to Muhammed, which became the Holy Quran and started the religion of Islam. In just over two decades, the Prophet Mohmmed successfully converted the nomadic and warlike Arabs that lived in small family and clan groups throughout the Arabian Desert.

Ethnic groups that call Iraq home today are Arab, Kurdish, and several smaller minorities including Assyrians. Each group remains devoutly religious, with most of the populace following the Prophet Muhammed's teachings as either a Shia or Sunni Muslim. Several other minor religions, to include Christianity, round out the country, but the two primary branches of Islam are Shia in the majority and Sunni in the minority. Though there are fierce tensions between the two branches of Islam today, both claim their lineages back to the Prophet Muhammed.

Indeed, upon Muhammed's death, the newly formed religion of Islam fell into discord over the line of succession. The branch that became Sunni chose to follow an elected successor. Initially, the Prophet Muhammed's close personal advisor and friend Abu Bakr, whom Muhammed had chosen before his unexpected death. Whereas the branch that became Shia, chose to follow the direct descendants of the Prophet Muhammed. Initially, his cousin and son-in-law Ali, and Imams (Religious Leaders) appointed by Muhammed or God himself. The two branches developed different practices over the years, but both continue to observe the Quran and the teachings of the Prophet Muhammed as the basis for their faith.

Foreign Rule

Mesopotamia spawned the civilizations of Babylon, Sumeria, Assyria, and others until the area was conquered by the Persians around 7 BCE. Mesopotamia remained an undeveloped Persian territory for the next 1,400 years, until the Arab invasion of the mid-7th Century. After the invasion, Baghdad became a major city of Arab culture and refinement. Important mathematic and geometric discoveries were made, and classic Greek and Roman scholars were translated into Arabic. These texts, which laid the groundwork for modern Western philosophy, were rediscovered by Western Europe during the Renaissance.

The Mongols destroyed Baghdad in the mid-13th Century, and Mesopotamia was once again a rural region controlled by local tribal sheikhs. In the 16th Century, the Ottoman Turks conquered most of Anatolia, before turning their attentions to the Byzantine Greeks and the Roman Empire in the east. The Ottomans divided Mesopotamia into three main regions: Mosul, Baghdad, and Basra. Kurds primarily occupied Mosul, while Arabs inhabited Baghdad and Basra.

Even under the Muslim Ottomans, Mesopotamia, which was on the periphery of the Ottoman Empire, was ruled by local governors and tribal sheiks. The Arab Shia of Baghdad and Basra disliked the foreign Sunni Ottomans' governance, and the Mosul Kurds maintained continued resistance in the face of foreign occupation. Iraq remained tribal. Although some scholars place emphasis on religion, family and tribe were more important than the branch of Islam each group followed during this period. Against this tribal backdrop, the contemporary view is that Iraq was never effectively brought under Ottoman control in nearly four centuries.

The Ottoman Empire was disassembled following World War I. Modern-day Turkey became a state, while the Allies took responsibility for the different regions of the Arabian Peninsula under mandates. France was given the mandate for Syria and Lebanon, and Britain received the mandate for Egypt, Palestine,

Iraq, and Jordan. In 1920, the state of Iraq was recognized as an official League of Nations mandate under British control. In the oil age, Britain quickly divided Iraqi oil equally between the Netherlands, France, the United States, themselves, and a small percentage to a private oil company. This oil arrangement provided no oil revenue for the Iraqi people, and remained in effect until 1958.

The British instituted a colonial model in their newly acquired Middle East territories, and in Iraq, established the Hashemite Monarchy under King Faysal. Social unrest and distaste for the British occupiers were widespread, but resistance was limited. The lack of resistance may be due to the absence of a unified Iraqi identity at this time. In the end, Britain withdrew from Iraq in 1932, thrusting the weight of self-governance on a struggling monarchy that just lost its benefactor.

Self-Rule

Politics in Iraq revolved around military coups, Arab and Kurdish coalitions, and general unrest for the next few decades. But even with enormous political instability, the successive governments somehow managed to place an emphasis on basic infrastructure improvement throughout the country. On July 14, 1958, Iraqi junior military leaders seized Baghdad, executed most of the royal family, and declared the country a republic within a greater Arab Nation. But the republic, was a republic in name only. Violent regime change was the status quo during this period, as politicians and military leaders continued to transfer power based on force.

Saddam Hussein grew up a poor farm boy in the small village of Auja, Iraq. He drew inspiration from his politically motivated uncle, Khayrallah Tulfa, an officer in the Iraqi Army and staunch believer in the concept of a united Arab community. At age 19 Saddam joined the Ba'ath Party, and three years later in 1959, he participated in an unsuccessful assassination attempt against the Iraqi prime minister. Young Saddam was wounded in the leg and fled first to Syria and then Egypt for several years. By 1968, the Ba'ath Party was able to overthrow the Iraqi government, bringing General Ahmed Hassan Bakr to power at the head of the party and the country. Saddam Hussein returned, and for his efforts in the revolt, he was rewarded with the position of vice-president. A prominent position that allowed him to build a network of secret police to suppress opposition for years to come.

By 1979, Saddam was done being second in command. He used his firm grip on the country to remove Bakr from power. As is the case in many totalitarian regimes, Saddam quickly consolidated power and purged any Ba'ath leadership not loyal to him. His secret police brutally suppressed dissent from the Iraqi people, as Saddam sought to bring to fruition his uncle's elusive vision of a unified Arab community.

Saddam's broader vision couldn't be realized as the Middle East was extremely volatile during this period. Views on the state of

Israel, rising fundamentalism, and deep-seated hatreds, prevented the development of a unified Arab community. The year prior, at the request of the Shah of Iran, Saddam evicted the Ayatollah Khomeini from An Najaf, and assassinated his Iraqi Shia counterpart, Baqir al-Sadr. Both Iran and Iraq were extremely worried about the fundamentalist preaching of the Ayatollah, a concern that proved to be correct shortly thereafter.

Iran-Iraq War

On September 22, 1980, Iraq invaded Iran. This decision cost a tremendous amount of pain and suffering for both countries over the next eight years. It also set in motion the conditions for Saddam Hussein's ultimate removal from power. The Middle East was in a state of chaos as the Soviets invaded Afghanistan, Iran took and held the American Embassy in Tehran with hostages for 444 days following the overthrow of the Shah, and intermittent fighting raged in Lebanon between the Israelis, Syrians, and Palestinians.

The Iran-Iraq flashpoint was claimed to be a dispute over control of the Shatt-al-Arab waterway and its access to the Persian Gulf. But experts suspected that Saddam feared the non-secular fundamentalist threat in the form of Kurdish support, and possible militant Shiite uprisings mirroring the overthrow of the Shah in Iran. Given these possible threats to his power, Saddam decided the sooner the attack, the better, since the Ayatollah was still consolidating power in Iran. Saddam also calculated that a war with a long-standing enemy like Iran, would solidify his authority within Iraq.

The Iraqi Army initially penetrated deep into Iran, but by 1982, the Iranians gained the offensive and drove the Iraqi Army back to the border. The Iraqi Army shifted to the defensive, and repelled deadly Iranian human wave attacks. These tactics contributed to extremely high casualty rates that were felt for generations.

Iraq severed ties with the United States in 1967, after the Arab-Israeli War where the U.S. supported Israel. But following the Iran Hostage Crisis and the possibility of a victorious fundamentalist Iran over Iraq, Iraq suddenly appeared to be a possible U.S. ally in the region. Officially, the United States maintained a position of neutrality. But by 1982, Iraq was removed from the State Department list of known states sponsoring terrorism, and in 1984, Donald Rumsfeld traveled to Iraq as President Reagan's special envoy.

U.S. involvement in the Iran-Iraq War was complex. While relations improved with Iraq, the United States quietly provided both Iran and Iraq arms just as the other showed signs of success. By 1987, the world was tired of the costly conflict. Fueled by worries of instability in the region, should either make a significant gain, the final straw of international patience broke when the Iraqis engaged the *USS Stark* in the Persian Gulf. Iraq immediately apologized, and there were no further attacks on American ships, but the United Nations Security Council drafted a resolution several weeks later that called for an end to the conflict.

The two Arab nations fought to a costly stalemate that finally ended in 1988. Human losses were staggering, with an estimated 400,000 Iraqis, and as many as 1,000,000 Iranians dead or wounded. Many of the social programs Saddam had enacted, or wanted to initiate, were terminated in an effort to continue fighting a war estimated at an Iraqi cost of $300 billion.

In 1988, Iraq's ability to export oil was severely degraded because of crumbling infrastructure, and the country was drowning in debt. Iraq owed billions to numerous countries that included many of their Muslim neighbors. Saddam owed more than $13 billion to tiny Kuwait alone. With decreased export capacity and falling oil prices, he had little hope of repaying any of these debts.

The Iran-Iraq War ended August 20, 1988, and the Iraqi invasion of Kuwait commenced on August 2, 1990. In just under two years, Saddam concluded that he had no other option available to avoid loan repayment default. Like impoverished Germany following World War I, Iraq was swimming in a sea of debt. But unlike post-World War I Germany, Saddam remained in power and was already in command of a highly trained million-man military.

First Gulf War

Saddam decided his best, and maybe seen as his only, course of action was to resuscitate age-old territorial arguments that much of Kuwait was rightfully part of Iraq. The British were vague when they initially defined the borders of Saudi Arabia, Iraq, and Kuwait in 1922, but further definition and recognition was provided later. Kuwait was a thorn in the Iraqi side and several regimes had planned invasions in the past to assert Iraqi claims. But it wasn't until 1990, that any Iraqi leader acted on these age-old border arguments.

It may seem irrational, but Saddam saw the invasion of Kuwait as a way to employ his army and relieve some of the debt pressure from his previous conflict. He didn't simply decide to invade, rather he utilized a deliberate planning process. This process identified three main deterrents to the success of a potential invasion: 1) Iran wouldn't act, 2) the Kurds, who had revolted during the Iran-Iraq War, would remain quiet, and 3) the United States wouldn't get involved.

He took care of the first two issues by agreeing to a mid-channel boundary for the Shatt-al-Arab waterway. Yes, the very reason used for going to war with Iran in 1980, was the carrot that kept the Iranians from arming and inciting the Kurds. Saddam engaged the United States in private discussions with President Bush's representative in Iraq to resolve whether the U.S. would get involved if an invasion of Kuwait took place. Saddam was repeatedly reassured that America had no opinion of Arab-Arab conflicts and that Kuwait was not associated with the United States. With all three conditions addressed, the invasion began in August of 1990, when a sizeable portion of the Iraqi Army advanced into Kuwait City.

Indifference to Saddam's intentions was exactly the opposite of the world's response to the invasion. Saddam Hussein had miscalculated again. President George H.W. Bush immediately established an opposition coalition, with the goal of removing Iraqi forces from Kuwait. The United Nations likewise condemned this action and called for the immediate withdraw of Iraq from Kuwait. By late August, Saddam realized the world was against him. He attempted to negotiate a withdrawal from Kuwait in exchange for the lifting of U.N. sanctions, Gulf access, and control of the Rumalyah oil fields.

The coalition responded by deploying 230,000 troops to Saudi Arabia as part of Operation Desert Shield. Instead of attacking immediately, both sides continued to build forces in theater until the next phase of the war. After the United Nations passed a series of resolutions against Iraq, President Bush defined his political objectives as: 1) Unconditional Iraqi withdrawal, 2) restoration of Kuwait's government, 3) protection of Americans abroad, and 4) promotion of security and stability in the Persian Gulf.

The United States wasn't prepared to push the coalition past the Kuwaiti borders or take responsibility for the reconstruction of Iraq. While there was a coalition behind the removal of Iraq from

Kuwait, the Arab-West coalition wouldn't support a follow-on invasion of Iraq. Just as hawks in the U.S. Senate called for the invasion of the Soviet Union following World War II, the Senatorial hawks of this period advocated for the continued push into Baghdad and the removal of Saddam Hussein from power.

Saddam allowed the coalition to deploy ample forces to the region, and by January 1991, they were prepared to remove Iraq from Kuwait. Following the expiration of the United Nations Security Council deadline, coalition aircraft began to bombard Iraqi forces on January 17, 1991. While waiting for the air war to soften Iraqi Army defenses, the two unknowns for the coalition forces were: 1) Would Saddam attack Israel and weaken the coalition, and 2) would he employ nuclear, biological, or chemical weapons?

Iraq launched conventional Scud missiles at Israel and Saudi Arabia, but casualties were minimal, and the Israelis remained on the sidelines throughout the war. Although Iraq was working towards nuclear weapons, intelligence suggested Iraq was several years away from nuclear capabilities in 1991. Saddam had previously used chemical weapons against Iran and the Kurds during the Iran-Iraq War, but the coalition used diplomatic channels to dissuade their use in 1991.

The air war continued for a month. Coalition aircraft pounded Iraqi targets, and Saddam appealed to the world for mercy through the media. While the air war raged, coalition ground forces repositioned to attack the Iraqis from the rear of their fortified positions.

The 100-hour ground war commenced on February 24, 1991. The swiftness of the attack shocked the world as ground forces met weeklong march objectives in a matter of hours. The isolated Iraqi Army was caught off guard by superior maneuver and technology. The air war left most Iraqi units leaderless and badly in need of basic supplies, such as food and water. Coupled with the overwhelming technical superiority of the coalition weapons systems, the battle-hardened troops of the Iraqi Army were helpless as the United States engaged targets at ranges beyond the human eye, and further than any weapon system in the Iraqi arsenal.

When there was resistance, the Iraqis, to their dismay, watched as their main tank rounds failed to penetrate the armor of the American tanks. The main issue quickly became prisoner of war collection and care, rather than combat. After months of air bombardment and the lightning-fast attack of the ground war, highly demoralized Iraqi troops surrendered in mass. Some units, such as Saddam's elite Republican Guard stood and fought, but the coalition forces were too much for them.

As quickly as Operation Desert Shield became Operation Desert Storm, Desert Storm transitioned to Operation Provide Comfort. The legitimate government returned to power in Kuwait, and Iraqi forces withdrew. In Iraq, both the Kurds and the Shiites rose in opposition to Saddam, but the Iraqi Army crushed these rebellions. Saddam solidified his power while the coalition was preoccupied restoring Kuwait, and processing Iraqi prisoners and refugees. After the coalition identified what was happening in Iraq, they established the northern no-fly zone to protect the Kurds in April 1991, and then a southern no-fly zone to protect the Shiites in August 1992.

Historians from each camp involved in the Persian Gulf War went to work describing the remarkable victory of their patron. In most of the world, the coalition forces were the victors of grand proportions. But in Iraq, the history lessons of the First Gulf War were painted as a picture of a victorious Iraqi Army led by their remarkable president Saddam Hussein.

For the next decade, American planes monitored no fly zones, while United Nations sanctions starved Iraq, and the International Atomic Energy Agency looked for weapons of mass destruction. The oil-for-food program provided some respite for Iraq. But the most impoverished portions of the country lived in abject poverty, as Iraqis watched their country deteriorate even further from the penalties of yet another costly war.

Second Gulf War

On September 11, 2001, elements of the terrorist organization al Qaeda attacked the World Trade Center, the Pentagon, and failed in a third attack on the White House that crashed in the Pennsylvania countryside after passengers confronted the terrorists. In response to these terrible attacks, President George W. Bush declared a Global War on Terror. America responded by invading Afghanistan a few weeks later.

As Operation Enduring Freedom forces swept the mountains of Afghanistan for al Qaeda leader Osama Bin Laden, a familiar despot sounded off on the periphery. Over the previous decade the world softened its stance on Iraq. Most members of the United Nations no longer saw the need for sanctions, and several nations resumed trade with Iraq, in violation of standing United Nations resolutions. The United States, however, remained steadfast in its position on Iraq. Considering the recent terrorist attacks, America was not prepared to stand by idly as another threat identified itself.

There were discussions of the Iraqi problem from the very beginning of the second Bush administration. The United States and United Kingdom attacked military targets near Baghdad in February 2001, and the United States attacked again in August of 2001, after the downing of an American aircraft. Immediately following the September 11, 2001, attacks, the Bush administration directed an examination of all possible links. Findings included the Taliban in Afghanistan and Saddam Hussein in Iraq.

While the Taliban safe haven link in Afghanistan was clear and had immediate global support, the involvement of Iraq in the 9/11 attacks couldn't be directly established. But this was a new era where traditional domestic and foreign policy barriers were temporarily suspended. An era where an emerging national security strategy argued the United States wouldn't wait to be attacked. Instead, the United States would now preemptively pursue terrorists around the world.

The situation deteriorated for the next two years as President Bush declared Iran, Iraq, and North Korea the Axis of Evil. Saddam Hussein refused to abide by United Nations resolutions and blocked International Atomic Energy Agency inspectors. He abused the oil-for-food program, instead buying weapons and other banned items. Largely based on faulty human intelligence sources, the United States was led to believe there was political opposition to Saddam by Ahmed Chalabi, and that new weapons of mass destruction were being produced by Ihsan Saeed al-Haiberi. Unfortunately, both sources were unreliable Iraqi expatriates with personal agendas.

Additional faulty intelligence attempted to link Mohamed Atta of al Qaeda to a meeting with an Iraqi diplomat, and the attempted Iraqi purchase of uranium and centrifuge material from Africa, but both were later disproven. The latter led to the political scandal of an outed Central Intelligence Agency officer, and its bitter legal aftermath. As the United States made their case to the world, Saddam continued to posture in opposition. The Bush Administration pressed the United Nations for a resolution on Iraq, but French and Russian diplomats, both countries having large trading interests in Iraq, vowed to veto any potential Security Council resolutions.

Instead, the United States established a "coalition of the willing," and prepared for war based on three main arguments: 1) Iraq had weapons of mass destruction, 2) Iraq provided safe haven for terrorists including al Qaeda, and 3) Iraq was in violation of United Nation sanctions. When weapons of mass destruction are broadly defined as chemical, biological, radiological, and nuclear, then yes, Iraq did have old chemical and biological weapons dating from the Iran-Iraq War, but they weren't producing new weapons at the time of the invasion. Some chatter about acquiring nuclear technology was mentioned, but Iraq failed to initiate a successful nuclear weapons program during the 1980s and was no further along at the beginning of the new millennium.

On the second point, a link between al Qaeda and Saddam was never established. Other than their disdain for the United States, neither leader shared the same goals. One was a terrorist chieftain determined to expel the infidels from the Middle East and the other a totalitarian despot, focused on remaining in power at any cost.

There's little debate that the third point was untrue. Iraq was in violation of the United Nations sanctions, but the United States was the main backer of continued sanctions, while the remainder of the world looked to or had resumed trade with Iraq. As such, the United Nation Security Council refused to pass an Iraq invasion resolution.

One U.S. administration official to counsel caution was Secretary Colin Powell. As a senior general during the First Gulf

War, Secretary Powell revised the post-Vietnam Weinberger Doctrine to read:

- Is a vital national security interest threatened?
- Do we have a clear attainable objective?
- Have the risks and costs been fully and frankly analyzed?
- Have all other non-violent policy means been fully exhausted?
- Is there a plausible exit strategy to avoid endless entanglement?
- Have the consequences of our action been fully considered?
- Is the action supported by the American people?
- Do we have genuine broad international support?

Most won't remember Secretary Powell's speech to the United Nations General Assembly with Director of Central Intelligence, George Tenet, sitting just behind him, but he gave a succinct warning about Iraq using a Pottery Barn analogy, "You break it, you buy it."

Nevertheless, on March 19, 2003, a coalition of the willing initiated air strikes against high-value Iraqi targets. Shortly thereafter, ground forces maneuvered from the south as the United States announced a strategy of "shock and awe," the massive bombing of Iraqi command and control elements, and other military targets. Just as they did in the First Gulf War, the U.S. Army blitzed through Iraqi opposition, even as the Iraqi Minister of Information reassured the world that coalition forces weren't in the country.

In the aftermath, there was massive looting and breakdown of social order that U.S. Secretary of Defense Donald Rumsfeld described as untidy freedom. By May 1, 2003, President Bush declared, "Mission Accomplished" from the *USS Abraham Lincoln*. But unlike previous conflicts, there wasn't an armistice or unconditional surrender signed by the Iraqi government. Saddam went into hiding as coalition forces dispersed throughout the country in preparation for occupation duties.

In U.S. military operations such as Just Cause or Desert Storm, there was a legitimate government waiting to step into the vacuum in Panama and Kuwait. But in Iraq, there wasn't a legitimate government in exile, or even viable political opposition in the country prepared to take control. Contrary to the faulty intelligence provided by Ahmed Chalabi, President of the Iraqi National Congress, there were no indigenous elements of political opposition prepared to assume power.

In fact, anyone in a position of authority in Iraq prior to the invasion was affiliated with the Ba'ath party. Instead, a Coalition Provisional Authority was established under U.S. Ambassador L. Paul Bremer with the intent of handing power to an interim Iraqi government within a year. Like the initial denazification program following World War II, the Coalition Provisional Authority made a critical mistake of removing all former Ba'ath party members from their positions. With a single policy decision to exclude previous Ba'ath members, the majority of prominent Iraqi citizens --

professors, engineers, bankers, business owners, bureaucrats, etc. -- were prohibited from participation in the reconstruction of a new Iraq. This decision severely hindered efforts to initially secure, stabilize, and rebuild the country, and had lasting effects that hampered Iraq long after the withdrawal of major combat forces.

As the dust settled, America had achieved regime change in Iraq, but they also inherited decades of war debt, and centuries of violent political, religious, and tribal infighting. The country was relatively quiet for the first few months, while Iraqis attempted to make the best of their new situation. Occupation forces provided large sums of captured and donated funds for economic stimulation and reconstruction, and worked diligently to improve the quality of life in Iraq.

But by July 2003, the U.S. Department of Defense realized Iraqi reconstruction wasn't as easy as the war advocates thought, and announced one-year rotations. Following initial periods of calm, former regime loyalists regrouped, and disaffected Iraqi citizens joined forces to fight what many now saw as Western occupation. At this point, combat forces were still searching for Saddam as daily attacks steadily increased.

It's against this backdrop that the 3rd Brigade, 2nd Infantry Division made their final preparations for deployment from Fort Lewis, Washington. Although wheeled personnel carriers have been used for many years in other armies, U.S. proponents of tracked warfare vehemently opposed this concept well into the early 2000s.

After numerous debates, and prophesies of failure, the 3rd Brigade, 2nd Infantry Division was named the interim combat force of a transforming post-Cold War U.S. Army. The Interim Brigade Combat Team (IBCT), later known as the Stryker Brigade Combat Team (SBCT), and finally the Arrowhead Brigade Combat Team (ABCT), was designed and equipped with the eight-wheeled armor personnel carrier that became known as the Stryker.

The vehicle symbolized a vision of a lighter, more mobile force, capable of deploying significant combat power anywhere in the world in 96-hours. The brigade underwent training exercise after training exercise, completing each with the highest marks for deployment and tactical proficiency. Despite these high marks, naysayers continued to question the unit's readiness as they prepared for combat operations. But, with the latest equipment, sufficient resources, highly trained soldiers, and seasoned leaders, the Stryker Brigade proved them wrong in its first call to arms.

II. 5-20 Infantry in Iraq

The Arrowhead Brigade Combat Team (ABCT) closed on Udairi Training Area, Kuwait, in mid-November 2003. The brigade received the equipment they shipped from America while the soldiers acclimated. Excited to finally be deployed to a real-world conflict, the soldiers of the Stryker Brigade conducted updated training based on new threats identified in Iraq, executed final rehearsals, and prepared their equipment.

Retrofitting the Stryker Fighting Vehicles with slat armor to defend against rocket propelled grenades (RPG) was one of the important tasks the brigade needed to complete before advancing into Iraq. The new Strykers were good, but engineers identified the need for an additional bolt on armor system for the vehicle. This "slat armor" was designed to detonate rocket propelled grenade warheads before they could impact the organic armor plating. In the year to come, the afterthought armor proved invaluable, as it saved numerous lives and protected vehicles from serious damage.

The Udairi Training Area was little more than a large expanse of desert. It was poorly maintained and ill-prepared to receive the entire brigade combat team. In fact, the camp cadre were in the process of eliminating Operation Iraqi Freedom I expansion camps and were unaware of the size of the Stryker Brigade -- in excess of 6,000 soldiers. Facilities included large host nation tents with cots and intermittent heating and cooling units. Temperatures varied, and wind and sandstorms made life interesting in Kuwait.

A large dining facility with foreign workers provided meals for the entire camp. There were a few morale phones and computers, a small gym, morale welfare and recreation center, and small post exchange. There were several little restaurants, an internet cafe, a barber, and sewing shop. That was the extent of Camp Udairi's Spartan amenities.

The ranges and live fire shoot house were non-existent or in disrepair. As a result, the advanced torch party of the brigade contracted to build small arms ranges and improved the live fire shoot house. The indirect fire and convoy live fire ranges were utilized in their existing state, facilitated by civilian trainers.

Of note was the Mini-Military Operations in Urban Terrain (MOUT) site, actually a state-of-the-art training facility constructed in SEA-LAND containers. This facility came complete with real-time video after-action review capabilities, remote targetry, and multiple scenarios. It was maintained and run by a cadre of professional civilian contractors.

After a few weeks, the brigade moved into Iraq by ground assault convoy to a forward operating base (FOB) just outside of Samarra. The troops were filled with nervous anticipation as commanders delivered their final instructions prior to movement. The 5th Battalion travelled from Kuwait to Samarra over a three-day period. This was the first glimpse of Iraq for many of the soldiers in the battalion, and was marked by long movements, little sleep, and lots of mud along the way. In early December 2003, Saddam was still at large and the coalition focus was nation-building in all but a few contested areas like Samarra and Falluja. There were extremely long hours, but little contact along the route, as the battalion absorbed the sights, sounds, and smells of Iraq.

Samarra

The brigade was initially attached to the 4th Infantry Division for operations in the historic city of Samarra. Samarra is a city of approximately 200,000 people, with a long history of religious prominence, and anti-authority behavior. Centuries ago, the city was considered the center of the Muslim world, and is home to the remains of the famous Great Friday Mosque. There are also several Imam tombs, and the remains of the Abbasid Caliphate residence along the Tigris River. Even during the height of Ba'ath party rule, Samarra was considered a trouble spot for the government. Now, the Americans inherited the city's issues.

Upon arrival to FOB Pacesetter, a former Iraqi air base just a few miles from Samarra, the 5-20 Infantry "Sykes' Regulars" settled into locally sourced Bedouin tents and began planning and preparing for their baptism by fire. The battalion operated out of a tactical assembly area (TAA) just outside of the city, and was responsible for operations in the northeast portion of Samarra. The soldiers were ready as they waited for the order to execute. But just before movement, Ambassador Bremer announced the capture of Saddam. All operations were suspended for 48-hours, so the battalion settled back into their tents to wait a few more hours. With time for one last rehearsal, the battalion continued to refine the attack plan, only to be interrupted by actionable intelligence, and the order to immediately deploy one company.

24-hours prior to the scheduled hit time, soldiers from B Company found themselves engaging the enemy. The remainder of the battalion deployed to TAA Regular (formerly TAA Warhorse) and began offensive operations in Samarra on the following day. Over the next several weeks, the soldiers of the 5th Battalion, 20th Infantry experienced the shock of combat, and the wonders of an army Christmas in a tactical assembly area. Young men that had wondered about how they'd perform in combat had their answer, superbly.

The numerous veterans of previous conflicts in the ranks understood that this was only the beginning of a long year in the Middle East. In Samarra, the Stryker vehicle was proven and the Arrowhead Brigade earned the name, "Ghosts," from a local Washington newspaper. The nickname referred to the stealth approaches and infiltrations facilitated by the surprisingly silent vehicle.

The large Strykers ably maneuvered through the streets of the city and repelled small arms and rocket propelled grenade fire. The vehicles also provided advanced optics for day and night operations. More importantly, the Stryker provided unparalleled-armored protection and support for the infantrymen that it carried. This allowed gunners to use the Remote Weapon System (RWS) to engage mounted .50 caliber machine guns and 40-millimeter grenade launchers in support of dismounted maneuver elements. This considerable mobile firepower was unmatched in Iraq.

Northern Iraq

In mid-January 2004, the battalion staged and prepared to execute another ground assault convoy further into Iraq. The destination was another forward operating base called Q-West, just 45 minutes south of the northern city of Mosul. The town of Qayyarah was the location of another former Iraqi air base that hosted the 1st Brigade, 101st Infantry Division (Air Assault) and 101st Aviation Brigade. Several other civilian agencies and Department of Defense contractors were also there. The population on Q-West surged from 6,000, to over 8,000 people when the Strykers and the Air Cavalry arrived.

The Stryker concept of independent brigades centered around lone operations or operations as a plug and play attachment to other organizations. This concept was new to the army at the time. The army structure previously put a major general in command of a division of three or more brigades. Without a general officer to command and control the brigade, there were questions as to how the Stryker brigade would be tactically employed.

In Samarra, the brigade was attached to the 4th Infantry Division, and in northern Iraq the brigade was initially attached to the 101st Infantry Division (Air Assault). But these units were scheduled to rotate home. Where could the army find a spare general officer to put in command of an oversized brigade? The solution was to deploy part of the I Corps staff stationed at Fort Lewis, Washington, to northern Iraq, and form Task Force Olympia commanded by the deputy corps commander Brigadier General Carter Ham. Several other coalition forces were task organized under the nascent Task Force Olympia, but the Arrowhead Brigade constituted the majority of task force combat power.

The big question initially confronting the brigade was, "how does a 6,000-soldier brigade transition with a 15,000-soldier division and still remain effective"? The 101st is an air assault division containing nine aviation battalions and three infantry brigades. Helicopter assaults and missions are fine for rapid mobility from point A to B, but soldiers are reduced to light infantry once they reach point B.

The 101st was supplied with additional wheeled vehicles in Iraq to increase their mobility, but these assets were limited. Amazingly, the Stryker concept and its unrivaled mobility allowed the brigade to cover even more area than the 101st had previously occupied. Yes, there was less human interaction with local leaders, but the sustained, rapid, armored personnel carrier mobility of the Stryker made this transition possible in early 2004.

The transition of authority (TOA) between 1st Brigade, 101st Airborne Division (Air Assault) and 5-20 Infantry went well. The 101st was tired after a year of combat, and ready to go home. On the other hand, Sykes' Regulars were ready to have a home of their own and conduct operations without the interference of another unit. There was some animosity as the 101st Airborne played the role of grizzled combat veteran, overlooking the reality that the Regulars had already been in theater for three months. Worse, because the army is not manned at 100%, the personnel policy at that time was to move soldiers from returning units, to units that were about to deploy. That meant some of the Regulars had already been deployed to Operations Enduring and/or Iraqi Freedom, and were now returning with the "new" battalion. It was difficult for many of these soldiers to be lectured by know-it-all veterans on their way home.

The base saw a massive outflux of population when the 101st convoyed for home in late January and early February 2004. Where there'd been disagreements over space, now there were empty buildings. The battalion settled in and reduced its footprint to a smaller area to improve security. Areas once occupied by 600-soldier battalions were now occupied by 170-soldier companies. When the aviation brigade was taken into consideration, you now had company commanders responsible for areas once covered by as many as two battalion commanders. This left large areas sparsely patrolled by the Arrowhead Brigade.

Q-West itself was a small city. It required water from the Tigris River to be pumped and purified, power generated, waste managed, food shipped and prepared, and other personal services provided on a large scale. Many things that are taken for granted in the Western world, took hundreds of contractors and servicemembers to provide.

The majority of contractor support was provided by known companies like Kellogg Brown and Root (KBR) or L3 Communications, with a heavy sub-contracted labor element of third-country nationals from outside the United States or Iraq. Local Iraqis also provided shops, restaurants, internet and phone cafes, and base services such as fire protection, augmented security, and so on. Many of the former Iraqi engineers and commanders assisted the U.S. Army from the beginning. Whether it was pipeline security, formation of the new Iraqi Civil Defense Corps (ICDC), base functions, or translation, there were dedicated Iraqis ready to lend a hand. Dedicated professionals, such as Hakeem Lukeman and Bashar Shakar, were invaluable to the civil-military effort in the region. Using these two examples, you can see a positive aspect of Iraqi society that was willing to accept great personal risk to get their country up and running again.

Hakeem Lukeman was the base manager for Q-West during the transition of authority with the 101st. He was the chief engineer of the base prior to the invasion and was slated to be promoted to brigadier general in the Iraqi Air Force in the summer of 2003. But, because of the invasion, his promotion never happened. During the initial invasion he cut power to the base and waited for the coalition forces. Having been educated in England, he spoke excellent English, and was instrumental in the reception of the 101st and the other units that followed. Unfortunately, he lived in a constant state of fear. He was threatened and attacked to the point that he had to move his family out of country before returning to support American efforts. In such an explosive environment, he lived with the reality of death on a daily basis, and the unenviable task of constantly proving his loyalty to rotating American forces.

Likewise, a younger and deeply devoted Kurdish translator was Bashar Shakar. Bashar received his law degree from the University of Mosul prior to the war and spoke Arabic, Kurdish, and English. Originally from the small town of Ugba, just outside the base gate, he worked much more than anyone would expect of a poorly paid translator. Again, based on death threats, Bashar eventually moved on base and provided 24-hour support. With his verbal and professional skills, he was able to operate well above the level of translator. When the battalion received orders to move, Bashar threw a few things together and accompanied Task Force Arrow to the south. Bashar had never been further away from home than Mosul and this was a huge sacrifice that we're sure his mother never forgave. Thanks to the brave and professional support of these two men, and many others like them, the battalion and other coalition units were able to operate inside Iraq.

The base was renamed FOB Regulars, but is more commonly referred to as Q-West. While at Qayyarah, the battalion was heavily involved with civil-military operations. Army and Iraqi leaders met regularly, as U.S. Army officers became political experts in the region. Companies conducted security patrols and operations in search of Anti-Coalition and then Anti-Iraqi Forces, and other high-value targets, while simultaneously supporting civil affairs and other nation-building efforts.

Because the Coalition Provisional Authority was the recognized government in Iraq at this time, company commanders held a dual role as the political leaders of designated sectors, and the battalion commander governed a space equivalent to the state of Rhode Island. In addition to military and political tasks, the headquarters company commander held the additional role of unelected base mayor, responsible for the administration of the small city known as Q-West. To say the battalion was busy is an understatement.

Another complication was the currency of Iraq, as the country transitioned from the Iraqi dinar with Saddam's image, to a new dinar that the people referred to as the Bremmer dinar. To avoid confusion, armed contractors shipped the old Iraqi dinars out of Q-West to be destroyed. The area was also home to a large munitions stockpile, with tens of thousands of pounds of explosives and other ordnance destroyed daily by another group of contractors.

The battalion conducted security patrols and other military operations, but the number of additional tasks was staggering. U.S. Army personnel paid the Iraqi Civil Defense Corps, supervised reconstruction and maintenance, trained, equipped, and fortified Iraqi military and police forces, established medical support, and responded to the ever fluid political and security situations of the region. It was still relatively peaceful during the winter of 2003-2004, but there were enough tasks to require 18-hour workdays for much of the battalion.

The battalion's area of responsibility extended north to the outskirts of Mosul. In addition to the base, the battalion manned a communications re-transmission site, and a separate company compound known as Objective (OBJ) Aggie, near the town of Hammam al Alil. C Company was detached from 5-20 Infantry and attached to the 1-14 Cavalry in Tal Afar. A Company and B Company rotated in and out of OBJ Aggie approximately every month.

OBJ Aggie was an old agricultural college, but was completely run down and provided no amenities for the line companies. Hammam al Alil and the adjacent town of Qabr Abd were easily the worst areas for the battalion at this stage in the deployment. There was also a platoon leader course established there known as the Northern Iraqi Regional Training Center, where

Iraqi officers studied basic leadership and infantry tactics in preparation for service in the civil defense force and later the Iraqi National Guard (ING).

Task Force Arrow

As winter turned into spring, life was busy, but stable. That was until mid-morning on April 7, 2004, when the brigade issued a hasty order for the formation of a battalion task force to reinforce coalition forces in and around An Najaf, Iraq. Moqtada al-Sadr and his Mahdi Militia had fortified the holy city. This was a delicate political situation, as pilgrims dressed in black and green made their annual pilgrimage to An Najaf for entrance into paradise. An Najaf is a city of nearly 600,000, and recognized as the Shia birthplace under Ali, the 4th Caliph of Islam, and the 1st Imam of Shia Islam. There's a famous shrine to Ali located in the city, and it's said that 70,000 Muslims will gain access to paradise following their visit to An Najaf.

5th Battalion, 20th Infantry, under the command of Lieutenant Colonel Karl Reed, was tasked with providing one infantry company and the headquarters for the task force. The task force was eventually named Arrow to symbolize the blazing speed with which they were shot across Iraq. The other two infantry battalions in the Arrowhead Brigade, 1st Battalion, 23rd Infantry, and 2nd Battalion, 3rd Infantry, were each tasked with providing one infantry company.

By early afternoon on April 8th, 2004, all elements of the newly assembled Task Force Arrow closed on Q-West. The task force commander issued his guidance, operations order, and conducted rehearsals in preparation for the early morning movement scheduled for the following day. Vehicles were staged in the order of movement, and final inspections completed as task force soldiers stayed glued to the news for uprising updates.

The entire country of Iraq erupted in violence during April 2004. The usually calm northern region even exploded with violence in Mosul. This prompted the brigade commander, Colonel Michael Rounds, to request an extension for Task Force Arrow, and a potential change to the original Combined Joint Task Force-7 directive. If deployed as directed, one third of Task Force Olympia's combat power would be sent to the other end of the country.

A one-day extension was granted, but on the morning of April 10, 2004, the task force deployed as ordered for An Najaf and a potential rendezvous with Al Sadr's Mahdi militia. The first day's movement came to an end at Forward Operating Base Warhorse, the Iraqi home of the 1st Brigade Combat Team of the 1st Infantry Division. The 1st Infantry Division was tasked to provide the headquarters for the brigade task force being dispatched to An Najaf.

Late that afternoon, Task Force Arrow received orders to move the next morning and provide security for the brigade logistical elements and transportation trucks. The movement was extremely difficult since many of the bridges along the route had been blown by the enemy. Unlike previous months, the insurgents were also prepared to stand and fight instead of detonating improvised explosive devices and disappearing into the countryside like before. As a result, the task force fought several major engagements, and endured long hours and harassing fires throughout the movement.

The following account is an after-action report for two major Headquarters Company engagements en route to An Najaf:

Headquarters Company 5-20 Infantry Task Force Arrow Convoy Highlights

At approximately 0200 hours on the morning of April 11th, 2004, the Scout Platoon of 5th Battalion, 20th Infantry departed Forward Operating Base Warhorse as the lead element for the Battalion Task Force. The Scout Platoon was comprised of four Reconnaissance Variant Strykers that carried nearly 30 Battalion Scouts and Snipers. The Reconnaissance Variant Strykers are equipped with special optics at the expense of a front Squad Leader's Hatch and Remote Weapon System. Instead of a Remote Weapon System, the Reconnaissance Variant gunner must expose himself to enemy fire with only a small shield provided for his protection.

The Scout Platoon moved in column from intermediate objective to intermediate objective, clearing the designated route for Task Force Arrow. Not more than an hour into the movement, the platoon was moving near a little village named Ad Diwaniyah, when a large explosion ripped through the trail vehicles of the column. Non-Compliant Forces initiated a complex ambush with four volley fired Rocket Propelled Grenades, that were impacting on and around the trail Scout Strykers.

The trail vehicle was temporarily immobilized, losing a tire and its electrical system. The Scouts and Snipers in the exposed hatches were blown back into the vehicle, as the shock wave of multiple exploding Rocket Propelled Grenades viciously engulfed the last two Strykers in the order of movement. The initial blast was immediately followed by a second volley fired Rocket Propelled Grenade attack from the same area.

Simultaneously, several separate irrigation ditches to the right, front, and rear of the ground assault convoy, erupted with small arms fire while machine guns fired from an elevated support by fire position located approximately 200 meters to the two o'clock on a slight rise. A Rocket Propelled Grenade impacted the Slat Armor of the trail vehicle, and exploded just below the vehicle commander's hatch, while a second Rocket Propelled Grenade impacted and destroyed a tire. Another Rocket Propelled Grenade ricocheted safely off the Slat Armor of the next to last vehicle, and the remaining Rocket Propelled Grenades sailed clear or impacted into the ground to the front and rear of the two vehicles caught in the kill zone.

The two trail Strykers were caught directly in the center of a well-laid ambush. The two lead Strykers were forward of the ambush and able to quickly accelerate further from the attack. There were no communications with the disabled trail vehicle, and the next to last Stryker was still recovering from the blast as the lead vehicles sped clear of the kill zone by about 400 meters. The Non-Compliant Forces continued to pour accurate machine gun and small arms fire into the kill zone as the infantrymen secured their bearings. After a few moments, Sergeant Hudgeons, the vehicle commander for the next to last Stryker, was able swing his .50 caliber machine gun in the direction of attack. Rounds were impacting both vehicles. They tore through the exposed gear, but were not effective against the armored Strykers. Scouts and Snipers sprayed suppressive fire from their hatches, as the crew of the last vehicle quickly composed themselves and returned fire.

Sergeant Walden, the vehicle commander of the trail vehicle, manually traversed his .50 caliber machine gun to bare accurate suppressive fire upon the enemy. Scouts and Snipers in the trail vehicle sprang into action from the rear hatches as Staff Sergeant Horton, the acting Scout Platoon Sergeant, took charge of the engagement from the next to last vehicle, and ordered the Strykers forward. Specialist Thompson, the driver for the trail vehicle, was able drag his wounded Stryker onward, as the trail vehicles began to push out of the kill zone.

The Scouts continued to receive accurate fire as the trail vehicles withdrew from the kill zone, and attempted to make their way to the remainder of the platoon. Lieutenant Hicks, the Scout Platoon Leader, attempted to consolidate and reorganize the platoon at his location, approximately 400 meters forward of the ambush site. From there, his vehicle was able to provide suppressive fire as the trail vehicles made their way forward.

Upon consolidation, the trail vehicle crew immediately began to assess the damage sustained to their vehicle, while the remainder of the platoon provided mounted and dismounted security and accounted for personnel. Sergeant Galka, a Battalion Senior Sniper, noticed armed movement through his thermal scope and engaged additional Non-Compliant Forces while they attempted to maneuver on the regrouping platoon. The enemy immediately returned small arms fire and broke contact, but their actions forced the Scout Platoon to suppress and move further south.

The platoon moved to a service station, approximately 500 meters further from the ambush site and again attempted to assess the damage. As the platoon dismounted and cleared the area, Specialist Thompson restarted his electrical system and isolated the blown tire. In the distance they could hear the next element in the Task Force order of movement, Bravo Company, 2nd Battalion, 3rd Infantry, in contact in the same area. The company made their way through the ambush to the service station and assisted the platoon in securing the area. The Scout Platoon hurriedly mounted their Strykers, and provided a situation report to the Task Force Commander. Lieutenant Hicks led his platoon to the next intermediate objective, a blown bridge along the route, and coordinated for maintenance support to repair his damaged vehicle at the next security halt.

The Scouts performed magnificently during this movement. They received additional contact, and later in the movement linked up with the Headquarters Company convoy that now consisted of nearly a hundred vehicles. En route, the convoy had absorbed two 1st Infantry Division convoys carrying tanks, Bradleys and other vehicles and equipment on HETTs [heavy equipment and truck transport] and other cargo vehicles. Many of the new vehicles were from the reserve component and lacked radios and armor.

The Scouts returned and led the convoy through an urban area, as the vehicles crawled along at a snail's pace through the tiny street and narrow roads. Just as the convoy cleared the urban area several large explosions tore through the night followed by small arms and return fire. Without adequate communications and based on the size of the convoy that spanned over a mile, it took the convoy leaders some time to check the status of the men, weapons, and equipment. Several soldiers were wounded, one severely, and two HETTs were badly damaged and could not immediately move. It was pitch black on a single lane highway with poor communications.

Captain Vogt, the convoy commander, directed the vehicles to pull security, dispatched troops to clear the buildings where the attack appeared to come from, and called for MEDEVAC [medical evacuation]. The transportation crews performed brilliantly and were able to patch together the HETTs good enough to move as the MEDEVAC helicopter landed and evacuated the severely wounded soldier. As the convoy prepared to move the head count came back as one contractor missing. It was between 0300 to 0400 and after an extensive search there was no sign of the contractor. Eventually, the MEDEVAC unit confirmed that the contractor had crawled into the helicopter and hidden until they arrived back at the hospital. With all men, weapons, and equipment accounted for, the Headquarters Company convoy continued to move and eventually closed on Forward Operating Base Duke later that evening.

Tobias Vogt

Captain, Infantry, U.S. Army

Task Force Arrow went on to participate in multiple engagements as they closed on FOB Duke, just outside the holy city of An Najaf. After conducting several days of reconnaissance patrols, Task Force Arrow received a change of mission order. Insurgents were targeting civilian logistics trucks headed north to resupply American bases that were now running short on food, water, and ammunition

As a result, the task force quickly headed north to Logistical Support Area (LSA) Anaconda for Operation Road Warrior. The April uprisings brought ground logistics support to a screeching halt, and the Strykers were needed to open main supply routes and secure critical rations and supplies to central and northern Iraq. From LSA Anaconda, Task Force Arrow provided security for theater logistics between LSA Anaconda and Convoy Support Center (CSC) Scania. Escort duties exposed the task force to daily firefights and explosive ambushes, as they moved through Baghdad for the next few months.

Tal Afar

Just before Iraq was scheduled to transition to control of the Interim Iraqi Government, Task Force Arrow and the 5-20 Infantry received another change of mission order. This time they were to move to Tal Afar and replace the 1-14 Cavalry in northwestern Iraq. Tal Afar was an active city on the Syrian border, and the cavalry didn't have the manpower to engage such a hostile area. Tal Afar is home to approximately 250,000 people and was a known waypoint for smuggling and insurgent entry into Iraq. The new task organization reunited C Company with the rest of the battalion.

C Company, originally detached to 1-14 Cavalry, spent most of the deployment operating out of Rock Base in the city of Tal Afar. This forward firebase allowed them to deploy rapidly throughout the city and demonstrate presence, but exposed them to harassing and coordinated insurgent attacks. C Company was ordered to move to FOB Fulda, later renamed FOB Sykes, where they returned to the battalion for combat operations in Tal Afar. A Company was still detached to Hammam al Alil (Objective Aggies), and later Mosul. In place of the battalion's organic A Company, 5-20 Infantry received A Troop, 1-14 Cavalry for operations in Tal Afar. Civil-military operations were still the focus, but since April, the brigade was consumed with combating the deteriorating security situation throughout the country.

The task force conducted another ground assault convoy to Q-West to collect their equipment, sign over the base to the 1-37 Field Artillery Battalion, and move to Tal Afar for immediate combat operations. Politically, little had changed following the transition of sovereignty. The beleaguered Iraqi government forces were unable to establish order and the countryside still looked to the Americans for answers, direction, and security. The battalion did far less political interaction in the hostile city of Tal Afar. The environment was completely different than Qayyarah. At this point, the battalion engaged in one combat operation after another as the insurgency gained momentum in northern Iraq. Insurgents were more willing to stand and fight, and had increased the frequency and intensity of their attacks.

Parts of battalion continued to train Iraqi National Guard forces during the Task Force Arrow period. With the change to Iraqi sovereignty, these Iraqi National Guard forces found themselves incorporated into more coalition combat operations. American advisors from the battalion lived and ate with the 102nd Iraqi National Guard battalion, which was co-located on the base with the rest of the 5-20 Infantry.

During rehearsals, Iraqi leaders participated in rock drill exercises to prepare for combined combat operations. Iraqi National Guard leadership was normally integrated with the companies or task organized to the scout platoon to ensure communications and support. Unlike the Americans, these men deployed into urban combat on the back of a pickup truck with little more than an AK47s and a vague idea of what they were supposed to do.

Death threats, attempts, and successful assassinations of Iraqi's supporting coalition forces is incomprehensible to most outsiders. These courageous men and their families lived in constant fear, not just during combat operations, but at home and on their way to and from work as well. Imagine commuting to work with the knowledge that you may be ambushed. Arriving at work to take part in a combat operation and returning home to find your scared family threatened or murdered.

Combat operations in Tal Afar were intense, as patrols were frequently engaged with rocket propelled grenades and anti-tank hand grenades. For the next several months the battalion worked diligently to identify and crush insurgent elements in and around the city. The detention facility on FOB Sykes remained at capacity with insurgents, as the companies continued to raid and capture high-value targets and known insurgents. Operations Assyrian Drifter and Black Typhoon highlight the intensity of operations in Tal Afar.

Operation Assyrian Drifter was a several-day battalion operation designed to pressure and clear insurgent forces from Tal Afar. On day two of the operation, a Kiowa Warrior, OH58D helicopter from the 3-17 Cavalry was shot down. The battalion scouts reached the scene first and secured the helicopter, while B Company and the battalion tactical group sped to the crash site.

C Company, back on the base, was alerted to prepare a quick reaction force with Headquarters Company recovery and resupply assets to retrieve the downed helicopter. This operation lasted several hours, with the scout platoon nearly overrun by insurgents, and B Company and the 102nd Iraqi National Guard sustaining several wounded each. The crew and the aircraft were rescued, but the fighting intensified to the point that a 2,000-pound bomb was dropped near friendly units to turn the tide of the fight.

The battalion followed Assyrian Drifter with a brigade level operation that targeted the insurgency and evicted everyone from Tal Afar. Operation Black Typhoon opened when the battalion mortar platoon fired a 300 round, 120mm mortar preparation on key insurgent targets within the city. Companies of 5-20 Infantry, 1-23 Infantry, and the 102nd Iraqi National Guard moved into assault positions, as AC130 Spectre gunships engaged preplanned targets.

The fighting and cordon lasted for several days and bore witness to further U.S. Air Force munitions employed in support of coalition forces. During this five-day period, residents of the city weren't permitted to return to their homes. The brigade and battalion commanders negotiated with the mayor of Tal Afar, and eventually permitted the residents to return to their homes. With pressure from the greater populace, Tal Afar didn't return to its previous level of hostility until after the brigade departed.

The following account is an after-action report from the incoming brigade commander that was observing the operation:

Observations on the Battle of Tal Afar, Iraq

4 September 2004

Operation Assyrian Drifter Day 2

On 4 Sep 04 I (COL Stephen Townsend) accompanied the Regulars of Company B, Task Force (TF) 5-20 on what was intended to be a quick Cordon & Search in Tal Afar, Iraq on the second day of Operation Assyrian Drifter. The TF, with an Iraqi National Guard (ING) company, crossed the SP [start point] at the FOB [forward operating base] at 0730 and by about 0800 had closed with their three objectives in Tal Afar city (B Co. Objs Jonah and Nimrod in the northeast sector of the city and Scout Platoon Obj Gilgamesh on the eastern edge of the city).

Though we were slightly behind schedule due to the slowness of the ING jeeps, many of the Iraqis at the objectives still appeared surprised at our arrival. The operation progressed smoothly, netting several detainees from each objective, and by approximately H+30 minutes [Bravo Company Commander] CPT Mason was discussing with his leaders if any more intelligence value could be gained from the objectives and when to posture for the planned withdrawal. Up to this point the operation had encountered no enemy interference.

Then at approximately H+35 minutes B Co. elements at Obj Jonah received 1-2 incoming RPGs [rocket propelled grenade] from the south which wounded three ING soldiers, two seriously. The RPGs were accompanied by a fusillade of enemy small arms fire but I was unable to determine the source or target of this fire—it just seemed to crackle all around. B Co. was already in a hasty perimeter defense at its two objectives but the platoons strengthened the southern perimeter to address this emerging threat to the south. The company commander requested air evac of the two ING casualties and this was executed from the TF's pre-planned evac HLZ [helicopter landing zone] North IVO [in vicinity of] B Company's objectives. The initial flurry of small arms fire had abated but more persistent fire, including sporadic RPGs, began to build slowly though, at this point, it was not interfering with B Company's operations. CPT Mason continued to move about supervising the actions of his Soldiers, while remaining exposed to this increasing fire.

The air evac of ING casualties was nearing completion as CPT Mason issued orders to execute the planned withdrawal and elements began moving to their vehicles. At approximately H+50 minutes, just as the air evac was completed, I was listening to the TF command net on CPT Mason's command Stryker when I heard someone make an urgent call, "An aircraft is down, Crazyhorse 25 has gone down..." I was surprised but not shocked at this news as the Kiowas had been operating at very low altitude over the small arms and RPG threat. I looked to the south and could see a single Kiowa Warrior in a tight orbit about a kilometer away.

Captain Mason immediately ordered Company B to REDCON 1 [readiness condition] in anticipation of an order to move to assist at the crash site. During the TF rehearsal, the Battalion Commander, LTC Karl Reed, had directed that in the event an aircraft was downed in the city, the entire force should be prepared to rally at the crash site. The platoons began to reposition to load their vehicles and prepared to move.

As we waited, I continued to discuss the situation with CPT Mason as we monitored the command net—I was conscious of the fact that CPT Mason was trying to command his company and he didn't need a lot of "help" from the strap-hanging Colonel in back. We heard several transmissions about the incident unfolding. I cannot recall the exact source, sequence or wording of these transmissions but the gist of them, as I recall it, was:

- The other Kiowa has eyes on the crash site...requesting ground forces to assist
- The Scout Platoon is en route to the site

- *The Scouts have secured the site and two pilots...one pilot shaken up and one with injured back*

- *The Scouts are getting increasing pressure at the site...requesting reinforcements*

At some point during this, the Battalion Commander gave B Co. the expected order to move to the crash site. Even with the preparation we had done, it took a few minutes to load the remaining dismounted security elements and get into order of march. As we uncoiled and headed south on Route Corvette, the fire around us began to slowly increase.

As we moved south, I didn't realize that there was no good route straight to the site. As it turned out, we would be forced to drive along Corvette beyond the site to the south, turn back to the east, turn back to the north and make our way to the site—a "fishhook shaped" route of almost 3 kilometers. For the first 500-800 meters, the fire directed against the column was steadily increasing but not yet, in my opinion, to the point that our movement was affected. Captain Mason rode exposed to the fire in the leader's hatch of his Stryker.

Suddenly, the fire seemed to dramatically pickup in intensity, with continuous small arms and RPG fires seemingly being focused directly on our column (I later learned that some of these fires were probably targeting the Scout Platoon at the actual crash site and we happened to be driving through the enemy's line of fire). At almost every intersection we passed you could hear the boom and whistling whoosh of RPGs adding to the constant crack of AK fire—the RPGs impacted on nearby walls and airburst overhead in small black clouds. I heard someone warn the column that the enemy was tossing hand grenades at the column from the upper floors of the flanking houses. I looked to the rear and the ING soldiers behind us were hunched over in their little open jeeps as if they were driving in a hailstorm and firing madly to both sides. At this point, every weapon in the column was firing to each flank and I began firing my M4 at muzzle flashes and suspected enemy locations on upper stories, rooftops and down alleyways—until then, I had refrained from firing my own weapon as I had not seen clearly identifiable targets. However, the enemy fire was now so intense that I felt compelled to do my part to lessen it in any way possible. Captain Mason continued to ride erect in his hatch returning fire while he worked to maneuver his company to the crash site.

At some point during this move, we took a short halt in the street—in order to ensure the entire company had uncoiled from the objective and was following. Captain Mason gathered reports from his platoons during this stop. Sound bites I remember hearing over the radio during this move:

- The Scouts were under heavy fire and severe pressure on their flanks

- LTC Reed requested permission to use CAS to suppress the enemy's assault

- *If unable to use CAS, we would likely have to destroy the aircraft and/or abandon the site*
- *One of B Co's platoons (3d I think, but I can't recall with certainty) was unable to move due to the intensity of enemy fire*
- *One of B Co's vehicles had been struck by one or several RPGs and required recovery*

After a few minutes, we began to move again.

I could now see that we were approaching an intersection ahead. Just when I thought we might make it through the gauntlet of fire relatively unscathed, the column again ground to a halt—though we could see our destination on FBCB2 [Force XXI Battle Command Brigade and Below], we were backed up trying to locate a trafficable route to maneuver the company into the crash site. CPT Mason's command Stryker was parked in the middle of the intersection and subject to RPG fires from down several long streets—we repositioned to get at least partially out of the intersection and next to a building. Someone then shouted over to warn us that we were now parked just beneath the windows of the building the grenades had been thrown from—we repositioned again, again exposing a flank to a street—there was just no good spot to be. Every 20-30 seconds an RPG burst overhead or smacked into a wall—my impression was that the enemy was lobbing them over the block of buildings to our west. I cannot state with any certainty the number of RPGs that had been fired at us up to this point. I had attempted to count them for some reason but stopped when I hit 10 and began firing my own weapon—about halfway thru our movement. A conservative estimate for this part of the battle is somewhere between 20-30 RPGs.

While we were halted in the intersection, I suggested to CPT Mason that we deploy infantrymen to clear the immediately adjacent buildings and seize the urban high ground on the rooftops around us...he agreed, having already had the same thought, and issued the orders—we all began to feel better as we started seeing teams and squads of Regulars on the nearby roofs—though this did little to lessen the incoming RPG fire. CPT Mason again gathered reports from his platoons. Sound bites I remember hearing around this time were:

- The "pinned" platoon was now able to move

- Several vehicles had been damaged but the one struck by the RPG could make it to the main intersection we were currently at to be rigged for towing

- The CAS strike had been approved

We remained halted at this intersection, under almost constant fire, for what seemed like 15-20 minutes. I was unable to monitor the radios during this entire period so I'm not certain as to why but I believe it was to insure we had recovered all vehicles. During this time, CPT Mason continued to direct the company with an emphasis on insuring 100% accountability of his Soldiers and the ING Company as well.

Finally, we were able to move, though it took several minutes to recall and account for all the deployed infantrymen—CPT Mason had a lot of concern that we not leave behind any of the ING soldiers and accounting for them probably added a few minutes as well. We rounded the corner to the left (east) and after a short sprint we again turned left (north) and suddenly, we were at the crash site. LTC Reed wanted us deployed on the western side of the site but, due to the routes from our current position and the enemy fire, we couldn't get there from where we were on the eastern side. LTC Reed directed B Co. to halt in place until he could bring in the CAS to suppress the enemy fire--we took a hasty herringbone halt along the eastern side of the crash site.

While we waited at this halt, for what was probably five minutes or so, the Battalion TAC [tactical group] directed the fast movers onto their target. Enemy small arms fire continued to crack around us and RPGs continued to explode in and around the crash site— both air and ground bursts. I had the impression that the first enemy mortars impacted during this time but it can be difficult to tell the difference sometimes between RPGs and 60mm mortar bursts. LTC Reed was very concerned with limiting the potential collateral damage of employing JDAMs [Joint Deployed Aerial Munition] in the city but something needed to be done so we could maneuver. LTC Reed directed that the strike be targeted at an obvious marker, a tall column of black smoke billowing near the center of the enemy activity along Rte. Corvette that we had just traveled down. Everyone was ordered to take cover in their Strykers or behind walls or terrain. Finally, a few hundred meters away to the west, a huge column of dirt and smoke shot straight up into the sky. I was surprised by the amount of dirt that was thrown into the air and that the explosion was not louder as close as we were. I assumed the JDAM fuse had been a delay fuse to reduce collateral damage and the danger to friendly troops in proximity.

As we had hoped, the enemy fire lessened dramatically and almost immediately after the bomb's impact. CPT Mason had already directed his lead platoon to find the quickest route to the west side of the crash site as soon as the bomb impacted. The company quickly moved north a few streets and then turned left (west)—intending to come into our planned blocking positions from the north. What followed next seemed almost surreal—like something I had read in "Blackhawk Down." As we probed for a suitable route, we zig-zagged west through a maze of streets and alleyways until we emerged…back on Route Corvette! We happened to turn south back onto Corvette right where the bomb had landed. The bomb looked like it fell into or near a depression or wadi on the west side of Corvette. The area was blackened and smoking—there were few people visible and almost no incoming fire at this point. The B Co. Soldier riding air guard/flank security with me (a SGT Kellar or Kellam I think) asked, "Didn't we just come through here?" I confirmed we had as we turned left (south) back onto Corvette and began to run the gauntlet again.

I admit wondering myself, at the time, why we were re-covering this same ground and only later learned that the lead platoon could not find a suitable route back to the west side of the crash site. But, unlike the previous journey, this time we traveled the route quickly and with little enemy interference—a few scattered shots and one or two RPGs. We turned left again at the grenade thrower's house and left again to head back north to the crash site arriving at a suitable place to deploy the company around the downed helicopter within probably 8 or 10 minutes after the bomb's impact. The platoons maneuvered to the sectors CPT Mason had assigned them and immediately began occupying a hasty defense in and on top of the surrounding buildings.

The respite brought by the CAS probably lasted another 5, maybe 10, minutes...the whole period being just enough for B Co. to reposition and create a perimeter around the crash. Then the enemy fire began to build steadily until it returned to its pre-strike levels. After a few minutes in position, I decided to dismount and find LTC Reed to see how he was doing. CPT Mason was concerned for my safety and insisted on sending his RTOs [radio teletype operators] along with me. It wasn't hard to find LTC Reed. He was standing erect with a very small TAC in the center of the site as small arms fire cracked overhead and RPGs began whistling in again.

After linking up with the Regular TAC, I directed the B Co. RTOs to return to CPT Mason in case he should need them. After we shook hands, LTC Reed and I exchanged views on what had happened from each of our perspectives. We discussed the cordon and search, the events ensuing since the crash, his decision to employ CAS and his plan and our prospects for recovering the aircraft and extracting the force. LTC Reed was very calm and focused as we moved about the site—I thought he had an excellent feel for the battle and what potentially lay ahead and his plans were very sound. I also thought he was, without being conscious of it, providing a superb leadership example to the Soldiers of his battalion as he moved about openly and calmly directed the fight. We moved to HQ63 and talked with his S3, MAJ Doug Baker, who was implementing LTC Reed's plans. After a few minutes, I left them alone to their fight.

I moved over to the ING Company Commander, crouching near a building about 25 meters away and congratulated him on the bravery of his soldiers. I was amazed at how light his casualties were…they had sustained three in the initial RPG attack at Obj Jonah and I couldn't believe they hadn't sustained more as they ran the gauntlet down Corvette. They had moved through that fire in open jeeps, helmetless and wearing only body armor and were now pulling security on the eastern flank of the crash site. He pulled me over to a nearby ING truck containing detainees from Obj Gilgamesh and said something, in a mixture of Arabic and broken English, about his three casualties and the five bound detainees in front of us. I didn't quite get his meaning until he made a gesture like he was firing a tommy gun from the hip towards the detainees— his meaning became clear. He wanted my permission to execute the five detainees in retribution for the loss of his three soldiers. I told him no as clearly as I could—that the Coalition did not execute prisoners. He either wasn't understanding or choosing not to—he again fired his imaginary tommy gun towards the detainees.

LTC Reed's interpreter was nearby and I called him over to assist. We again told the company commander to not execute the detainees. Satisfied that we had bought the prisoners at least a few more minutes of life, I walked over and relayed the exchange to LTC Reed. He immediately directed some nearby troops to move the prisoners and take them into protective custody and effectively solved the problem. Less than five minutes later the first of a series of distressingly accurate 60mm mortar volleys landed right where we had been arguing about the detainees, wounding several ING. These rounds landed within meters of LTC Reed's TAC. Over the next couple of hours as we fought to secure the site and extract the aircraft, these mortar volleys would flatten tires on several Strykers and wound more ING and some Regulars as well. We were grateful they were 60mm and not 82's.

It wasn't too much longer when the 5-20 QRF [quick reaction force], Company C, arrived with a recovery package including a HEMTT [heavy expanded mobility tactical truck] flat rack. I stayed in the area of the helicopter to observe the actions of the recovery team. 1SG Mapes, the C Company First Sergeant, oversaw the efforts there—the recovery team effectively and quickly disarmed the Kiowa's weapons systems and removed the rotor blades by cutting them from the mast with a quickie saw. Finally, using the HEMTT, a Stryker winch and cable and old-fashioned manpower, the Kiowa was loaded and strapped into place on the HEMTT.

This entire recovery effort was executed under a slow drizzle of 60mm mortar rounds that consistently fell only about 70 meters away to the east and RPGs bursting overhead. By a happy accident of slope and construction, the Kiowa had come to rest in an area that was, for the most part, somewhat protected from direct small arms and RPG fires. The Regulars all around us continued to fight fiercely from the windows and rooftops as the insurgents continued to advance from the west and made attempts to envelop the site to the northern and southern flanks. You could tell where the enemy pressure was greatest at any given moment as B Co's fires would crescendo and ebb periodically at various points around the perimeter. B Company's MGS (ATGM) [mobile gun system] platoon fired several TOWs [tube launched optically tracked wire guided missile] during this engagement which effectively neutralized enemy automatic weapons that were firing from positions in buildings. LTC Reed could be seen throughout the recovery effort walking around upright inside the perimeter—leading his Soldiers through both his orders and his personal example.

With the Kiowa lashed to the truck, LTC Reed issued the orders for the battalion to begin its extraction from the city. We departed the city into the desert to the east and then turned south on the outskirts of the city to make our way back to FOB Sykes. We continued to attract small arms, machine-gun, RPG and mortar fires as we left the city proper and skirted its eastern edge. The battalion suppressed these fires with return fires from their Strykers as they moved and by calling in close combat attack fires from the Kiowas overhead.

The leaders collected personnel, ACE [ammunition, casualty, equipment] and BDA [battle damage assessment] reports by voice and FBCB2 as we rolled back to the FOB. Once back inside the wire, the Battalion's leadership focused on tending to the casualties and insuring 100% accountability of the ING soldiers. Two to three hours after our return, the battalion Task Force conducted an After-Action Review to develop a complete picture of the events that had unfolded and identify lessons learned and TTP adjustments.

Based on my observations of their actions and leadership example on 4 Sep 04 at Tal Afar, Iraq, I recommend:

LTC Karl Reed, Commander, TF 5-20, 3-2 SBCT, be awarded one of the following in priority: the Bronze Star with V for Valor, the Army Commendation Medal with V for Valor, or the Bronze Star for Heroic/Meritorious Achievement for his actions on that specific day.

Captain Damien Mason, Commander, Company B, 5th Bn, 20th Infantry, 3-2 SBCT, be awarded one of the following in priority: the Bronze Star with V for Valor, the Army Commendation Medal with V for Valor, or the Bronze Star for Heroic/Meritorious Achievement for his actions on that specific day.

I further recommend that LT Rob McChrystal, Platoon Leader, Scout Platoon, HHC, 5th Bn, 20th Infantry, 3-2 SBCT, be also considered for a valor award for his actions on that day. Though I personally observed him only briefly on the battlefield, I know from what I observed and heard that his quick thinking, decisiveness and inspirational leadership example was central to the unit's success that day.

Stephen J. Townsend

Colonel, Infantry, U.S. Army

Transition of Authority

By this point, it was mid-September, and the battalion was not long from rotating back to the States. Several smaller operations followed Black Typhoon, but nothing of that magnitude as the battalion prepared to leave. The 1st Battalion, 24th Infantry "Deuce Four" from the 1st Brigade, 25th Infantry Division, was scheduled to assume responsibility for Tal Afar and relieve the 5-20 Infantry in place. This relationship was short lived. Before the property was transferred, the Deuce Four was reassigned to Mosul. They went on to distinguish themselves in Iraq, but in the meantime, the Regulars adjusted to this last fragmentary order and handed over the base to the cavalry instead.

In the end, the battalion redeployed without Strykers and equipment. 1st Brigade, 25th Infantry Division, the second Stryker brigade to be created by the U.S. Army, relieved the Arrowhead Brigade in northern Iraq. 1st Brigade signed over their equipment to the 3rd Brigade rear-detachment before deploying to Iraq. This eliminated the need to ship their own equipment to the region. After handover, the Regulars were left with only small arms, optics, and some miscellaneous man-portable equipment to carry home.

Fighting still raged, and Iraqi elections loomed in the near future as commanders exchanged property. For the men of the 5-20 Infantry, signing for their traded equipment, refitting, and reorganizing for their next deployment was far from their thoughts. After a year in combat, the war weary soldiers prepared to board C130s to Kuwait, where they would catch "Freedom Birds" home to Fort Lewis, Washington, and reunite with loved ones. Next year could wait. Right now, everyone just wanted to go home.

60 | Tobias Vogt

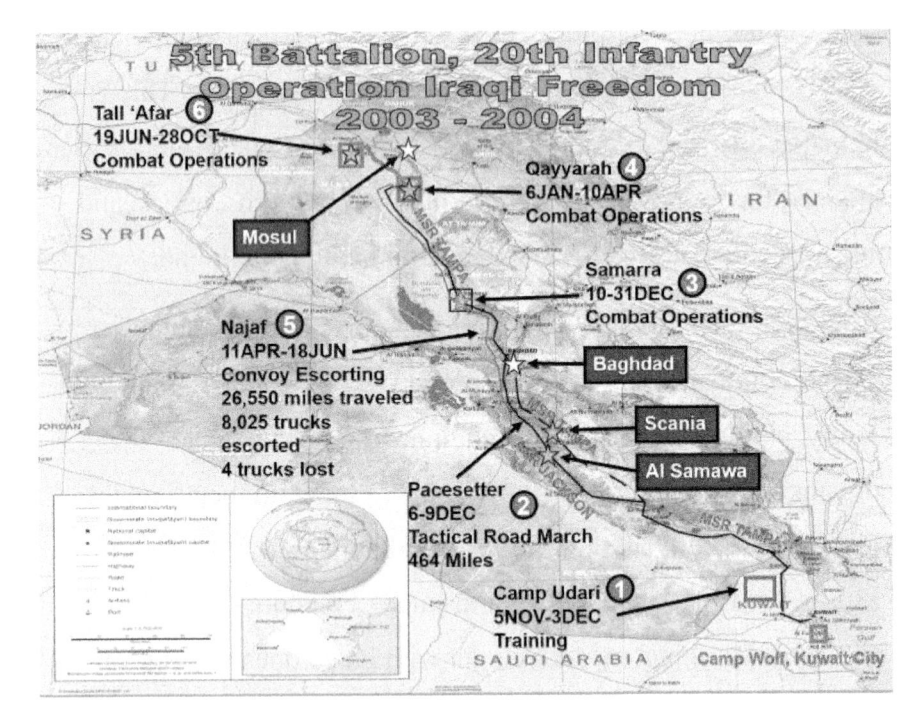

(Sparks)

III. In Their Own Words

Timothy Bennett

Alpha Company Platoon Leader and Headquarters Company Executive Officer

My name is Timothy Bennett. I originally served as the platoon leader for the mobile gun system platoon, Alpha Company, 5-20th Infantry, before moving to Headquarters Company as the executive officer. I was born in College Point, New York. After high school I went to college at Colorado State. I eventually joined the army in 1999 as an enlisted soldier. After my enlisted time in military intelligence, I was commissioned from the officer candidate school in Fort Benning, Georgia, and then assigned as an armor platoon leader in Alpha Company 5-20th Infantry.

November 13, 2003, I boarded a plane en route to Kuwait. Once we got to Kuwait, we were shipped to Camp Udairi, that's when our deployment began. It was uncertain when we got to Camp Udairi, what our future plans were and where and who we'd be assigned to after our move into Iraq. I do recollect a lot of sand, a lot of tents, and a lot of nervousness and uncertainty by the soldiers. Again, it was uncertain about what the near future had in store for us. We knew we had to convoy into Iraq, and the soldiers prepared their gear, and their equipment, and vehicles for that movement. Our primary mission at Camp Udairi was to train and acclimate to the climate. We continued to do physical training, and we worked on continued weapons maintenance and maneuvering skills while they put slat armor on our Strykers, the RPG [rocket propelled grenade] repelling cage around the original armor of the Stryker. We were there for a couple weeks.

It took several days to outfit the entire brigade, particularly my platoon took three days to outfit the three vehicles that we had for the slat armor. Once the slat armor was installed, we continued additional preparations on the vehicles, inside and out, securing load plans and preparing equipment. Within about a week and a-half to two weeks, we had finished all the training at Camp Udairi and we were prepared to move north into Iraq.

We received numerous briefings about the convoy order, about the time frame, and the way we were to move into Iraq. On the first day of the convoy, we traveled through Kuwait and stopped just shy of the Iraqi border. The soldiers that night, were getting nervous about the initial move into Iraq. It was my platoon's first combat experience for most everyone in the platoon. The following morning, we got up and moved into Iraq. At the border of Kuwait and Iraq, it was quite a demonstration with the arrival of U.S. forces and vehicles unknown to the local population.

Certain things that you'll never forget about the initial crossing at the border, one of them was a gentleman waving an AK47 in strong protest, which was not lightly received by the rest of the platoon. Although movement through the area was slow and tedious, we moved through without complications and I believe nerves began to calm down after that. It took three to four days to move into Iraq with minimal contact between Kuwait and Samarra. While passing through Baghdad, we were approached with large amounts of traffic and large demonstrations, there were some complications with vehicles getting too close, and tensions were pretty high moving through the city of Baghdad.

My platoon sustained no contact while moving through Baghdad, although the company encountered various types of contact. The road march in my opinion went pretty successful, no loss of vehicles or personnel. It was pretty calm for the majority of the trip as we moved into Camp Pacesetter with minimal difficulties. We arrived late at night and were attached to the 4th Infantry Division. We were just a brigade, so I don't think they knew how they wanted to use us in the beginning.

Samarra

Once we arrived at FOB [forward operating base] Pacesetter, we were preparing for operations in the city of Samarra in conjunction with 4th Infantry Division from Fort Hood Texas. Our initial mission at Pacesetter, that I understood, was to quell any uprisings from insurgents in the city of Samarra. When we first got to Pacesetter, it was an abandoned airfield, not much there, although a lot of the soldiers were excited to finally be in Iraq, and begin to do what we were training to do.

The first couple of days we were in Pacesetter we were outfitting the vehicles again, getting prepared for actual combat inside the city of Samarra. Our initial mission was to move into the city of Samarra on the eastern side, and the 4th Infantry Division was going to be on the western side, divided by the major street that ran down the middle of Samarra. We initially moved in, as the MGS [mobile gun system] platoon leader, I was responsible for establishing an outer perimeter on the east side of Samarra, as the rest of the company prepared to infiltrate. We first established three vehicles outside of the city in an outer perimeter, and were observing the activities, which we could see on the east side of the city, before any initial movements into the city by our guys.

I remember standing there that day, shortly after arriving in country, and a group of television reporters came up to my platoon compromising our position. With concern, I got off the vehicle and addressed the reporters. They were from an Italian TV news station. With their broken English, they were trying to explain to me that they were trying to figure out what we were doing there. I very clearly told them that we were conducting traditional operations, and they were to vacate the area immediately. With a little bit of difficulty, they had a hard time understanding me, they eventually moved away from the vehicles and we continued our observation of the city.

About an hour or two after our observation had ended, the company began to move into the city of Samarra from the eastern side. Bravo Company was the initial move, and Alpha Company would be second. Once Bravo Company moved into the city, they immediately received contact in the form of small arms and machine gun fire. I remember moving directly in after them, coming into a narrow street and hearing the gunfire, although uncertain from which direction it was coming from. We quickly moved into a small clearing inside of the city by some rubbled buildings, buildings that had been knocked down, and set up headquarters security in the middle of the city with Captain Bachelor, the company commander, and the company medical vehicle.

Actions that day were pretty hectic in the city; it was uncertain what was going on at the time. The primary task at that point was for Bravo Company to break contact, and we were to secure the route outside of the city. Confusion was high between the company commander and the platoon leaders, about which directions to go, which routes to take, and how to be able to set the EVAC [evacuation] plan for Bravo Company.

I'd say within 30 to 40 minutes we had established our foothold in the city, and began to set the EVAC plan for Bravo Company. Although never seeing Bravo Company pass by, we were able to set up security for the headquarters and eventually moved the entire battalion in and out of the city. I know the soldiers were pretty nervous that day, since that was our first day of combat and we had a lot of contact, although my platoon never received direct fire from what I recall. Once outside of the city, we did a debrief and moved back to FOB Pacesetter.

Back at FOB Pacesetter we prepared for additional operations in Samarra. The next operation was an entire clearing of the city of Samarra in conjunction with 4th Infantry Division. Clearing all insurgents out of the city took approximately two to three days, and I think the initial movement was to move in, set up an Alpha Alpha, an assembly area, outside of the city, and then conduct operations from the assembly area. My platoon was assigned the responsibility of moving the battalion into the Alpha Alpha.

I remember it was late at night when we were to move with the battalion scout platoon, we had staged at FOB Pacesetter to set out on the mission. Minutes before we were to SP [start point] from FOB Pacesetter, we received a radio transmission from the battalion to halt the SP and wait for further guidance. After 30 minutes to an hour had passed by, with many questions as to what was going on, we were informed that Saddam Hussein had been captured, and that we were on a 48-hour stand down for all offensive operations in the country of Iraq, primarily in the city of Samarra.

During that 48-hours, many soldiers were unclear of our future, whether that was the end, whether we were gonna go home, or if we were going to continue operations in Iraq. Then we were notified, we were to continue operations. The previous mission had been put back on, and we were to receive the battalion and establish the Alpha Alpha. We moved into the Alpha Alpha late at night, it was a farmer's field. It was very rainy that night and very muddy, we had a lot of mud during the winter over there. Myself and my eight other soldiers were responsible for cordoning in the entire battalion. Three companies, well four companies in total, and almost 200 hundred vehicles.

Once we got in the Alpha Alpha operations ceased for that evening, as soldiers prepared to conduct operations within Samarra for the next couple days. Primary operations for us in Samarra were to establish outer checkpoints, and my primary mission as the MGS platoon leader was to establish outside observation, to sustain checkpoints, to inspect the coming and going of vehicles inside the city of Samarra. Not much else is clear about what we did in Samarra. It seemed like a sustained operation of checking coming and going vehicles, running observations, moving back and forth between the Alpha Alpha and FOB Pacesetter. I mean after about two weeks we were notified that we were no longer continuing operations in Samarra, and we were to move further into Iraq.

Qayyarah

After finishing up operations at FOB Pacesetter we were moved further north to the vicinity of the town of Mosul. From what I recollect, the road march was to be about seven to eight hours, and we left mid-day from FOB Pacesetter and arrived at Q-West late in the evening. I just remember it being rain, very cold, and very muddy as we pulled into FOB Q-West in conjunction with 101st Airborne Division. Once we got there that evening, our primary objective was to ensure the soldiers got their rest from the previous day of driving, and the following day we began to figure out what our responsibilities were going to be. We were linked up with the 101st units that we would be relieving of their responsibilities.

My primary responsibility was to link up with the company of the 101st that was running checkpoints and traffic control points on the main highway, as well as conducting operations in small villages along the highway. I spent about two weeks, myself and a few soldiers from my platoon, my platoon sergeant, and my gunner running co-op operations with the 101st Airborne, running rolling TCPs [traffic control point], static TCPs, and frequenting small villages along the highway.

The highway was referred to as MSR [main supply route] Tampa. It was the main highway that ran all the way through the city of Qayyarah, with adjacent villages within a quarter mile off of each side of the highway. The primary objective of running the rolling TCPs was to stop cars and ensure that they were following the guidelines set up by the command there in Iraq. Checking vehicles for identification, verifying names against the blacklist, as well as vehicles and license plates.

As I mentioned, we also were responsible for running frequent stoppings, if you will, of the local villages. Talking with the mukhtars and the Imam's, religious leaders, of the town to see if they had any information to report about activity around the highway, within the vicinity of their villages. After a couple weeks of co-op operations with the 101st, my platoon was responsible for taking over the mission in its entirety. Primarily, we would run two to three patrols a day around the base perimeter of Q-West, checking for activity outside of the perimeter, as well as conducting traffic control points, and rolling traffic control points on the highway, investigating vehicles.

Hammam al Alil

Shortly after being at Q-West, Alpha Company 5-20th was assigned to FOB Agees, which was a small agricultural college that had been abandoned in the city of Hammam al Alil. When we first got there, it was a two-story building, and the initial mission was to conduct operations in Hammam al Alil. The facility was run down, with no water and no electric. We relied on MREs [meals ready to eat] for food, and bottled water, and primarily flashlights for lights within the building. I remember the necessity to black out all the windows. No lights were to be used in the hallways and if lights were to be used in the rooms, they would be with blacked out windows to ensure that the people of Hammam al Alil were not necessarily focused on the location of coalition forces within the city.

The company's primary mission was running patrols within the city and investigating certain houses, but my initial mission while at FOB Agees was to continue checkpoints along MSRs Flagstaff, Atlanta, and Dallas, in and around the firebase Agees. Actually, it was a firebase, not a FOB. One of the villages I spoke of earlier, that I was responsible for by firebase Agees, was aptly name by my platoon as Shadyville. It was a small village, probably a couple hundred people, where the mukhtar always had weapons, as long as we had money to give him for those weapons. I remember running a couple of operations out there, where he would have mortars, RPGs, and at the time we were still able to give him money for those weapons. Because of his constant availability to weapons, we referred to it as Shadyville. He wasn't trying to help the country. He was just making money by selling weapons. I was always uncertain what would happen when we went there, although most of the time though it was pretty quiet when we went in. We'd do the exchange, and talk with the mukhtar and the Imam, and continue operations without much complication.

While at firebase Agees, there were two stories that I remember vividly, that I'll probably never forget. One of them, during regular operations at firebase Agees, we had received a call from battalion or from the company commander, that we were to investigate the products pipeline that Iraq had underground for possible leakage. I got the coordinates for the pipeline, and we moved out to the pipeline and discovered that a part of the pipeline had been exposed and it was fuel, benzene, or unleaded fuel running all over the countryside. When we got up there, we found security forces that were responsible for the pipeline and without a translator, using translation cards and broken Arabic that I had learned up to that point, we tried to figure out what had happened at that site.

They said throughout the night, Ali Babbas, they referred to bad guys as Ali Babbas, came up with a fuel tanker, uncovered the pipeline and tapped it. They put in a hose and were filling up their fuel tanker with the fuel. At the time, fuel was a rare commodity there in the country, and it was extremely expensive with limited availability to the citizens. So, this was a big deal, that somebody was stealing directly from the pipeline. Well again, through broken translation I tried to identify why they didn't try to stop the insurgents from their activities. They said that they engaged in a firefight with the operators of the fuel tanker, which I thought to be peculiar, because firing at a fuel tanker could never be a good idea. And the lack of brass or evidence of a gunfight at that scene also led me to believe that their story wasn't necessarily true.

I had called back to the company commander and notified him that there was a leak at the site, and the leak was persistent as a garden hose, and needed to be stopped because the fuel was pouring out all over the countryside. After some waiting, I got a radio transmission back that he had called brigade and that brigade engineers were in a different part of the AO [area of operations] at the time. They couldn't alleviate the problem, and probably wouldn't be able to for quite some time. Once he told me that I tried to figure out how I was going to take care of the situation, at least a temporary fix it until the brigade engineers could get on site.

Inside of each Stryker we were issued a Stryker BDAR kit, Battle Damage Assessment Repair kit, to repair the Strykers from small bullet holes or shrapnel wounds, or additional ways to fix tires or small engine problems. It had some epoxy tape, different types of glue patches, and what not. After speaking with my gunner and my platoon sergeant, we identified a way that we might be able to stop the leak. After persistent measures and different techniques, we finally were able to patch the part of the hose that was leaking out, enough that we reduced the flow of the fuel to a minimal drip from the persistent flow that it had already been doing.

When I called the company commander and told him that we had done this, it was actually kind of a humorous thing [laughs]. I told him we had stopped the leak, he asked me how, and I said we used a Stryker BDAR kit. He said, "You did what?" I said we used a Stryker BDAR kit to stop the fuel from flowing out, and he said make sure you bring pictures and come on back to the firebase. So, we took pictures with the digital camera that the platoon had and went back to firebase Agees. I showed him the picture, and in astonishment he was amazed at the success, that we were actually able to stop the fuel leak. After time, they were able to get the brigade engineers out there to cover it up. During a normal mission we were to drive the pipeline, and we went out there and checked, and made sure that the fuel had been stopped, and it was covered properly. Never had any other problems along the pipeline, but it was kind of an interesting part of being at Agees.

One other mission I won't forget at Agees was when we were running a traffic control point in the city right next to Hammam al Alil called Salhiah. We were just on a traditional traffic control point, checking vehicles coming through it at nighttime, checking names on the blacklist, when we identified one individual that was on the black list. My platoon broke down the checkpoint, and took him back to firebase Agees, and this was one of the first guys that my platoon had actually taken from the blacklist back to the base, so everyone was pretty excited.

Once we got him back to firebase Agees, it was late at night, traditionally the commander takes the initial interview with detainees before they're sent up to the brigade detention center, but the commander was out on another mission at the time, so it was my responsibility to conduct the initial interview with this detainee. I just remember the uncomfortableness of being in a small room with a detainee, my translator, myself, and then I had my gunner there for additional security. I asked the detainee general demographic information, and information about where he lived, and his activities in the area. I never saw him after that evening, he was shortly moved to the brigade detention center up the city of Mosul. But I just remember the unease of dealing with somebody I had just taken off of the street, and interviewing him before I knew he was going up to the detention center.

I was a platoon leader for six months in country when I received word from my company commander that I was being transferred to be the executive officer of Headquarters Company 5-20th. I remember that being very hard, because I had made promises to the families of my soldiers that I would bring them home safely, now they were bringing in a new guy from West Point to take over my platoon, 612, to take over combat operations. It was extremely difficult for me to go. I had many talks with my commander about desiring to stay in the platoon, but he said it was my time to move onto bigger and better things. He said to trust in my platoon sergeant, and he would watch over my guys.

I talked it over with my platoon sergeant a lot, and my gunner. They said they'd do their best to watch over the guys. I just remember having to leave the platoon, it was probably the hardest thing I did in country. Guys that I trained with for a year and a half up to this point. I spent six months in combat you know, sleeping next to everyone, waking up to them every day. Working with the guys every single day, you know a lot about your guys when you're in combat together, and I was being moved out of there to be an executive officer of a new company. Again, it was one of the hardest things I had to do especially, because I knew the guy that they were bringing in was green, straight out of West Point, no training or combat experience, so it was extremely disheartening for me.

Even as the XO [executive officer] I was able to meet up in different locations like FOB Marez, on supply runs and what not, and I would run into my old platoon. I'd talk with the guys, and they'd tell me how it was going, and how operations were going. They used to tell me stories about the new platoon leader, and they always made me feel better about my existence in the platoon, the fact that my ingenuity, my creativeness, and leadership was missed by the platoon certainly made me feel a lot better about, you know, my success in the platoon as a platoon leader.

Qayyarah

But that was behind me now, it was time for me to move to the executive officer position and move back down to FOB Q-West with Headquarters Company. Right before the time that I got to the company as the executive officer, the company was split for Task Force Arrow. I had worked with Captain Vogt on FOB security as one of our missions back at Q-West, but he was down south when I got back from Agees. Half the company went down to An Najaf, and the other half stayed at Q-West and formed what they called Task Force Sykes, or excuse me, yeah, Task Force Sykes, because of the civil war commander. My primary mission then at Task Force Sykes was to assume command of the remaining elements of the Headquarters Company there at FOB Q-West, as well as pick up the responsibilities as the FOB mayor and battalion S4 [logistics officer]. I just remember as a lieutenant, the job load was a lot, the responsibility was a lot, but I was ready to take on this mission, accept the challenge, and fulfill my duties as the executive officer.

Operations at Q-West were pretty mild compared to what I had been used to up at FOB Agees as a platoon leader, as far as combat operations are concerned. It became our primary objective to train Iraqi soldiers on Q-West for the new Iraqi National Guard. I remember the training was extremely challenging, although I myself was not responsible for the training of the soldiers, I was responsible for the building of and maintenance of the facilities for them to train, as well as providing the logistics for them to train, so that the other companies that were there training soldiers had the assets necessary to conduct the training. I remember building three different ranges, an obstacle course, making housing arrangements, food arrangements, dining facility, and what not, for the Iraqi National Guard to come in. People take utilities like clean running water, electricity, bathroom facilities, and other things we're used to for granted, but being the mayor of a FOB is just like being a mayor in the U.S., minus the election part.

At Q-West we had to pump the water from the Tigris River and purify it, we're talking about hundreds of thousands of gallons to run a small city, and people just turn on a tap, or flick a light switch, and don't even think about it. Anyway, we were there for about three months running field operations. Primary objective while at Q-West was remain training the National Guard, which went well, and once that job was resolved, Task Force Arrow started coming back and the company was reunited at Q-West as we prepared for operations to move up north into the city of Tal Afar.

Back as the executive officer of Headquarters Company, my primary mission to prepare for the move to Tal Afar was to get all the vehicles serviced and maintenance up on them, as well as figure out how we were going to move the necessary vehicles to Q-West, excuse me to Tal Afar, with the minimal manning we had at the time. People don't realize how big a Stryker Headquarters Company is in combat, I seem to recall at that time we had about a hundred and fifty pieces of rolling stock, that is trucks, trailers, Strykers, and other wheeled stuff. We had many meetings about the move, getting vehicles up there, preparations of getting the equipment up there, how we were gonna move all of our equipment, our food, our water, our supplies, and eventually we made the move up to Tal Afar. At the same time, we were signed for Q-West, so everyone was looking for equipment so the commander could sign over all the base property. Luckily, I was able to take a couple weeks leave about that time.

Tal Afar

We got to Tal Afar, it was another airbase up north. It was kind of secluded from the town, the town was about two miles away from the actual base, and I picked up operations there as the executive officer. My primary objective again at Tal Afar was to conduct and mediate ground support from the city in Mosul, where we ran supplies back and forth between Mosul and Tal Afar to sustain operations out at Tal Afar. Those supplies included all classes of supply from barricades, concertina wire, food, fuel, ammunition, and everyday necessities. We had numerous convoys back and forth between Mosul and Tal Afar, and it seemed that anytime we conducted an op, a supply convoy between the two cities, we always received contact at the city of Tal Afar. While at FOB Sykes we conducted a lot of missions inside the city of Tal Afar.

    I remember distinctly one day we were gonna run about an eight-hour mission inside of the city. We had Kiowa support to conduct surveillance and overwatch from the air, and I remember receiving information that one of the Kiowas had been shot down and the mission turned into an EVAC of the Kiowa in the middle of the city. The original mission was to take four- to six-hours which in turn, turned into a four-day mission cause as soon as the Kiowa was shot down, pardon the expression, but all hell broke loose inside of the city as we tried to get to the Kiowa and get it out. Our primary mission at that time was to get the recovery crew together, including wreckers, support vehicles, and emergency ammo resupply, to go in and get the downed helicopter. I did a lot of logistics at Tal Afar, but for this mission, I led our recovery assets as part of the quick reaction force. I remember the battalion scouts cleared the area, secured the helicopter, and then we were able to move in and recover the downed aircraft.

Once we got the aircraft back on the base, the battalion planned and conducted a clearing operation in Tal Afar where our primary mission was to continually re-supply the troops that were fighting inside of the city. After two days, soldiers were running out of ammunition, water, food, and fuel, so it was our responsibility to take out a re-supply to the soldiers in the city. It was going to be a battalion resupply. I had two fuel trucks, two food trucks, a truck full of water, a truck full of ammunition, and various cargo trucks and support trucks.

The objective was to set up a static retrans, not retrans, but static tailgate re-supply inside the middle of the city where each company would come through and re-supply with all their necessary ammunition, fuel, water, food. I remember getting into the city, you could hear it crackling from gunfire throughout the Tal Afar. Initially we didn't receive any direct fire, and the re-supply seemed to be going well, but within about a half hour, when we were static in the one location doing re-supply, we began to receive sniper fire at the location. One of our support vehicles was able to identify where it was coming from, and they were able to move in and destroy the enemy. From that point on, the re-supply went without much complication. We got the battalion completely re-supplied and moved back in. After about four days it all became quiet inside of the city, and we continued with traditional operations again in Tal Afar, and continued with regular resupplies from the city in Mosul.

After traditional operations in Tal Afar for a while, our deployment was coming to an end. 1-24 Infantry Battalion of the 25th Infantry Division was going to take over our responsibilities in Tal Afar and Mosul, in particular 1-24 was going to take over Tal Afar. Our primary responsibilities at that time were to enable 1-24 to transition well, and to account for all company equipment, conduct inventories, and ensure that 1-24 was comfortable with the equipment they were receiving. We did our best to hand it over to them with little difficulties.

The hand over went over pretty smooth. They came in, they transitioned, spent a couple days getting acclimated to the area. I worked with the XO of 1-24, Jeff Smith I think his name was. He came ADVON [advanced party] so we conducted inventories of all the equipment, ammunition, vehicles. We went over vehicle services, we went over operations as far as how logistics packages were run back and forth between Mosul and Tal Afar, how refueling operations went, how operations went with other units on Tal Afar, and it all went without complication. Then it was time for us to leave. I will say, the Headquarters Company 1-24 XO was very competent, and their battalion commander, Lieutenant Colonel Kurilla, seemed like a real leader, from what I saw of him.

We waited at Tal Afar, where we were going to be flown from Tal Afar into Mosul, or excuse me, directly down into Kuwait by C130s. I remember all of us anxiously waiting for the aircraft to arrive. We got onto the aircraft, where we flew down to Kuwait, and spent about a week in Kuwait waiting for an aircraft to go from Kuwait to home. Once we got home, there were small ceremonies at the local gymnasiums, families united with their soldiers, and then everybody was released and able to go out and do what they did.

Final Thoughts

My big activity when I came home is I went to McDonalds with my friend, grabbed a couple cheeseburgers, and then established myself back in the civilian world. The entire experience of Iraq will never be forgotten, I'm sure, and after my schooling, I'm sure that I'll be able to experience it yet again. The first combat will always be what you remember most I believe.

I had gained a lot of experience as a platoon leader, company commander, and Headquarters Company XO. I received the Army Commendation Medal for my actions while serving in Iraq. Our unit didn't give very many Bronze Stars, and maybe only one Silver Star, but I'm not sure. I'm preparing to move on in my career as an infantry captain, and be a company commander, and continue my military career.

While I was in Iraq, I spent a lot of time at Tal Afar with Captain Vogt and First Sergeant Wabinga. They talked to me about the army, and changing branches from armor to infantry. I had been a Stryker platoon leader and headquarters XO, serving only with the infantry as a lieutenant. It took several months, but finally the

Department of the Army approved my branch transfer to infantry before we left Iraq, so hopefully I'll be able to return to a Stryker battalion, and command a line company in the near future.

Matthew Dabkowski

Headquarters and Alpha Company Commander

My name is Matt Dabkowski, I'm a captain in the United States Army. I was born and raised in Pittsburgh Pennsylvania, actually, just south of Pittsburgh Pennsylvania in a suburb called Apple Park. I spent the better part of my life there, until I went to West Point immediately following graduation from Apple Park Senior High. At the United States Military Academy, I studied and majored in operations research, and received my bachelors of science and a commission in the infantry in 1997.

From that assignment I went to Fort Benning, Georgia, for the Infantry Officer Basic Course, Airborne School, and Ranger School. While I was at Fort Benning, Georgia, I met my future wife Nicole Gabriel Fonsworth, now Nicole Dabkowski. My first assignment was in Vicenza, Italy, with the 1/508 Airborne Battalion Combat Team. I spent two and a half years there. Pretty momentous two and a half years. Beyond military aspects, I married Nicole and we had our first son Isaac who is now five years of age. Following this assignment we returned back to the United States, attended the Infantry Captain Career Course, again in Fort Benning, Georgia, and then moved from there to Fort Lewis, Washington, where I spent the remainder of my time until just this past year.

I moved immediately into the 5/20th Infantry, which was at the time, the Interim Battalion Combat Team, not the Stryker

Brigade Combat Team, and went through all of the initial transition into the Stryker Brigade. Literally, we started with the Marine Corps LAV [light armored vehicle] and then worked our way up to the actual fielding of the equipment. I spent almost two years in the 5/20th Infantry under Lieutenant Colonel Rob Choppa, as part of his S3 [operations] shop working under initially Major Barry Huggins, who eventually became the brigade S3, and then the brigade XO [executive officer], and then following that, for a short period of time under Captain Travis Rooms, until finally under Major Mark Landis. I guess, I spent a few weeks under Major Tom O'Steen. After that, I took command of Headquarters and Headquarters Company 5/20th on July 25th, 2003, and that is where I remained up into our deployment to Iraq in November of 2003.

I was the commander of the Headquarters and Headquarters Company for the 5/20th Infantry when we arrived in Kuwait. In that capacity, I had the standard compliment of SBCT [Stryker brigade combat team] Headquarters Company units. Specifically, a reconnaissance platoon, mortar platoon, medical platoon, the battalion sniper squad, and all the staff sections, S1 [personnel], S2 [intelligence], S3 [operations], S4 [logistics], S6 [communications], my company headquarters, and then a lot of additional attachments. In particular our CRT [combat repair team], basically our mechanics, our FFT, or field feeding team, and as well as the ICLS, our civilian contractors that worked on the Stryker vehicles and made sure that those things kept running for the entire year. There were two reporters that were also attached to the company at that time from the *Army Times*. There was Matt Cox and his cameraman.

The total unit size we deployed with from Fort Lewis, Washington, and landed with in Kuwait was 222 soldiers. I remember when we landed in Kuwait, getting off of the chartered government aircraft, which was actually relatively nice. I think it was a Northwest 747, and I actually got to sit in first class on the second level. So, I was thinking that this particular hardship deployment to Iraq was going just about right at this point in time. I remember getting off the airplane with our equipment, and the first person that I saw, which was kind of nice because it's also the first person that I saw when I returned home, was our Battalion XO at the time, and a great friend of mine Major Mark Landis. I was thinking to myself, how nice it was just to see a friendly face on the other side of that long journey, and immediately put me, and the gentlemen around me, specifically Captain Damion Mason was with me at the time if I remember, put us at ease immediately, when he showed us into a car that was waiting for us.

He got us moving and made sure that we were taken care of, and that we got billeting for our soldiers. When we left the airport, I remember thinking that it was unusual that there wasn't any kind of an armed escort, because at the time we didn't have any ammunition. Not knowing much about Kuwait in terms of its threats or what we could have expected in terms of any kind of an attack, I felt a little bit nervous because I didn't have the means really to defend myself, beyond some kind of hand-to-hand combat, which certainly would not have been my strong suit.

In any event, I remember driving down a bunch of dusty roads and we eventually came to one of the camps, Camp Udairi, which is surrounded by a series of other camps. I believe Pennsylvania, New Jersey, New York at the time. Driving onto the post, and I remember just seeing tent after tent. It was just extremely hot, when we got off the airplane, and we got out of the vehicle at Camp Udairi, it just felt like you got hit by a hair dryer or you were standing behind a jet engine. The wind was blowing about 30 miles an hour, and I'm sure that ambient temperature was somewhere north of three digits, 105 or something around there in November. I was thinking to myself, this is going to be a long year because the heat is almost unbearable.

As we entered the camp, we were immediately shuttled towards a receiving tent, and I was not surprised that the first person we talked to from the brigade was the brigade command sergeant major. Command Sergeant Major Du was just an absolute rock throughout the deployment. He always had a smile on his face, was always good for a couple of laughs, and made sure that we understood the rules, what we could and could not do, and what was expected of soldiers in the 3rd Stryker Brigade Combat Team.

During our deployment I remember it really set the right kind of tone, it was light, but it was also pretty direct in the sense that we were obviously here for business, and that while we were in Kuwait, we needed to make sure that we took all steps necessary to get our equipment, our men, and our weapons prepared. Because heading north into Iraq meant we were obviously going to be heading into harm's way, and we had to do everything we could between now and then to make sure that we were prepared. God forbid that we ever lost a soldier for lack of adequate preparation, or for not giving a hundred percent when it came to the training before we crossed the border.

As we began to settle ourselves at Camp Udairi, I remember trying to figure out what my role was going to be as the headquarters company commander in this environment. Taking command only on 25 July, and deploying in early November, we had basically two opportunities for me to take my company to the field. The first being at the Yakima Training Center, where I had the opportunity to plan and execute scout break contact live fires, and in this particular exercise, I made an effort to integrate our mortar platoon, and our medical platoon, as well as the sniper sections, so that I could exercise all the elements in my company in order to make some assessments as to their proficiency. Which I determined was fantastic at the time.

That question actually bore itself out throughout the entire deployment. The second opportunity was during the brigade FTX [field training exercise], and I remember that during the brigade FTX, I was in charge of the field trains, and I was really more of a maintainer or an additional administrator. Trying to make sure that the battalion's parts were being placed on order, and our equipment was being fixed, and making sure that our LOGPACs [logistical packages] were assembled and delivered on-time, and that the mechanics were staying on task, and all of the things that you would do in a field training environment. At the time we had our combat trains more or less co-located, so I was kind of in charge of both of those nodes.

I remember when I got to Kuwait, it seemed like a lot of the responsibilities that I had during those exercises were, more or less, beginning to be directly managed by some of the higher-ranking officers around me, as they were obviously a little bit more concerned, maybe not more concerned, but it was now a little bit more important that the equipment was actually being turned around and fixed on-time. So, there was a lot more support emphasis from my superior officers, and it seemed like many of the tasks that I would normally perform back in the rear, were now being double tapped, or even initially tapped by people who weren't necessarily executing those tasks before.

In any event, I was trying to define my role as the Headquarters Company Commander, and my boss, Lieutenant Colonel Karl Reed, the Battalion Commander, would help me define that role. Specifically, Lieutenant Colonel Reed charged me to work with the MPRI [Military Professional Resources Inc.] civilian contractors to execute quality convoy live fire exercise at Camp Udairi, and make sure that we ran all of our elements, all of our

MGS [mobile gun system] platoons, and other attachments through convoy live fires before crossing the border into Iraq. Additionally, as part of this training, we also executed pretty good close quarter marksmanship training, and were able to basically gain more familiarity, and really more confidence, with our weapon systems before we actually made our deployment into Iraq.

So, we executed the convoy live fires over a three-day period. We left the camp, it was approximately 45 different vehicles, about 300 soldiers, and myself, and we moved off into the desert to link up with our MPRI contractor friends. When we got there, we went through a standard compliment of classes, and I remember assisting the contractors and making sure that the soldiers were staying on task. We executed some basic drills and planning considerations for convoys. This was based off specific information that was gathered from sources and lessons learned down range. So, it was current and consistent with the contemporary threat of IEDs [improvised explosive devices], and other insurgent or guerrilla type tactics, as opposed to some of the more walk-step, conventional threats that would often be encountered and planned for at some of the dated combat training centers.

In any event, we proceeded on day two to do a lot of shooting, zeroing of weapons, qualification of weapons, and a lot of what I would consider non-traditional firing. Things that you normally wouldn't find state side at some of the training facilities, like firing out of the windows of vehicles on the move, and off handed firing. A lot of things that were just not typically taught, were being brought to us by these contractors who had done a lot of research, a lot of talking with soldiers that were coming back through Kuwait after their deployment in Iraq, it was very useful stuff.

Maybe a little high on the end of the risk assessment that you would except if you were in the United States, but right on the money for the stuff that we were going to be doing once we crossed the border. So, I remember feeling very comfortable with the level of expertise that those contractors provided, and I know that the soldiers got a lot out of it. Phase 3, which is really kind of like the last day, we executed our convoy live fires. There was not enough time in the timeline to execute a night live fire, even though that was kind of one of my training objectives. It turns out that no one really executed at night, because we were a little bit crunched for time.

In any event, I can remember dividing up all the vehicles and the soldiers into essentially six groups. Basically, we had one that simulated a LOGPAC scenario, one that simulated a vehicle recovery, another one that was essentially the battalion aid station, and the remainder of the staff. Not a very realistic convoy, but one that would force the soldiers that normally do not get an opportunity to lead in that kind of environment, to basically dust off their nerves and work through their lack of experience. To at least develop some proficiency, and a little bit of confidence.

After that, we ran through each one of the rifle companies with their mobile gun system sections, as well as their medical evacuation vehicle, some of their company headquarters elements, their company trains and separate elements. I thought that the exercise was very well done, we got to fire a lot of ammunition, that doesn't necessarily mean that it's good training, but it certainly makes soldiers a lot more confident with their weapons systems, cause we had plenty of jams. All in all, I think it was very worthwhile.

A lot of the soldiers that were being trained would often be forced to support training back in home station in the continental U.S., so I think that it was a very valuable experience. That the soldiers that were involved certainly felt more comfortable with their abilities, and with the ability of their equipment to function under stressful conditions. If nothing else, it kind of put some fears at ease, I think maybe, and made them realize that even though they were staff soldiers and not infantrymen, that they were capable of defeating the enemy if they came into contact.

Following this event, the battalion commander, Lieutenant Colonel Reed, then tasked me with writing the battalion's convoy SOP [standing operating procedure], which I did and presented to the officers of the battalion. It was relatively well received. It kind of gave the template for task organizing your convoy, accounting for the distribution of your weapons systems, having a primary and an alternate aid and litter team, having a primary and alternate enemy prisoner of war and search team, so more or less, organizing a convoy as a combat patrol as you would learn in Ranger School.

I think that it was good refresher for a lot of the people that received the instruction, and I think that it kind of refocused everybody that the initial convoy into Iraq was not something to be taken lightly. That contact was in fact probable, and that we needed to be prepared to evacuate our wounded, engage the enemy, return effective fire, and basically just make it to our final point in Samarra alive. So, I think that the instruction was well received. All in all, it gave me something to do, and helped me refocus myself when I was maybe kind of searching for what I should be concentrating on when we initially arrived into Kuwait and Iraq.

Now looking at some, less specific aspects of things that occurred at Camp Udairi. One of the things that I remember is that the relationship between my first sergeant, Sonny Wabinga, and myself really began to become one of a mutual understanding, [Pause] just an excellent command team. I can remember that he and I would talk for probably several hours a day, right around when we went down prior to going to rack at night and obviously in the morning. Just kind of reprioritizing ourselves, figuring out where we were going to cover down to make sure that all the tasks were being accomplished in terms of command circulation. Figuring out which platoons or which sections we were going to visit with that particular day. So, I remember thinking that the opportunity in Udairi was, especially for a brand-new commander, extremely useful time for me to really develop and build a strong, and what would turn out to be effective, relationship with my first sergeant.

Another thing that I remember feeling is, that I was really kind of taken aback by not really having the opportunity to brief all the soldiers in my company daily, certainly not daily, and not even when scheduled in mass, when it came to crossing the border. This is a function of having a lot of the soldiers in my company, nearly 300 at that time, being task organized essentially out of my tactical control for the operation, and even in terms of training. I remember feeling very frustrated because that is not necessarily the way that you're taught at the Infantry Captains Career Course, when you practice giving orders to a rifle company.

Normally you have your platoon leaders present, your FSO [fire support officer], and your RTO [radio teletype operator] there. You're able to give the order and do your rehearsals, and complete all the steps of the troop leading procedures. The military decision making process (MDMP) that seems so natural, had to be adjusted, manipulated and molded in order to get the information out. I found myself probably doing a little bit more typing and Power Pointing than I would have liked to. But it was really one of the only ways for me to at least make sure that they had seen the information, and be able to talk to them very briefly about the information that I was putting out.

There were an incredible number of administrative tasks that had to be accomplished for all the soldiers in the company. Tracking all those folks down and then just keeping track of who had not completed those tasks turned out to be practically a full-time job for myself, my first sergeant, and my company executive officer. That's basically what I did at Camp Udairi, Kuwait.

Towards the end of our time there we received an operation order for crossing the border. I remember thinking that this was the most important thing that I've written in my life. I went down to actually think about and do my courses of action, and figure out how I was going to lead a relatively large convoy, and a convoy that consisted of an incredible number of attachments all the way from Kuwait to Samarra. We spent the majority of our final days there executing rehearsals and making sure that everybody understood exactly what we were going to do if we made contact, and if we took casualties. Making sure that we understood the route.

I remember feeling not necessarily nervous, not scared I think, those are not good words to express the emotion that I was feeling at the time, probably a better word would be just a little bit anxious, because I just wanted to get started with the reason that we had deployed. The reason that I was being taken away from my family for a year wasn't to sit in Kuwait and enjoy their fine food in the mess tent, and develop battalion SOPs, it was to go to Iraq and execute the missions that were given to me to the best of my ability. I basically remember being somewhat anxious, and ready to get started.

For the ground assault convoy phase going into Iraq, the marshalling and staging of the convoy vehicles seemed like they were just endless. Tons of heavy equipment tractor trailers with drivers that were often difficult to find. I can remember vehicles that didn't have any kind of radio communication, and soldiers that didn't have any kind night vision devices, and just the cross leveling of equipment across all those vehicles. Cross leveling of personnel to make sure that all vehicles obviously had at least two soldiers. All the final preparations, and the stragglers that kind of trickled in at the final minutes in Kuwait, before we got on the road and started to move up to our final staging point at Navstar, just seemed the most stressful ten hours of my life at that point. You obviously don't want to leave without all of the stuff you need to have, or leave anyone behind.

In any event, the trip from Kuwait up to Samarra, I think was supposed to last, to the best of my recollection, like two and a half days, or maybe three days. I remember that the weather was terrible, and we made some progress, maybe a little slower than we would have liked, and it basically took us an extra day to get there. In any event, I remember throughout that particular convoy into Iraq, thinking that I was almost overly concerned. That's not a good way to put it, maybe just on edge, because every time you drove by a piece of trash on the side of the road, or every time you drove by an abandoned structure, anytime that you went underneath a bridge, and anytime that you saw someone that appeared to be suspicious, I remember thinking that we're about to hear an explosion and be in a fire fight.

The reality is that my particular serial, and my march unit had absolutely no contact. We didn't hear any contact, we didn't see any contact, and it was a relatively pleasant journey. The only real difficulties that we encountered during our trip from the Kuwaiti border up to Forward Operating Base (FOB) Pacesetter was a couple of vehicles that broke down. All of these problems were fixed in a timely manner.

The majority of that credit has got to go to Major Mark Landis, who was in the final serial with extra HETTs [heavy equipment and truck transport] and extra mechanics. He basically had the best four days of his life, as he continued to police up all the vehicles that fell by the wayside, as they found a way to get all of our stuff from the Kuwaiti border up to Samarra. I don't think that our problems were exceptional or uncommon. I think they were the norm, but I think that the unit really did an exceptional job getting all of our stuff there, and keeping all of our soldiers accounted for, and getting to where we needed to be. Which was FOB Pacesetter.

There is one anecdotal note here about the convoy into Iraq, I remember thinking, because at the time I was the Headquarters Company commander, and I was in what looked like a vehicle out of Beyond the Thunder-Dome or Mad Max. I mean it was a HMMWV that had a bunch of external machine gun mounts attached to it, and all kinds of special modifications, and we didn't have any doors on it. It basically was not the prettiest thing on the road, but I remember thinking as we began to move up the road, maybe several hours into the trip, how much nicer it actually would have to been to have been in a Stryker [Small exhalation of breath, laugh] for the extra protection and amenities that that vehicle offers. Typically, in a herd of gazelle you don't want to be the lamest looking piece of prey out there, or else the lion is going to target in on you and take you for a meal. I remember feeling like I was the weakest gazelle in that particular herd in that HMMWV. In any event, it was nice when I finally got a Stryker.

Samarra

I remember arriving into FOB Pacesetter, we went down what seemed like an endless road to the entrance of the FOB, and when we got there, we were greeted by Sergeant Major Overbey, who was our operations sergeant major at the time, now retired. He immediately grabbed hold of the convoy, made us feel at home, took us directly to where we needed to be. He put us into the motor pool and we began to realize that life at FOB Pacesetter in Iraq was not going to be half the pleasurable living experience that we had in Kuwait.

The tentage had just recently been set up. The conditions were terrible. They were nothing but port-a-Johns. There was no mess hall facility, we had to use our own field feeding teams. There was no maintenance facility, we had to set up our maintenance tents. There were absolutely no soldier comforts like phones to call home, or any kind of computers to check our e-mail, no TVs to watch a movie during your down time, or anything like that. Not even any showers, with the exception of one on the far side of camp. You basically needed a vehicle to go to it, to take a freezing cold shower. I mean it was Spartan, the living conditions were terrible to put it bluntly and I remember thinking this ought to make it easy to focus on our job because there's really nothing else here to distract us.

Again, when we got to FOB Pacesetter, I was just trying to figure out what my role, again as the Headquarters Company commander, was going to be. I can remember during the first battalion operations order that I was essentially given no instructions whatsoever. I mean there were no instructions given in the written order, there were no instructions given essentially verbally. All that could be intuited from the order from my perspective, was that there were some administrative tasks for the soldiers that were on my unit-manning roster (UMR) to perform, and it was my job to track those tasks and make it happen. It got as bad as during the rehearsal for the first operation that we were going to do in Samarra, that I actually didn't have one word to say. There was no prompting, there was nothing on the combined arms rehearsal script that would basically have me speak.

So, I remember feeling extremely frustrated, basically useless for lack of a better way of putting it. Really kind of struggling with what the next year was going to look like as the Headquarters Company Commander, and that I had better figure it out or else it was going to be a long 365 days. Yeah, at this point I remember going to the battalion XO, and talking with him about the situation, and talking with the battalion commander about my frustration. In any event, again I talked to battalion commander about my frustration, and I was eventually given charge of the combat trains command post, which was a much better billet in my eyes at the time, because it meant I actually got to leave the FOB. I got to go forward to the tactical assembly area and would at least be able to manage parameter security and help lead and take charge of combat recovery, as well as any medical evacuation situations that may arise.

So, in this particular capacity, I began to plan for our initial operations in Samarra, which I remember as a series of direct-action raids on some targets in the town. During the combined arms rehearsal for our first operation, there was a sudden scattering of personnel, and the battalion commander was eventually intercepted, and then came back into the combined arms rehearsal, and basically informed us that a vehicle from 1-14 Cavalry, who was our Reconnaissance Surveillance and Target Acquisition (RSTA) squadron, had been struck by an IED [improvised explosive device] outside of Samarra. They were conducting an initial area reconnaissance and the vehicle was essentially destroyed and it was gonna have to be recovered.

I looked at Captain Damion Mason and said, "Hey Damion, will you guys be ready to go" and Damion said "Sure," they'd do whatever we need to do. Then the battalion commander had to leave to go talk to the brigade commander about the course of action to recover that vehicle. In any event, the situation eventually was resolved and just prior to us conducting our initial combat operations, everybody got the word that Saddam Hussein had been captured, and we were delayed a day or two.

At that point in time, I was somewhat intrigued as to what this would mean in terms of our role in Iraq during our year there, and how this would change the way that the U.S. was asserting itself in that area. Obviously, what the trickle-down impact would be on the soldiers under my command. I was just basically waiting for some information from my higher, and of course they had no idea either. No one really knew what the impact of that was going to be, and the reality is, there was very little impact at all. There were probably some changes in the message threads that were being distributed by the PSYOPS [psychological operations]. There were some adjustments to our standard themes, and what we were supposed to be saying to the Iraqi population, but in reality, there was, I think, probably very little impact on how we conducted ourselves.

We immediately went out with the 4th Infantry Division and conducted raids in Samarra. We changed headquarters several times, in Samarra we were part of the 4th Infantry Division. In any event, I remember thinking that Saddam's capture was incredibly good news, but that I didn't know what it meant. Only time would tell whether there would be any impact. I remember thinking that it would be real nice to go home right now, that maybe they'll send us home, but obviously understanding that that wasn't going to happen.

On the initial assault into Samarra, I was in charge of the combat trains and we were essentially trailing the battalion. The battalion moved out, and I remember the weather was not very good, to the point it was literally almost treacherous. The clay sandy loam type roads of the area to the to the east of Samarra, was essentially as if you were driving on ice, and this is in an eight-wheel drive vehicle with an inch and a quarter deep tread. The better part of that first night I spent with our combat recovery guys, pulling one vehicle after another using winches, and HEMMT wreckers, and every other possible ingenious idea that they had to pull Strykers out of the mud.

In terms of the sights and sounds of this particular evening there were quite a few explosions, not so much on the gunfire side, it was basically a lot of ballistic and explosive breaching of the of the targets inside of Samarra, by elements of our Bravo and Charlie Companies, which were to our immediate front during a lot of the recovery. I remember hearing the passing of fixed wing aircraft over my position, and I remember that there was a lot of chatter over the battalion command net as well as the admin and logistics (A&L) net for recovering down vehicles, but it really didn't seem as if there was much in the way of significant activity. Although, we were apparently making significant progress.

I think it was probably a feeling out operation, really for the battalion. I mean it was the first one that we had conducted in Iraq. It was the first combat operation for probably 95% of the battalion if not more than that. Tensions were high, but confident execution in a lot of ways. If we had sat back at the end of our deployment in Iraq and looked back at that first operation, probably a lot of botched execution, and some really foolhardy tactics, techniques and procedures (TTPs) that were executed. But in any event, successful from the sense that we didn't lose any soldiers, and all in all, it wasn't a bad operation. Following the nights festivities, the battalion began to move itself towards a tactical assembly area (TAA), which at the time was called TAA Warhorse.

TAA Warhorse was essentially a burned-out area, probably a half mile in diameter, if it was that big, almost a perfect circle that had been constructed by the 1-14th Cavalry Squadron. That was going to be used as our staging area for additional strikes into Samarra over the course of the next couple of days. At least that was the information we had at the beginning of the operation, that was what we believed would be our home, before we made it back to the illustrious and deluxe accommodations of FOB Pacesetter, that's what the soldiers had planned for. That's how much they had packed in terms of extra gear, sundry items, and their basic load of the stuff that was required, and not a lot else.

In any event, we took quite a while that evening trying to find this place. It was basically a road or a field that had been grated by the attached heavy engineers, and it was very difficult to find when we finally straggled into this location that evening. I'm sure that our security wasn't the best, because soldiers were tired, and there was really a lack of structure to the base. Kind of reminded me what you might remember from a Ranger School patrol base before daylight, when you could adjust the parameter. We trickled in there and basically got as much sleep as we could, while maintaining adequate security and preparing to get more information about follow on operations.

During our two days, which turned into I believe close to a three week stay, in TAA Warhorse, the battalion conducted a series of company level raids, or what we were calling armed reconnaissance at the time, into Samarra to develop the situation, engage local population, and react to contact if required. I remember that things were moving at a reasonable pace, but it didn't seem like anything significant was happening. There are two significant events though that obviously occurred.

One of them was Bravo Company was executing an armed reconnaissance in Samarra, and had moved into, not really an open-air market, but a large courtyard type area on the eastern, northeastern side of Samarra where they were ambushed. When they entered this area, it basically turned into a coordinated ambush, and the soldiers from Bravo Company obviously understand all the particulars a lot better than I do, but it was the first contact that had been made by the entire brigade in Iraq, and the first contact that any Strykers had ever been involved in. During this action, Captain Damion Mason and First Lieutenant Robert McChrystal, Sniper Davis, and the soldiers of Battle Company did a fantastic job putting down the enemy that attempted to inflict harm on them. Battle did it in a manner that was precise, and literally verified, I think on the spot, that the Stryker concept was one that was well conceived, and the soldiers that were charged to prove that, were trained, and executed very well, and in a manner that made the entire brigade extremely proud.

I can remember being in the tactical operations center (TOC) at TAA Warhorse talking, I think it was with the battalion XO or maybe it was Captain Bob Leseman at the time, when those radio calls started to come in. Damion coming over the radio, "In contact, out." As the situation developed, getting his battle damage assessment (BDA) coming in, "Drop two more, took two RPGs, drop three more enemy," etc. etc. I think that one of the things that we realized during this particular contact, me listening to the radio, and things that came out later in the after-action report, was that the enemy was not really willing to leave its dead behind, this situation played itself out time and time again.

Getting an enemy body is difficult, you got a better shot of making contact and killing some enemy than you do of actually recovering one of their bodies. They made a lot of effort to pull their wounded and their dead off the battlefield, and they did it well enough that we had no body in hand to show for the contact that was made in Samarra. Not that we're in the business of policing up enemy dead, but it was just a realization that if you shot some man and you killed him, you could expect maybe a slightly more sustained contact as they tried to recover their wounded and dead.

During this time, another situation that occurred, and I believe this was actually on the night of the first operation, although I really don't remember, was when Attack Company flipped a Stryker into an irrigation canal. The vehicle flipped completely over and was covered in water, the only thing that was showing was the very bottom of the vehicle and half of its tires. I remember, as we were moving out with the recovery team, just being amazed that nobody had lost their life, or was really even wounded in this particular roll over. About two weeks prior to this, I believe it was Bravo Company from 1-23 Infantry Battalion, had a Stryker roll into a similar irrigation canal, and I believe two or three soldiers drowned. I remember thinking that it was just an absolute miracle that God had been on our side on this one, because we lost nobody.

Staff Sergeant Lucas, who was one of our chief recovery guys at the time, a mechanic, was amazing. I was just amazed at his ability to pull this vehicle out of this ditch. He used two HEMMT wreckers, had both winches working, and was probably using something that is not recommended in any kind of a technical manual (TM) for fear of snapping cables. But he managed to right the Stryker in the canal, and eventually pull it out of about a ten-foot canal with steep banks. I was absolutely amazed that he was able to accomplish that.

I also remember hearing for the first time, that there was some really heroic actions that took place on the scene. There were two soldiers in particular, Staff Sergeant Rowes and at the time Corporal Moore from Attack Company, that were in a few vehicles to the rear of the vehicle that flipped in the canal. When they saw the vehicle flip into the canal they immediately hopped out of their vehicle, in full gear and ran, then jumped into the rushing canal, and somehow managed to open the back of the vehicle. They then waded inside the vehicle and essentially saved the lives of all the men inside, as they got the door open, pulled the guys out of the driver seat, and cleared all of the men out of a Stryker that was completely blacked out and full of water in the middle of the night.

I remember that was my first time, that I realized that these ordinary men that we trained with day-in and day-out back in Fort Lewis, were capable of really extraordinary things under stressful circumstances. In this particular instance, saving the lives of one of your comrades at the risk of your own life, is probably the most incredible thing you can ever do as a soldier. For that particular action they were recommended for the Soldiers Medal, and unfortunately, that award was still pending when I left the unit, so I'm not sure if they'll get the recognition that they deserve.

After having been in the TAA for a few weeks, and after this rollover incident occurred, I can remember that there started to be some rumors that one of the rifle company commanders, Eric Bachelor, was going to be counseled. A series of events transpired over the course of about a 24-hour period unbeknownst to me, and the next thing that I knew, I was essentially back at FOB Pacesetter talking with our brigade commander, Colonel Mike Rounds, and he was telling me that I was going to take command of Attack Company.

I remember at the time, I told him that I would do the best that I can, and that I was ready to lead those men, and it was my honor to do so, and that he had given me his full confidence. I also remember thinking that it was kind of a bittersweet moment, because the company that I had taken command of, Headquarters, and I thought that I had led relatively well up until that point in time, and the company that I had told their families I'm going to bring these men back, was not the company I was going to return with. So, there was a bitter aspect to that event.

I had to leave First Sergeant Sonny Wabinga, the Scout Platoon Leader John Hicks, all the other guys, the platoon leaders, the platoon sergeants, the soldiers that you work with every day. You develop strong relationships in training, and obviously ten-fold in combat. You learn about where they're from, and what their fears are, who their girlfriend is, what the name of their dog was when they were four, and anything else you can say to pass the time. By going to Attack Company, I was no longer going to be with these guys, and it was a kind of stark realization that that was unfortunate.

On the other hand, I remember thinking this was just an incredible opportunity for me professionally, and it was something that really gave me a cause to smile, in the sense that I was finally going to get a chance to lead a rifle company in combat. I don't think that any infantry captain would be telling the truth if they said that they did not want to lead a rifle company at some point in time. Whether it was as a second company, if they took a Headquarters first, or whether it was their first company, I mean that is what you train for, that is the doctrine that you study, that is the buildup, and is supposed to be the climax essentially of your military career.

Every battalion XO or S3 that you talk to would confirm that that's the best job of their lives, and in many ways a lot of battalion commanders would tell you that they wish they were commanding rifle companies again, because it's a very rewarding experience. I remember feeling thankful that I was going to have the opportunity to do this. I also remember feeling bad for Captain Bachelor, and I hoped at the time, that there would be no hard feelings between he and I, because I had no idea that this was going to happen, and I told him as much. From where I sat at the time, besides a couple of missteps, but everyone has missteps, I wasn't aware that maybe he was in that kind of predicament, that he might be removed from command. So, in any event, I moved from commanding the Headquarters Company and I was put in charge of Alpha Company.

In the middle of TAA Warhorse on a cold, muddy morning on the 25th of December 2003, I remember having two change of command ceremonies in about 15 minutes, where the only distinguished guest was my battalion commander and obviously my outgoing company first sergeant, Sonny Wabinga, and my incoming company first sergeant from attack company Greg Littinger, who turned out to be just as capable and just as fantastic as Sonny had been. The moment was almost surreal.

Toby Vogt, I didn't know Toby all that well, he had just come into the battalion about three weeks before we deployed. He'd just returned from Operation Enduring Freedom with Special Operations Command, deployed ahead of the battalion with the Torch party to Kuwait, and was the battalion TAC OIC [tactical group officer in charge] for the first month with Lieutenant Colonel Reed. In any event, at dawn I was handing over the Headquarters Company guidon to Lieutenant Colonel Reed and minutes later receiving the Alpha Company guidon from Lieutenant Colonel Reed. No change of command inventories or expectations from the chain of command, simply a hand over of the guidons and planning for the next operation in Samarra.

Approximately five hours after taking command of Attack Company I got to lead my first combat operation into Samarra with my new company. I remember when I issued them the operations order for this particular action that it literally reminded me of a Ranger School patrol. Beyond just the names of folks, and knowing who's who in terms of their face, and that only for the senior leadership within the company, I was basically giving an operations order to a group of strangers. It really reminded me to focus on the basics, to be specific about my instructions. To be clear when it came to explaining what I meant by certain language, or what I wanted first platoon to do, so that second platoon can do this. Really nesting my efforts in focusing on just the art of writing an operations order, and more importantly issuing that operations order and doing it in a time constrained environment, when the chips are really down and there are very real consequences for a poor plan. In any event, I think it kind of set the tone for the company, that I was going to be someone who focused on planning, thought it was important, and that I would expect the same from them.

We embarked on our first armed reconnaissance of Samarra with me as their company commander at approximately ten o'clock that morning. I remember going into Samarra as we penetrated the outermost row of buildings into that town, just thinking wow, this is probably one of the greatest moments of my life, being out here, doing a real rifle company mission in a combat environment, with a group of men that are completely professional and capable of performing their jobs. Thinking this is about as good as it gets for somebody that does this kind of stuff for a living.

Then I also remember thinking wow, I really don't know what these guys strengths and weaknesses are, what the specific company SOPs are going to be if we make contact. Thinking that it's probably best to keep my eyes open, keep my instructions short, and do almost as much observing as leading here, because I need to try to figure out the organization, in addition to conducting this operation. We conducted the operation, made no contact, found absolutely nothing, but it was a good opportunity for me to get on the ground with my new platoon leaders and platoon sergeants, and just try to feel out the organization and see what our strengths and weaknesses might be.

Shortly after this first operation, the battalion gave me my first mission as the battalion main effort. The name of the operation was Operation Fort Apache, and basically the crux or the central concept of this mission was that I would take Attack Company into Samarra, pick a piece of defensible terrain in the middle of the square where Bravo Company had taken sustained contact, and reinforce the structure in about a ten-hour period. I would more or less sit like cheese in a mousetrap throughout the evening with my guys, in the hopes that we would be attacked.

Counting on a good engagement area, good sets of engagement criteria, and proper direct and indirect fire planning to eliminate the threat. Once again, this was an operation that bore no fruit with respect to making contact, but it was an operation again that allowed me to learn the people that were working for me, and kind of gave us a sense of accomplishment, because it was the first time that the company had been selected to be the main effort for the battalion, and it kind of renewed their sense of pride because Attack

Company was the first company to be fielded with Strykers during training when they were led by Captain Brandon Tegtmeier.

Tegtmeier was, I would say, widely regarded as probably like the go to company commander in the brigade while he had been in charge of the company, and it was kind of nice, I think, for the guys to see that we haven't been forgotten. We're still going to get the good missions, like the other guys, we can still accomplish them, and perform our job as well as anybody else. So, it was an operation with limited tactical success in terms of KIA [killed in action], or finding caches, or anything like that, but certainly one with a lot of psychological impact, and morale boosting for the soldiers in the company.

I guess it was on or about December 28th, 2003, when the battalion finally collapsed TAA Warhorse and moved back to FOB Pacesetter. We spent approximately one week back at FOB Pacesetter after returning from TAA Warhorse, although it was renamed TAA Regulars before we left. Basically, we were conducting sustained operations as a battalion, where we were assigned a battalion sector that was divvied up into company sized sectors, and we were responsible for patrolling those sectors, maintaining a quick reaction force (QRF), and actioning any kind of targets should they come down for the better part of a week.

Significant action during this week, was one day we were scheduled to go out on a normal patrol, when prior to leaving the FOB gate, we received information over the battalion command net that they had acquired a point of origin for a mortar or rocket south of FOB Pacesetter. More or less in the middle of an agrarian area. No real dense urban structure to it, and that they wanted us to go investigate the site. Because we were prepared, our response time was immediate. We immediately left the gate and did a successful job of navigating to the spot.

When we arrived on the site, there was a white pickup truck that immediately began to flee the area. My third platoon leader, Kevin Hutchenson, with his platoon sergeant, Sergeant First Class Ward, began to pursue the white vehicle. We followed that vehicle back to a nice, for the area I guess, a nice residence, and immediately began to have success in our search of that residence. We found multiple machine guns, RPGs, RPG rounds, and eventually a 60-millimeter mortar tube with bi-pod, sighting element, and various other propaganda and military paraphernalia.

I think that this particular chance operation was where we eventually got to integrate all aspects of the company, as we expanded our search, safeguarded the area, and took detainees. This was probably the operation where the company turned the corner, because it was the first score that the company had on a cache, it was the first detainees that the company took, and it was the first time that I really got to demonstrate that I had some proficiency in leading an infantry company. That I understood tactics, that I was able to make split second decisions.

It worked in reverse as well, as I was able to see my squad leaders and above within all the platoons and sections of the company. Verifying that they were just as capable as I in performing their jobs, and it was kind of like a great sense of calm, that kind of passed over me, as I realized that these guys are ready to really take the fight to the enemy. A realization that we're going to basically execute the remainder of this tour in the manner consistent with the excellence of the soldiers that are in the company. That is more or less our time in Samarra from my perspective as the Headquarters and Attack Company Commander.

The only other note that I'll have from Samarra is that during this time, we did not get to talk to our families. I remember the first time I talked to my family in a month was on Christmas day out at TAA Warhorse. The battalion commander lined us up and gave all the soldiers a short call. I was able to use the battalion satellite phone to call my wife. Nicole, she picked up the phone, and we were given basically two minutes to talk, no more no less, because there were obviously hundreds of soldiers that had to use the same line. I remember just being so happy to just hear her voice, and hear the voice of my children, I was elated that I had taken command of a rifle company, that everybody was still alive, and that it was the birth of our Lord.

I remember feeling also, like an incredible sense of, like, not melancholy, but an incredible sense of just incompleteness, not being with my family during the holiday season. My entire world is my family and the army, not having my family around me during the holiday season kind of hit me pretty hard, so it was great to talk to her, it was great to talk to the kids on Christmas day, but it was also a pretty stark reminder that we had a lot of work to do before I'd be back with them permanently, and didn't have to rely on a satellite connection in order for me to just see how they were doing. The other bright spot of Christmas 2003, is the food, the food was fantastic for Christmas day dinner. The cooks really outdid themselves. I mean we had some fantastic chow and there was plenty of it. I remember stuffing myself to the gills, drinking eggnog, and the phone call and meal just really ended up brightening everybody's spirits.

Qayyarah

Moving on to northern Iraq, it started again with the ground assault convoy. I remember again, planning the convoy operation up to the Qayyarah area, and thinking to myself, how nice this was to actually have a relatively standard task organization. There were basically two serials, I had one, and my company XO had the other. I was going to lead, and he was going to follow, he was going to have the maintenance assets, I had rifle platoons to distribute, as lead and rear echelon elements, and an MGS platoon to subdivide as required with their TOW missile [tube launched optically tracked wire guided missile] capability, and a mortar section to help pick up the slack at the company headquarters. I just remember thinking how nice it was to have a relatively typical task organization for this convoy up to the Qayyarah area instead of the non-standard Headquarters Company monstrosity that I had brought to Samarra.

Anyways, so the ground assault convoy into northern Iraq was planned in much the same manner that the ground assault convoy up to Samarra was planned. Taking count of actions on contact, actions on down vehicle, distribution of all the appropriate strip maps, the use of OPSKEDs [operational schedule], where all the treatment facilities were along the way, and what all the planned stops were going to be. Everybody had a good idea of what that operation was going to look like, the battalion was beginning to come into its own with respect to conducting combined arms rehearsals, and publishing orders, and we were wasting less time kind of spinning our wheels on things that were now generally kind of understood. Battalion and company SOPs were solidifying, and we were beginning to develop some TTPs, which was also good to see, and saved a lot of time. So, in any event, we made our trip up to, at the time it was called Q-West, but it eventually became FOB Regulars, Qayyarah West airfield, in much the same way that we made our trip to Samarra. No contact, at least from my element, no contact, relatively smooth sailing. Probably the biggest thing was drivers and TCs [truck commander] getting tired since now basically driving in Stryker became a very routine.

Rotation exercise, where we could put different guys in the hatches. We stayed a lot fresher than we were, say in a HMMWV, where you only had four guys, and everybody's either pulling security, or navagatin, or drivin. So, I remember that convoy seemed much easier, and I also remember how much easier it seemed, because of the distribution or the density of FBCB2 [Force XXI Battle Command Brigade and Below] systems within the unit. An FBCB2 is basically a military GPS that tracks you and all your elements.

When I was in Headquarters Company, we had a lot of attachments that did not have the FBCB2 capability, and as a rifle company commander, everybody did, so it was just a matter of following the line, and having situational awareness about your own elements, and the elements to your forward and rear. It was as simple as looking at a computer screen that told you exactly where everybody was. So, the idea of command and control was simplified greatly by the advent of the technology known as the FBCB2, and I finally had a chance to live it as we made this assault into northern Iraq.

We arrived at Qayyarah West airfield, I remember that once again, we were met at the main entrance, this time it was not by Sergeant Major Overbey, it was by Sergeant First Class Green in a pickup truck, and we followed him around the outer parameter of this monster, I mean it was a very big base. It housed an entire brigade of the 101st airborne division, and another brigade of 101st aviation, and a lot of contractors and Iraqis, but we kind of flowed into a holding area and made our way to the chow hall.

I remember the look on the soldiers faces when we went into that chow hall, it was something that would be difficult to forget, because guys saw that life was going to be way better than it was for the past month when we were eating out of tents and basically just kinda gettin the scraps of what was really available with respect to the food service in Iraq. The 101st had done a way better job than the 4th Infantry Division, as far as quality of life. I mean this was a first-class operation with full-service lines, and choices for the soldiers, and ice cream stands, and I mean it was just the best thing we had seen in quite a while. So, in any event, we kinda grabbed ourselves some food, and I eventually made my way down to a battalion meeting.

Major Mark Landis, I believe he'd moved ahead on this particular operation to talk with the brigade staff that we were going to be relieving, and get an appreciation for what the mission was going to be up here at Q-West. I think that obviously he saw the full support of this brigade, it was a great brigade, commanded by Colonel Hodges, who we had the opportunity to work for a couple of weeks when I first arrived at Fort Lewis. So, we got the full support of the 101st guys, and I found out, I don't believe it was this evening, but a couple of nights later, that basically our Charlie Company, Captain Eric Beaty and First Sergeant Jim Mapes, were going to be sliding over to the task organization for 1-14 Cavalry and moving out to a town much further to the west called Tal Afar. Then the remainder of the battalion was going to receive the attachment of Captain Eric McCallister and Charlie 1-14 Cavalry the "Crazy

Horse" troop, wait, that task organization may have taken place before we left Pacesetter?

Hammam al Alil

Either way, my company, Attack Company, was going to be assigned to our own company operating base, or company combat outpost, that was dubbed an objective even though it was more or less a forward firebase in a small town called Hammam al Alil. Hammam al Alil was approximately thirty kilometers as crows fly from Qayyarah West airfield. I remember at the time, it was briefed that I was not going to be the battalion main effort. The main effort was going to be Captain Damien Mason, with his Bravo Company at Qayyarah West airfield, because Colonel Reed wanted to develop the situation around his battalion FOB. That seemed a little off to me, because I remember being briefed that kind of the hub of insurgent activity in our region, was more or less based out of Hammam al Alil and the surrounding area. That my mission would be more of a direct-action combat-oriented nature, which was fine by me, because it was again a good opportunity as a new company commander to demonstrate proficiency, and just perform all the duties that I've been trained for since I've been in the service.

So, in any event, I immediately made contact with the commander from the "No Slack" battalion of the 101st. It was the "Cobra" Company of the battalion, the exact battalion escapes me, but in any event their motto was No Slack. Cobra company was commanded by a guy named Captain Matt Cohns. I had the opportunity to travel up to Hammam al Alil and meet with him, and do a good left seat, right seat ride. He was extremely knowledgeable, and in the area of socio-political issues, he had an extremely firm grasp of the enemy situation. He was an expert in every regard, on all the things that were going on in his area of operations, and he equipped me with all that information, and all the products that were required to be successful, to hit the ground running. So, I really began to make an impact right away.

So, I had an extremely favorable experience during RIP TOA [relief in place/transfer of authority], and something that kind of solidified in our own minds that this was not necessarily going to be the same fight that we had in Samarra. At least not for Attack Company. During our right seat ride portion of our RIP TOA with the Cobra Company, we were at the propane plant, there's a large propane distribution plant that was approximately three kilometers, I would say, away from the actual company combat outpost, which was based at an old agricultural college. It used to be a satellite of the University of Mosul, but we knew it as OBJ [objective] Agee.

So anyways, about three kilometers away from OBJ Agees, we're at the propane plant, and there was a very loud explosion. I see Captain Cohns kind of furrow his brow, and kind of move to his RTO. He begins to get information that one of his patrols has been hit by an IED, so we immediately respond from the propane plant, and this time it was nice for Captain Cohns, because he got to respond with more than just anti-tank HMMWVs, I mean he was actually with a full complement of Strykers, and an additional two platoons of combat power.

We moved to the scene of the explosion, which was on a route that we dubbed ASR [alternate supply route] Pittsburgh, and I believe that they had called it Dallas, but the name of it doesn't matter. So basically, what had happened was one of his patrols was out investigating a site that they thought, from their thermal sights the evening before, could have been an area where the enemy might have been digging an IED. The explosion basically confirmed it. I mean it was a very large explosion, probably a 155-millimeter projectile right next to the road, that was detonated within literally twenty meters of his soldiers when they were on the ground. By the grace of God alone, none of the soldiers were injured from the 101st, which was wonderful because they were about to redeploy.

And so, in any event we immediately assisted Cobra Company with searching all the houses within a kilometer, essentially a kilometer because it was a very agrarian area around the actual detonation site. I got to observe Captain Cohns firsthand conducting tactical questioning of Iraqis that would have been in the vicinity of an IED strike. Got to see a lot of the TTPs that his soldiers used, and just got to realize that the area that we were in, just like another area of Iraq, should never be taken for granted. That the threat was very real, and that we had to approach this business with the very serious nature that it requires. So, in any event, it was a good miss in the sense that nobody was hurt, and it gave us the opportunity to kind of see these guys in action, and really learn the area and the tools that they had been employing in what we eventually called AO [area of operations] Rose.

So, our RIP TOA with the Cobra Company basically occurred over a two-and-a-half-day period. We initially took the FOB security, which more or less consumed one of my platoons, then transitioned into utilizing another platoon for the patrols that occurred in the immediate vicinity of the base itself, and then another one of the platoons basically moved into a QRF mode. Once we had finally assumed that final part, Captain Cohns himself was delivered back to FOB Q-West, so that he could prepare his men, weapons, and equipment for redeployment back to the United States, and well-deserved break after a great job.

So, now Attack Company was where we would be for the majority of the remainder of our time in Iraq, which was OBJ Agees, more specifically Hammam al Alil, which was basically a town of thirty to forty thousand people. It was the seat of the Hammam al Alil district, which is one of the major districts of Mosul, just to the south of the city. It was complete with its own mayor and city council, and series of police stations and satellite villages like Salahia to its south, Gabarabet to its north, Ubware to its west, and eventually moving into the Assura district to its south.

One thing that's notable, is the area that my company took control of, was the area of operations for all of the No Slack battalion. So, a company of 177 infantrymen took control of literally an area of operations that was covered by a 650-man battalion from the 101st airborne division. They were big shoes to fill, it was a great unit that we were backfilling. But I thought, with our obviously much superior mobility, superior fire power, soldiers of just the same quality or better, although we were one quarter the number, that we could at least do a sufficient job of maintaining our presence within the area of operations, and striking with plenty of combat power when required.

OK, so in any event, Attack Company settled down into AO Rose in the middle of January 2004. AO Rose was about a seven hundred square kilometer area to the north of Qayyarah West airfield. Adjacent units, we obviously had Bravo Company and the rest of the battalion to my south, and then to the north of my area we had 1-23 Infantry, which was operating out of the western side and southwest side of Mosul. Then to my east, basically on the other side of the Tigris River, on the eastern side of the Tigris River, that area was more or less unassigned. I believe it was the specific responsibility of 1-23 Infantry, but was far enough to the south that they had limited presence in that area. Then to my significant west would have been Charlie 1-14 Cavalry the Crazy Horse Troop, kind of operating in a large show of force in the western side of the battalions AO.

Anyways AO Rose, again about 700 square kilometers. Some of the key terrain that we had to be concerned with in our area of operations was a large cement plant, roughly to the northwest of OBJ Agee in a little village called Alaraige, that almost seemed like part of Hammam al Alil. That cement plant was critical from the standpoint that it was going to provide a lot of the construction materials required to rebuild Mosul, and a lot of northern Iraq following the war.

Secondly, there was a fuel distribution and propane plant, which I had mentioned, that was approximately three kilometers to our northwest. That plant was actually located in Hammam al Alil, and was one of the largest propane distribution points in all of northern Iraq. We had a products pipeline that ran more or less through Hammam al Alil. That pipeline was active or inactive at various points during our deployment, and was supposed to be used to transport various types of liquid fuel across the country. There was a large sulfur plant to my south approximately 15 kilometers, in a little town called Mishrak. That particular site had been the target of some sabotage attempts during the 101st stay, specifically, 107-millimeter rocket attacks on that location.

As far as the towns were concerned, Hammam al Alil again was the district seat, and it was the large town where I was located. To my south approximately 20 kilometers was the city of Ashira and that was the district seat for the Ashira district. Basically, the Hammam al Alil and the Ashira districts kind of made up a large portion of my AO. Again, you had the town of Gabarabet that was an Ansar al Islam stronghold, and also the hometown of Mammad Ka'lat Shekara, later known as Abutalhul. 1-24 Infantry eventually captured him in Mosul. We also had Abuer village, which was a small village located to the south of the battalion's northern most retrans site, in the vicinity of the Flagstaff and Camp intersection.

As far as the major routes in my zone again, we had Route Tampa that was Highway 1. It ran from Qayyarah all the way up to Mosul. We had Route Atlanta, which was the Mosul Qayyarah highway, so basically the route that more or less paralleled the Tigris River on the eastern border of my AO. Then Route Flagstaff, which was the horizontal movement corridor that connected Tampa to Atlanta. Basically, the endpoint of that route was at OBJ Agees, in the vicinity of the Tigris River and Hammam al Alil.

As far as security forces or things that were key terrain with respect to security forces in my AO, we had the NIRTC, the Northern Iraqi Regional Training Center, which was located more or less in my immediate FOB area, and was serving as a major focus of the 101st Airborne Division, certainly the brigade that was stationed down in Qayyarah West. It was a training facility for ICDC [Iraqi Civil Defense Corps] officers and soldiers as they were attempting to stand back up the host nation security forces following the war. So, it was a site that was seen as being critical by General Petraeus and the rest of the 101st Airborne Division, and eventually by 3rd Brigade and Task Force Olympia.

As far as the political composition of the AO, again basically two sub districts being controlled by two separate city councils and municipality departments, etcetera, etcetera. Again, in Hammam al Alil, we had very ethnically diverse groups of people that were living in that area. Predominantly Sunni, but a lot of different tribes within the area, and tribes that didn't necessarily get along real well with each other. The most prominent was the Aiwowi tribe of the Algibori Clan. They were basically the folks that held the majority of the political power in the area.

The district itself consisted of 65 villages, and had roughly fifty sheikhs, about the same number of mukhtars, and all told, about 62,000 people. The southern district of the AO, the Ashira district, at that time, was controlled by a mayor that more or less embraced the 101st Airborne Division when they arrived. That gentleman was eventually, more or less, thrown out of office and replaced. But in any event, we had nearly seventy villages and roughly fifty to sixty sheikhs and mukhtars, much like the Hammam al Alil district with its slightly smaller population of about 47,000.

As far as host nation security forces in our AO, again we had the 5th ICDC Battalion. They had two companies that were located in my AO. The one was the Hammam al Alil ICDC Company, that was located in the NIRTC compound. Then there was the Mishrak ICDC Company that was located basically at the Sulphur plant. As far as police were concerned, Hammam al Alil obviously had a large police force. They were actually the district headquarters, and they basically controlled all the operations in my AO plus the Qayyarah area, so a relatively large span of control. And then there were basically four satellite police stations, again there was one in Hammam al Alil, not the district headquarters, there was eventually one in Gabarabet, and then there was one out at the Mosul Archen highway, one at the Shahadhimaq station, and then we also had the Ashira station.

As far as facility protection service, I think there were up to a thousand of those folks that were supposed to be workin at my AO. Basically, guarding the critical infrastructures that I mentioned before. But they were more or less a non-entity and didn't do much in the way of actually securing anything. Basically, they just drew a paycheck.

Now, as far as what our immediate tasks were going to be at FOB Agees, of course we had to secure ourselves within the actual compound. We were more or less running two civil-military operations centers in Hammam al Alil and one in Ashira. Both of these places, we had weekly meetings and spent time there. In Hammam al Alil it was basically Monday, between nine and noon, and then in Ashira, we spent between nine and noon on Wednesdays. We had to attend city council meetings, they were basically concurrent with our manning of the CMOCs [civil-military operations center], basically from ten o'clock in the morning until complete.

We had to basically maintain route clearance and TCP [traffic control point] operations, and force protection patrols for the agricultural college, OBJ Agees, in the form of counter-mortar OPs [observation post] and setting up ambushes. We executed village engagements in terms of just associating with the local populace, trying to hear what their concerns were, and getting them to open up. We distributed school supplies, or took care of any other type of critical needs that they would have. We would also run LOGPACs back and forth between Mosul, as well as south of FOB Regulars.

Then probably the most important function that we served in that area, was to attack high-value targets, and kind of targets of opportunity within our zone. Almost every single one of these targets was more or less HUMIT [human intelligence] driven, and basically, I saw my role in the brigade's framework as being more or less a disruption operation to the south of Mosul. To prevent the enemy from planning and operating from sanctuary, and then attacking north into Mosul, or south towards the Qayyarah airfield.

In any event, in order to accomplish all that stuff, I basically took the company and divided it up into four supporting efforts, and then a main effort. As far as the tasks of those efforts were concerned, the main effort was primary responsible for conducting direct-action missions, the mission one platoon. They also got assigned tasks in the way of village engagements, when we didn't have any pressing targets. Had another supporting effort number one, they would augment that mission platoon on the raid, or the cordon and search required if more than obviously a platoon size strength was required, which it almost always was. They would help augment host nation traffic control points, and execute flash TCPs, and conduct force protection patrols as required.

My supporting effort number two basically just secured the FOB. That was more or less a platoon sized mission, and took all that manpower to do that in an effective way. We had a supporting effort number four, which was my MGS platoon. Really, they became the MGS platoon with the assistance of the mortar platoon later in the deployment, but those guys were kind of like the jack of all trades. They could do route clearance, convoy escort, surveillance missions, any kind of flash TCPs, and were absolutely critical to the success of the company. A very independent group of cavalry soldiers, they did fantastic.

And then my last effort was my team CMOC, which consisted, basically, of my company headquarters section, as well as the company mortars. They would obviously get security augmentation, but the job of those guys was to do any kind of civil-military related action. Attend the city council meetings, man the CMOCs, deal with the myriad of folks that would come to OBJ Agees and try to make a claim against the U.S. government, or try to have us assist in the resolution of some kind of tribal squabble or whatever. Other non-combat related tasks that we had to achieve, basically, would fall under the purview of team CMOC.

Later in the deployment, we also stood up a team ICDC, that was, basically, the baby of First Sergeant Gregory Littenger. He would be assigned some additional security, as well as, obviously, a dedicated interpreter. The job of those guys was to, as we did time and time again, train platoon sized elements from the different ICDC companies in our AO, to work with the local police, and give them the fundamental fighting skills that would be required for those organizations to begin to slowly assume the primary role of general security as well as in direct-action missions. He did absolutely fantastically. I believe that our company actually trained the first platoon of ICDC soldiers. This would happen after we left OBJ Agees, and were stationed down at Qayyarah West airfield for about a month and a half, between roughly the middle of February and beginning of April. But anyways, I don't believe he ever really got the credit that was due for that.

In any event, moving onto the initial reaction when the company moved into the agricultural college. The 101st had done a fantastic job, they had kind of had the pleasure of rotating companies through there on more or less a monthly, and normally on a bi-weekly basis. It was clear to us right away that our stay was probably going to be longer, and that the actual company combat outpost itself was going to require some significant defensive improvements, as any good defense does. A good defense is never finished.

Then we were going to have to just expand the infrastructure of the facility to be able to accommodate the vehicles, and all the other things that we wanted to do there. With this in mind, kind of like the initial focus of the company was just getting the security details straight on the roof, making sure we developed good fields of fire, and had a good security plan. Working with the engineers and all the associated heavy machinery that the battalion had assigned us initially, in order to improve the force protection of the actual facility.

In this regard, I can remember one of my more amusing moments was when we had some attached Sappers, and the guys had basically showed up without the heavy machinery that was going to be required to perform some of the tasks, but they certainly didn't show up with a lack of ingenuity. There was a series of very large trees, I don't even know what type the tree is, but it seems that all of the trees that grow in very arid climates typically have wood that's about as hard as concrete. So anyways, there was a large row of these trees, basically, preceding from the northeastern side. I guess it was by a building down a road that kind of ran on the northern border of the agricultural college, and we wanted to remove these in order to have improved fields of fire.

So, we basically decided that since the chainsaws that they had brought with them were not functioning well enough to actually cut these suckers down, that we were going to go ahead and construct some timber cutting charges in order to drop the trees, which was like the ultimate in the life of a Sapper to conduct a very large demolition effort like that. Anyways, so they primed all the charges, and they got everything set up, and we started to drop the trees in sequence. But what we more or less had not accounted for, was the fact that the explosions themselves were gonna have a tremendous shock affect, and as these trees began to drop one by one, the windows on that side of the agricultural college began to explode along with the trees. So, in addition to dropping the trees to improve our fields of fire, we kind of opened up all the windows, permanently. So, then we had to figure out what we can do now to seal off these windows.

OK, so anyways, the building continued to improve with respect to its force protection, but not very much as far as quality of life. It was basically a company effort, when soldiers were not out conducting patrols or executing raids, we were busy just trying to improve as best we could with the limited resources that we had, the living conditions of Agees. Somethin that we realized when we got there, was all the elation of having a first-class chow hall down at Qayyarah was quickly smashed when we came to OBJ Agees, and realized that the 101st had been eating MREs [meals ready to eat] there for the entire time that they'd occupied the facility. So, we did not really have the means to make our own hot chow at the time. The battalion was doing the best that it could just to establish itself down at Qayyarah West airfield, and we basically ate MREs for the first month. It was kind of a good reminder in some ways, that the focus needed to be on the mission, all the amenities were nice, but our purpose in Iraq certainly wasn't to sit around enjoying good food, it was to be out and about on the countryside engaging the local population, and trying to do our part to create a secure and stable environment.

Anyways, rather than belaboring the first month anymore than I already have, I can kind of say that the company learned a couple of very important lessons during our first month at the Agees college. I think the first thing that we learned was, that the use of interpreters and the successful execution of tactical questioning was probably going to make the difference between capturing bad guys, puttin pressure on the enemy, um, and basically sitting idle. The targets that were going to be developed early on by the battalion, were going to be, basically, left over products from the 101st. It was going to take them a while, I think, to really get a handle on the enemy situation and develop the trust of informants that may have been working for the 101st.

Understanding this, and understanding our geographical separation from the battalion, and the idea that we were not the main effort at the time, I made a conscious decision as company commander to kinda continue on the tradition of Captain Cohns from the Cobra Company. To do the best that I could to be directly involved in tactical questioning, and really try to work the translators, or the interpreters, and gain their trust. So that I could extract valuable information from the walk-in informants that had been coming to the agricultural college and try to develop new sources as well.

This particular tactic would pay huge dividends when the company had what amounted to a local shepherd, or at least the story that he passed when he walked into the walk-in facility, and basically claimed that he had some information. We met with this individual on several occasions, and, basically, gathered that he had found some type of military ordinance somewhere south of the FOB. This was, basically, a situation where we were not going to be able to have this Iraqi be able to pinpoint on a map where we needed to go to exploit this information. Instead, we were actually going to have to take this individual with us, and protect his identity in a way, or assure him that we would protect his identity in a way, that his identity would not be revealed to the enemy and he wouldn't be murdered for helping coalition forces. So, this was the beginning of working through some TTPs that would be repeated over and over throughout the deployment, and obviously increasing their effectiveness as we gained confidence with our techniques.

We more or less disguised this individual. We had a link up with him at the FOB, and we left the FOB, and did the best that we could to have him get us to the right spot. When we finally got there, the gentleman led us to a spot in the middle of, basically, an open area that appeared to be a slight depression in the ground, with some large boulders and some scrub brush, and he basically pointed out what appeared to be a very small piece of fabric sticking out of the ground. After approximately an hour of excavation, we were able to remove about 700 pounds of artillery propellant from this particular hole.

Kind of acting on the instinct that, well if there's some stuff here, maybe there's some other stuff elsewhere close by. So, I more or less assigned a platoon to spread out and conduct a general search of the area. The platoon that was with me at this point in time was more or less my first platoon, and their platoon sergeant, Sergeant First Class Jones, as well as their platoon leader Umar Majeeb, did an excellent job of getting the squads assigned to specific sectors and continuing the search.

I think every commander realizes at some point during his time in command, that he's been blessed with a few individuals that clearly possess not only a tremendous amount of knowledge, but really a flair for the application of that knowledge. That individual in this particular instance, and many times over again in Iraq, would be Sergeant First Class Jones. He used experiences that he gained from fighting in Afghanistan with the 75th Ranger Regiment, as well as just a lot of common sense, and a lot of things he had picked up over the years by talking to other folks, to begin finding, and eventually safely recovering many caches that day.

We recovered anti-tank landmines, RPG launchers, warheads, an incredible amount of det cord, and hand grenades, and hand grenade fuses. I think, all told, we probably recovered somewhere in the neighborhood of six to seven separate additional caches from the one that we found with the help of the informant. It was an incredibly large score for the battalion, and it was a huge confidence booster for us, because that was intelligence that was completely developed at the company level, it was exploited at the company level, really only with what amounted to a casual note to our battalion saying that we were going to conduct this operation.

So, it was a company independent operation, and it was successful. As a company I think it kind of set the tone for many of the things that we would do over the course of the next year, kind of operating autonomously, or under the very loose control of a higher headquarters that would provide logistics, and check up on us, and make sure that we had everything that we needed to execute our mission to the best of our ability. So, the real lesson learned here, was that the mining of intelligence through tactical questioning was going to be key for us as a company, in order to take the initiative and hunt down the enemy.

OK, I think the second thing that we learned while we were at Agees during the 16 January to 14 February time period, was that regardless of how well that we would plan these missions, and I believed that we planned them in quite a bit of detail, was that we had to be prepared always for a variety of contingences that would occur during your typical cordon and search. Often the home that would be identified by an informant would not be the correct residence. It might be the one across the street. It might be a similar looking structure a street down. We also learned, like I said before, that they had no idea about how to read a map.

Often the individual that you are looking for would have a name that was incomplete by the informant's recollection, or would be using an alias, so how do you go into a house, conduct a thorough search, and begin to pick up clues or fragments of information that can eventually be assembled into a puzzle. How do you determine whether or not, A) you have the right guy, and B) if you have the right guy, whether or not that particular guy is actually someone that needs to be taken in because he's a threat? Whether he's an insurgent, or just a security risk, or whether or not this guy might have been framed by the informant, who might be of a questionable origin to begin with. So, really learning how to audible off of a very general, but exhaustive course of action. I think this was key, that is, the company maintaining controlled tactical flexibility when we went out on missions.

One example that comes to mind, is we were given a kind of throw back target from the 101st. It was one of the first missions that we executed, and I remember going to the house with the platoon leader that was executing the mission. We had gained initial entry, and, basically, cleared the house, or the structure of all immediate threats, and had begun our search and our questioning of the people there. I remember asking the individual what his name was, and he gave me a name that did not match the name of the person that we were looking for. Physical description was close, but not enough, in a way that there was a distinguishing birthmark or scar that would have clearly identified him as the subject of prosecution. So, we decided that it might not be a bad idea to check with the neighbors, and maybe check with the neighbors in such a way that the person that we were trying to get information about didn't know that we were at the neighbors, and that the neighbors didn't necessarily know that we were at that individuals house, because obviously, in either case it could be bad.

Maybe the guy that we're collecting information on takes some kind of revenge action against the neighbor, or if the neighbor knows he's a bad guy, maybe he's not willing to cough up the information as freely. It might not be good if they know that that's kind of the point of our particular outing. So, we eventually went to a series of neighbor's homes and asked about a lot of things that were completely unrelated to the reason that we were actually there, and in the course of a conversation. We were, basically, able to gather information that the guy that we had talked to earlier, and that we were still holding under suspicion, actually had a nickname. And that particular nickname matched the name of the individual that we were searching for. So, I think we realized that there was a need to maintain again, tactical flexibility, and that the plan could change very rapidly based off your ability to extract information, and that we had to be able to do that in an effective and efficient way.

Another one of the major things that we came to appreciate as a company during our first month at Agees was, that there was going to be a need to be patient with the development of intelligence, and, basically, be realistic with respect to our expectations of success on any given mission. Specifically, put in more colloquial terms, we needed to be prepared to expect a lot of dry holes. We had tons of information flowing through the company CP [command post], being an inexperienced intel guy as an infantry officer, it was my particular stance that we would pursue every one of those to the best of our ability. So, we stayed very busy during our first month there. I think we probably conducted in the neighborhood of 15 cordon and searches over a 30-day period, all HUMIT driven, probably only five of those 15 were throw back targets from the 101st.

So, we stayed very busy, and we had a lot of success. But, we had just as many dry holes as we had positive outcomes on cordon and searches. It became obvious that this was going to be hard work, and it also became obvious that this was not going to be a hundred-yard sprint. That we had to be, maybe a little bit more judicious in our prosecution of human intelligence as it came through the CP. This would really form the crux of an intellectual effort to figure out a way to organize information about potential enemy targets, to be able to sort it out, be able to analyze the frequency of information that was coming in, and be able to link the information that was coming in.

To, basically, begin to look at people not just as white, gray, and black, but look at them with respect to are they right for prosecution now, or is this something that we need to develop additional information on, that would end up paying dividends? I think we improved the number of successful cordon and searches we had, versus dry holes, by using that. By using a series of techniques that we developed to be more effective. More importantly, we weren't going to burn out our own soldiers, and we would be able to get much needed rest, and clear our heads. Clear heads normally result in better performance when you're out on the roads trying to perform a mission.

OK, so that pretty much takes us through our first month at OBJ Agees, it was a month where we grew tremendously as a company, began to form ourselves into a very cohesive team under a new company commander, and new platoon leader in the third platoon. Lieutenant Kevin Hutchinson and I really came into our own as part of a very capable combat infantry company that was going to make contributions to the success of the battalion, brigade, and into the overall mission in northern Iraq during the remainder of our time there. So, on or about February 15th, 2004, my company was relieved at OBJ Agees buy the Battle Company under Captain Damien Mason.

Qayyarah

We then proceeded south to Qayyarah West Airfield where we assumed the mission that Battle Company had. We remained there from 15 February all the way up to the 2nd of April when we returned to OBJ Agees and reassumed the mission that we had left behind. So, reestablishing ourselves from the rather austere environment of OBJ Agees, to the practical pleasure palace of Qayyarah West Airfield, was one that was absolutely positive for the morale of the soldiers. We had better food, we had better accommodations, we had access to gyms, we had better access to phone lines, and the internet, and everything else, but I think it was a six-week period where the company may have lost some of its edge with respect to closing with and capturing or killing the enemy.

I say that specifically because the company, and Battle Company, was under the same type of battle rhythm when they were there. The company mission was one that required really just almost one hundred percent involvement of all the soldiers in the company, and there were quite a few specified fixed site security or area security tasks. The mission at Qayyarah West Airfield really turned into one of trying to manage the number of troops you have, to the number of tasks that you had to accomplish.

As an example for our task organization when we were down at Qayyarah West, typical things that we would have to perform, we basically had one platoon at any given point in time that had a squad plus securing the southern retrans site, one squad that was detached to Headquarters Company to assist in FOB security, we had one squad that was detached to the Crazy Horse Troop out at the Jaguar ASP [ammunition supply point], and they were, I should say, actually to the west of that, more or less responsible for guarding a hole in the ground, where there was a suspected chemical site.

We had another squad that was basically training, or would augment the one platoon that I had on mission when raids that we would be assigned would require more than just the platoons combat power. I had my MGS and my mortars for a large portion of our six weeks there, basically, detached permanently to Headquarters Company again, to assist in the FOB security mission. I'm not saying that because I have any ill will towards the battalion staff for making that detachment, because that was an important mission that had to happen, and those were forces that we had to cough up. So, like I was saying, there was just a lot of stuff to do, and you only got so many guys to do it. I had an additional platoon that was kind of on a very short QRF string, and they were going to react to things to the south, as well as almost all the way to Mosul depending on how the company in Hammam al Alil was being utilized at the time. Then basically one other platoon that would be responsible for conducting area and route reconnaissance in and around the FOB Q-West.

Notice, nowhere in here did I really mention that I had any element that was available to conduct cordon and searches when intelligence came down at the FOB. It required a restructuring of the forces that I had available, and there was obviously a cost associated with the availability to go outside of the wire and close with the enemy. That cost was often the area reconnaissance security mission that did not happen that day, or whatever else didn't get done because of shifting troops around.

So, in any event, during our six weeks at the Qayyarah West Airfield, we conducted cordon and searches, and actual engagements with Iraqi population at a very reduced rate, and we were essentially not involved at all with the tactical questioning of any walk-in informants. Those types of activities obviously fall under the purview of the appropriate supporting staff, which would have been an attached unit team to the battalion, some PSYOPS folks, if they had some additional expertise, or time on their hands, and then obviously the battalion's S2 section. So, as a company commander, I was able to assume perhaps a more traditional role in just managing operations, spending more time with the soldiers, but not necessarily developing intelligence like was really required of me up in Hammam al Alil.

In any event, one particular raid however, that does kind of stand out during our time down in Qayyarah West Airfield, is when there was a tactical HUMINTer that was assigned to the battalion, who had been working with walk-ins. This walk-in, basically, said that he had gone through a series of steps to set up an arms deal with a relatively large or prominent trafficker for all of northern Iraq. Obviously, he met this information with some skepticism, it almost seemed too good to be true, and we thought that maybe the guy was, or we probably knew that the guy was going to be motivated by the promise of a reward. We were skeptical of his ability to actually produce the results, or get the big fish on the table to be captured.

In any event, on 18 February the informant did come back. We obviously maintained a QRF, but weren't on a very high level of alert. We had the forces available at the time to go out and conduct a mission, and we had been prepared for that. We'd done all the planning that we could, based on the information that was available. So, we followed, well we didn't follow, we had the informant ride with us in the vehicles. He got us to a small village that was approximately 10 kilometers to the north of Qayyarah West Airfield on Highway 1. Literally, it was just to the western side of the road, as we penetrated the outer row of structures of that particular town, it seemed as normal as any normal town would seem, or underdeveloped town would seem.

You had the typical mud building, or very simple construction. Basically, all buildings are one story high. A lot of the buildings in a town like this have animal pens and livestock living inside of the city walls. Nothing seemed out of the ordinary, as we turned the corner and began to close within 50 meters of the target house identified by the informant. We began to have people scattering in all directions, jumping off of roofs, over walls, and we immediately deployed to the best of our ability to intercept those folks and prevent their escape. Luckily, it was enough of a shock to the people that were at this particular arms deal, that there was no real early warning besides the fact that the people heard the vehicles coming from a short distance away.

They really didn't have time to arm themselves, or didn't foresee the need to arm themselves. So, the entire takedown was executed without firing a shot. But in any event, one of my squad leaders from my third platoon, Staff Sergeant Maury Jackson, chased down a slightly elderly man that seemed to be of quite good physical condition. He ran down an alley way and tackled, and detained him. It turned out that that individual, after a series of interrogations, and some dots were connected, that he was probably one of the most prolific arms dealers in all of Iraq, well, all of northern Iraq anyway. So, it was a great take down for the company, we recovered 700 mortar rounds of various sizes and dimensions from that particular raid, and it was really just an awesome synergy of human intelligence with quick flexible execution. It was probably one of the more successful raids that we executed during our time in northern Iraq, but in any event, that was kind of, like, the highlight of our time down in Q-west Airfield.

The other thing that we inherited, and kind of took on during our time there was the initial ICDC training. As I mentioned before, First Sergeant Gregory Littenger began to train an ICDC platoon from one of the ICDC Companies that was just north in the Tiger ASP. He wrote up a fantastic two-week plan that was, basically, hands-on training that accounted for everything from basic rifle marksmanship, to physical fitness, and simple enter building, clear a room drills. He really got them to a level of proficiency that was remarkable in a two-week time period. We then eventually began to take these soldiers out on missions with us, operating out of their vehicles, not out of our vehicles. This was the first time, to the best of my knowledge, that this had been done in northern Iraq. It was really hard work, and almost the sole effort of my company first sergeant, who did an absolutely great job. So, that was kind of another highlight of our time down at Q-West.

Just kind of a few personal anecdotes here, I remember when we returned from Hammam al Alil, I'd basically gone one month getting probably on average, I would say three hours of sleep a night, and on a suspect diet, so when I returned to Q-West it was a situation where my body just basically shut down. I got violently ill one evening. The first couple of days that we were there, I was essentially incapacitated, and had to be more or less put down for a 24–48-hour period by the battalion physician assistant. This particular instance was significant from two perspectives, one it was a stark reminder to me that I was not in fact superman. That I did have to take care of my body and myself. I had to make sure that I was getting adequate amount of rest, and it was a good reminder to me that I needed to make sure that my soldiers were eating properly, getting enough sleep, had a means of just kind of recharging themselves in-between the missions, and it made me a lot more sensitive to that.

The second thing of value to come out of my misery, was while I was laid up, the company got some intelligence, another walk-in informant, and had to execute another no notice raid with me being under the weather. This particular mission was given to my company executive officer, First Lieutenant Chris Sheehan, and it was up to him to organize the company, come up with the tactical plan quickly, and execute the target to the best of his ability. He did a fantastic job. They detained a few individuals, it wasn't perfect, but nothing you do fast ever is. It was a great learning opportunity for him, and a huge confidence booster for me as his company commander, that should I fall, the company XO would clearly be able to take the reins and maneuver the company, and lead the company in a way where they could be successful and continue to fight to the best of their ability. So, it's amazing how many things you can learn from an upset stomach.

Anyways, the second kind of personal anecdote here, is during our time in Hammam al Alil, we had no access to phones, internet, anything like that for the first month that we were there, so I did not have to opportunity to talk to my wife or my children. When we returned to Q-West, we were more or less surrounded by telephones and means of communication back to the United States, and it was a huge opportunity for me as a company commander, and for all the guys in the company, to reestablish at least a verbal relationship with their children, their spouses, their moms, and their dads, and everyone that they had left behind. You could really see an improvement in the day-to-day morale of the soldiers, and this was going to be very important as we passed out of Qayyarah West Airfield on the second of April, and headed back up to Hammam al Alil.

Hammam al Alil

So, moving from Q-West to the reestablishment of the company up at OBJ Agees. This happened on roughly 2 April, and we would remain at the agricultural college up until the middle of August. In any event, I can remember when we reassumed the mission up at FOB Agees, the first thing that I realized was what an absolutely fantastic job that the Battle company had done, with the assistance of the Headquarters Company, to improve the living conditions immensely. I mean it's difficult to describe in words how much the facility had improved from the time that we had left, to the time we returned. I mean the installation now had electricity, it had, you know, running water, it had a chow hall, it had operational phones, and an internet center. I mean, it was just such a morale boost for the guys to return to an OBJ Agees they remembered as being monkish, to come back, and all of a sudden, we really weren't giving up a lot by leaving Q-West and going to OBJ Agees, in terms of our creature comforts.

I can't say enough about all the support work that went on at OBJ Agees and Q-West, people take the most basic creature comforts for granted, but in Iraq, our people had to do everything if you wanted the most basic luxuries like electricity, food, water, sanitation, and so on. They don't get much credit, but I thought Headquarters Company really worked hard to improve our positions from a tactical and quality of life standpoint.

So, that was pretty much the first impression, and then the second impression was that we began to hear rumors, almost immediately upon our return to Hammam al Alil, that there was more or less a complete closure of all of the major lines of communication in and around Baghdad. That they were really looking hard at a Stryker force to go down there and help relieve the pressure on those lines, and reestablish the ability of the of the theatre commander to move his logistics and his soldiers around the country.

With this in mind, I remember thinking that there was a good chance that they would potentially take my company from Hammam al Alil, and reattach us to the battalion, and probably send the battalion to perform that mission. Because, I think everybody understood that the center of gravity from northern Iraq was in Mosul, and that mission was more or less being handled by the Tomahawks and the Patriots. I thought that there might be a chance that they would pull the 1-14 Cavalry specifically, because that sounded to me like a very cavalryish mission. But I also knew that they were in charge of an area in Tal Afar that was probably operationally important, in terms of maybe closing down some borders or the trafficking of foreign fighters or arms.

So, I thought that there was a chance that the battalion might go to the south, and I thought that there was a chance that we would go with them. I would even say that I thought it was likely that we would go with the battalion if the battalion went south, but that didn't happen. In any event, we eventually did get the word that Colonel Reed and the rest of his staff, and at least a portion of our battalion was going to spearhead an effort known as Taskforce Arrow. To go into central and southern Iraq, to basically reestablish the lines of communication, and we also kind of got the initial word from the battalion commander that more than likely, our company was not going to be part of that effort, and that they were going to pull a rifle company from each one of our sister battalions instead. So basically, this means that Bravo Company was going to move with the battalion, and my company, Attack Company, was going to stay in Hammam al Alil, OBJ Agees, and C Company, which was still attached to 1-14 Cavalry at the time, was going to remain in Tal Afar, in order to provide the only infantry presence in that town at Rock Base, and Headquarters Company would be split to support both Q-West and Task Force Arrow.

So, in any event, the decision was finally made that, that was in fact the case. I can remember feeling at the time, and it was an irrational feeling, since it was obviously completely out of the hands of my battalion commander, who would have loved to have had both Attack Company and Rock Company attached to him. In a lot of ways, it was out of the hands of the brigade commander, in terms of having the appropriate amount of forces in the appropriate places across the area of his operations. So basically, we were not going to be going with the battalion.

I know that was difficult for me to stomach at the time, but I quickly turned to my faith and said to myself, well this was going to be an opportunity for the company to really demonstrate that it was a great organization, and that the headquarters that I would fall under, really wouldn't make much of a difference. I only asked in my own mind, that whatever headquarters that was going to be, was going to give me the same amount of flexibility that my parent battalion headquarters had given me to execute the mission in the best way that I saw fit, and apply the expertise that we had gained in that area during our month or so between January and February.

So, in any event, I soon got the word that the company was going to fall under the control of 1-23 Infantry, which basically owned the western side of Mosul. I was stationed immediately to their south. I found out that, at least at the time, my company boundaries were not going to change. I would eventually lose a good portion of the Asura district, to include the actual town of Asura itself. But at the time, I was maintaining the same exact AO, the same mission set, and would be simply working for a different battalion commander and a different set of battalion colors. So, with this in mind the company basically reinitiated our time at Agees in the same manner that we had left.

We immediately got busy pursuing a lot of human driven targets, and did a great job, in my estimation, of haulin in a lot of bad guys quickly and effectively. In particular, I think the battalion, or the company rather, conducted somewhere on the order of seventy or seventy-five to eighty cordon and searches between the 2nd of April and, basically, the 2nd of August. I think we detained somewhere in the nature of 80 individuals, which was a very high number, and we also released a lot, before we pushed them to the brigade cage. We were doing our own screening at the company level to see whether or not folks that we had detained, had legitimate reasons to be pushed forward, or whether or not it was a case of mistaken identity. We began to understand in very specific terms, the kind of information, or the kind of evidence that was going to be required in order to make one of these detentions stick, and have these guys move along in the system. We captured numerous caches, consisting of literally, tons of ammunition and explosives. I mean, the average person just can't comprehend the amount of weapons and explosives floating around Iraq.

We also had our fair share of at least indirect fire contacts at the FOB. I can remember on one particularly noteworthy occasion; we received a pretty significant mortar barrage from a series of actually three separate mortar points around the FOB. This happened to be on an evening when we had been busy the night before, had a large number of forces outside of the wire, and had made a decision to kind of reduce our footprint outside of the perimeter that evening, in order to get the soldiers some rest. Now obviously, we didn't relieve any of the requirements for the folks that provided the immediate security, but with respect to roaming the hills surrounding the FOB, we had basically stepped back that evening.

Well not surprisingly, the enemy had good enough surveillance of our instillation to capitalize on this, and we began to receive a significant amount of mortar fire. I think it was somewhere in the neighborhood of twenty indirect rounds. In any event, at one point the explosions seemed within a hundred meters of the FOB, and then there was one that was particularly loud. Come to find out, that the sergeant of the guard that was on the roof at that time, Staff Sergeant Lynn from second platoon, had a 60-millimeter mortar basically [laugh] brush his helmet, and hit approximately five feet behind him. At the time he was manning a Mark 19 on the roof of the structure.

It obviously blew him off of his feet, disrupted his equilibrium, and the great story about this is, that undeterred, the almost deaf Staff Sergeant Lynn immediately reassumed his role on the Mark 19, and continued to direct his men in providing accurate, and very voluminous counter fire onto the indirect position surrounding us. He was able to, more or less, thwart any additional mortar attacks that evening. So, that was one example of an indirect fire contact where you had an NCO [non-commissioned officer] performing in an outstanding manner, irregardless, I should say regardless, of the threat to his personal security. He did so in a manner that brought pride, at least on me as his company commander, and certainly to the folks on the roof, that in many ways, probably owe their lives to him that evening as he maintained order, and provided accurate fires onto the enemy.

Another instance that kind of stands out, is an IED contact, luckily it was not an IED that exploded, rather one we spotted. It was very difficult for us to avoid establishing a pattern, with respect to having to attend the city council meetings in the Hammam al Alil and Asura districts. These meetings have to occur on some kind of a schedule, or at least the information has to be published, so that the people who need to attend the meetings can actually be there. So, in any event, we had traveled south into Asura and had taken, more or less, the one high speed avenue of approach to get there. That's really the only way to get there based off of the broken terrain from where we were living, and the area where we had to go.

We got done with the particular meeting, and we were coming back on the same route, and my particular vehicle at that time was probably traveling in the neighborhood of 35 to 40 miles an hour on this road, and my rear air sentry, or one of my two rear air sentries, Specialist Mickey said, "Sir, I think I saw a piece of red cord back there, approximately 50 meters." Now, I was looking over the same side of the vehicle as this soldier, but nothing out of the ordinary struck me as we were driving by this location, and I was paranoid enough to be looking all the time for that sort of thing. So, we eventually held up the convoy, turned around, and traveled approximately an eighth of a mile back to the location. We began to scan, and in fact, there was a very small, and when I say very small, that's exactly what I mean. Roughly an inch and a half long piece of what appeared to be a reddish colored cord emanating from a small pile of gravel. It was not something that certainly would have stood out. So, in any event, it was suspicious enough to basically seal off that particular site with the platoon that was attached to my company headquarters at that time, and to call EOD [explosive ordnance disposal] to investigate.

The long of the short, or the short of the long, is that once the EOD arrived, they eventually recovered that particular munition. It turned out to be two 155-millimeter shells that were fused together with a remote-control initiation device, and the red cord like material that been had been observed by the rear air sentry at 35 miles an hour, was actually a piece of the detonating cored that was going to be used as the primer charge, or the fusing charge for the IED. So, absolutely unbelievable attention to detail, and one that very likely saved the lives of other soldiers traveling that road, or even soldiers that were to the rear of my vehicle in the convoy. So again, amazed at the ability of just average individuals to perform extraordinary acts of either heroism, or concentration on duty related skills in a very stressful environment.

Actually, retouching some information about counter mortar operations. After receiving an attack at least two or three times a week, over the course of roughly a month, we began to realize that the traditional methods for conducting counter mortar operations out of our FOB were ineffective. The enemy could capitalize when we were not there, and I couldn't keep all of my soldiers outside of the wire all night to ensure that we weren't hit by mortars. So, in any event, there was a large push by 1-23 Infantry, and there was a lot of support from my commanding officer, Colonel Rounds, and all the way up to General Ham, that we actually be able to fire counter mortar fire at points of origin that we could identify.

Now, this plan was initially conceived as a more traditional application of counter fire radar, the use of the battalion's fire support element to generate the actual fire missions, and then the actual firing of the missions by my company mortar section. What it eventually morphed into was, basically, a slice of airspace that I would control, a slice of terrain where I was the ultimate clearance and fires authority. We were not going to be firing those missions with the assistance of the battalion fire supporters, or the counter fire radar, so this was going to be, more or less, an observed counter fire mission.

It is difficult to portray how effective this particular means of counter mortar operation was. I had the advantage, unlike many commanders in some of the more densely populated urban terrain of Iraq, to actually employ successfully and safely counter fire mortars. Probably fifty percent of the area that surrounded me was agrarian, it was visible, and visible to the point that you could clear the area that you were gonna fire into, of even the wondering shepherd, or the misplaced civilian vehicle. So, in any event, I remember one of the times that we executed this particular drill, we were hit by a barrage of mortars somewhere around midnight, and probably within literally twenty seconds of that incoming mortar fire, we had outgoing rounds heading in the direction of the point of origin.

That's not particularly impressive, I mean that's fast, but the thing that is impressive, is that the soldiers that were hanging those mortar rounds from my company were doing so in shorts, flip flops, boxer shorts, and probably no shirts, almost to the man. Basically, they had maintained a hot gun, they had the rounds already prepared, they had the tube kind of coincidentally laid already in the vicinity of the point of origin on the ridgeline where they were coming from. The soldiers heard the incoming mortar rounds and immediately scrambled from their bunks, and began to provide deadly accurate fire.

Now, we never actually killed an enemy mortarman firing counter fire, but the psychological impact on the enemy of having 120-millimeter mortar rounds impact in his general vicinity, kind of sent a very clear message that if you fire mortars at this FOB, you can expect to receive the same type of attack on your position, but just with ammunition that's potentially twice as big as the one you shot at us. That was enough, basically, to reduce those contacts, probably by seventy-five percent. When we did receive indirect fire contact after that time, it was typically one or two rounds out of a small caliber tube, that would allow the enemy to quickly get out of the area from where he hung the rounds, so as to avoid becoming the victim of our incoming rounds.

So, during our second stay at OBJ Agees, there was too many missions to list. But what we did as a company, was we really again established ourselves as being a force that could be counted on for developing the intelligence in its area, for understanding the socio-political factors, for having appreciation of how the enemy operated. This was particularly noteworthy, because the area that we operated in happened to be the hometown slash stronghold of a large number of operatives that were working kind of for the number one HVT in all of northern Iraq. This particular fact gave the company the opportunity to conduct joint operations with multiple entities and agencies from the special operations community. An awesome learning experience for everybody involved, at least within my company.

To be able to see NCOs and officers with unbelievable expertise and proficiency in their particular duty related skills, complete professionalism. To be able to operate alongside these guys, and do so effectively, and to gain their respect and trust as a unit. A unit that could be counted on to give good information, to execute violently, but under control. One that was willing to share ideas, and listen, and grow from the interaction with them. I think every soldier in the company will take to heart and remember this as being one of the highlights of being in Iraq. Obviously, I'm not at liberty to talk about any of those operations, or any ideas, or anything else that was really exchanged with those folks, but it was certainly one of the highlights of my army career, and the guys were thankful for that.

Another thing that I can say, and this time without reservation, is that the great support that the company received from 1-23 Infantry, and that support came from the top down. From their battalion commander, Lieutenant Colonel James, from their battalion command sergeant major, from the interim battalion commander when Colonel James was having surgery back in the United States. Also, the deputy commander of the brigade, Lieutenant Colonel Heinamen, and their battalion executive officer Major Rock, their S3, who happened to be an armor officer and is one of the best S3s that I've ever worked with, Major Aafe, all the way down to their company commanders.

The level of support, and the sense of belonging that they gave us was truly phenomenal, and was remembered by all the soldiers in the company. It made the time away from our parent headquarters certainly bearable, and it made the time fly. It was truly an organization of first-class personnel in every regard, and everybody in the company is appreciative for what they did for us. We would have an opportunity to work with these folks again when the 1-23 Battalion received word that they would have to go south in the middle of August, to a town called Al'Kut.

Al'Kut

Now, the background behind this was that the 5-20th Infantry Battalion had returned from Taskforce Arrow, and had reassumed the mission or assumed the mission of 1-14 Cavalry out in Tal Afar. Kind of concurrent with the return of 5-20 was roughly the time of the second Sadr uprising where the Mahdi Militia was beginning to run amuck in southeastern Iraq and southern Iraq, south of Baghdad, and there was basically a vacuum of coalition forces in that area. It got bad enough in the town of Al'Kut that the militia had essentially closed all the bridges, had run, at least what we had heard, had run a lot of the police forces out of town, or at least out of their buildings, and had more or less taken control.

The assigned coalition force down there were, basically, under specific orders not to leave the FOB. So, 1-23 got the call for the particular mission to go down to Al'Kut, relieve the pressure of the Mahdi Militia, and conduct operations as required to reassert host nation and coalition forces control in the region. In this capacity, it was decided that we would go with 1-23. We quickly transitioned control of OBJ Agees from our company to one platoon. So, now you're at the point where the area was controlled by a battalion of the 101st, it was eventually transitioned to the control of a Stryker company, and now it was going to be passed to one platoon. Needless to say, the platoon leader had his hands full, and it was basically his mission just to keep the place from being ransacked and attacked. That platoon from 1-23 Infantry did a fantastic job.

Anyways, so we quickly packed, we alert marshaled, and deployed in a period, I believe it was less than forty-eight hours.

Moved the company north to Mosul, and eventually departed, I believe it was the 13th of August or their abouts, with 1-23, and headed south to Al'Kut. This particular movement, approximately 300 miles, was similar to any other movement that we would conduct in Iraq over extended distances. There was always the large number of attachments, there was multiple refuelings, and this particular one was basically able to be conducted more or less in a day. So, off we went to Al'Kut. It was a relatively uneventful journey besides two particular incidences.

The first one involved a particularly ill equipped HETT driver that had been attached to the company for the movement. Basically, the situation was, we had left our final refueling and were on our way to the place where we would eventually base out of named Camp Delta. We had just left the refueling station, and the next thing I know, I'm getting a call over the radio from my rear-von element, essentially telling me that they were missing a HETT.

So, obviously my first question to this particular NCO was, "Well, did we have the HETT when we left the refueling base ten minutes ago"? His response was, "Yes, we had every single person that was assigned to us." We had taken role as per the manifest, and everybody was with us. He responded that we had just went around a traffic circle and believed that that particular HETT may have exited out of the wrong clock face direction. The problem was that the clock face direction that he believed that they had exited in would have taken him directly into downtown Baqubah. Not necessarily a nice town, and that is really not what I wanted to hear when I was trying to control a twenty-five-vehicle convoy on unfamiliar terrain and roads, trying to reach Camp Delta on what had turned out to be a very long day.

So, in any event, we turned the convoy around and we began to head back in the direction of the traffic circle when we saw the HETT coming in the other direction. So, we were able to link back up with this driver, and we came to found out that the soldier did not have a set of NVGs [night vision goggles]. When we had conducted our initial inspection of the march serial, there had been another soldier in the vehicle with them, and that soldier had NVGs. Somehow over the course of this trip, that soldier had jumped vehicles or moved vehicles, and now the vehicle could not see during the night. So, this was a stark reminder that the idea of having attachments in a convoy requires that the unit that is securing that convoy, obviously needs to take a very hands-on roll in making sure that they understand the standards of your organization, and that they know, basically, what the plan is. So, in any event, we were able to recover this this lost HETT.

Shortly after this, approximately fifteen minutes further down the road, I got the call, the crackle over the radio of a serial which was now to my front, which was a serial of my executive officer, and, basically, all I could make out of over the radio was, "Sir, I'm hit," and that was my company executive officer Lieutenant Sheehan's vehicle. Basically, traveling through an area that was very clearly one of the insurgent's favorite spots to IED, at least of all the roads that I saw during my time in Iraq, and that became evident during the daylight hours when we made our return trip from Al'Kut. Anyways, he was basically hit by a rather large improvised explosive device, and had peppered the vehicle with shrapnel, blown out a couple of tires, and caused him to lose consciousness, and scratched up the driver a little bit.

I remember that my heart completely sunk, I mean Chris Sheehan is a great man, he's married with a couple of beautiful children, and I remembered thinking at the time, how blessed the company had been to make it all the way to August without having received one purple heart. Which was remarkable from many different angles, and that my first purple heart was potentially going to be my company executive officer, and I was just praying that the injuries that he had sustained weren't going to be severe. As it turns out, the injuries were extremely minor, he lost consciousness for an extremely short period of time, and actually had no visible marks of the contact. The driver received very minor wounds, and so anyways, we were very lucky. They immediately loaded the vehicle onto a HETT, there was nothing to see in the area with the thermal sites, and they continued to march.

So, we eventually made it to Al'Kut, to Camp Delta, very early the following morning, and were placed in what amounted to a very large concrete aircraft hangar where the company would base out of during our few weeks there. The morning following our arrival we did all of the typical things that an infantry company would do when they change location, we PMCSed [preventive maintenance checks and services] our equipment, we reconfigured our vehicles to a more combat friendly mode, or a fighting mode. Stripping unnecessary gear etcetera, refueled, and basically stood by for information about the impending mission. When the mission eventually came down, we came to find out that our company would be responsible for leading the battalion out on their initial assault into Al'Kut, and that we would have to seize a bridgehead across a canal, kind of an offshoot off the Tigris River, so that the remainder of the battalion could flow through us, and begin what amounts to, an armed reconnaissance of the city itself, and the critical infrastructures, and police stations.

With this in mind, the company went into its standard battery of MDMP. We assigned efforts according to the strengths of the different platoons, and at this point, obviously, mid-tour leave was in full throttle, so we were operating up to ten percent shorthanded in some of the units. We took great care to make sure that the units that were understrength weren't given tasks that were, obviously, too difficult for them to accomplish based off the strength that they had. In any event, the task of my second platoon was basically to clear the bridge. I had my first platoon secure a large granary facility on the far side, and provide overwatch, and then my third platoon was going to flow through them and establish control of a few dominant pieces of urban terrain, in order to overwatch a follow-on bridge that would be crossed by the battalion main effort.

On the night of the actual mission, this was the first time that the company had been passed direct control of a Spectre gunship, and we were actually able to execute a preplanned target along the road immediately following the bridge that we had to secure. So, once the Spectre was on station, and we had the conditions set, we executed that preplanned target. I remember thinking that this was just incredible to have control of an asset of this kind, capable of firepower and precision engagement, that once again this was one of those dreams of every infantry officer, to have something like this work for them.

So, as the aircraft is servicing its target, we began to see a lot of emergency response vehicle lights off in the distance, and at the time, I had assumed that we had, basically, scared some of the host nation security forces out of hiding. That they were moving out of the area, because they were anticipating a more sustained contact following the seizure of the bridgehead, and they were just getting out of the area.

In reality what ended up happening was, one of the rounds from the Spectre gunship had errantly traveled into the courtyard of a structure outside, obviously, of the area that was targeted. That particular structure happened to be a police station. It was unfortunate, one of the police officers was hit in the leg and sustained obviously some significant injuries, and the lights that we saw were actually the vehicles taking that wounded Iraqi police officer to the hospital. So, not necessarily the way that I wanted to enter Al'Kut and seize my objective, but it was in many ways again, a reminder that everything doesn't always go according to plan, and that you have to be able to effectively deal with those situations when they arrive.

So, the company drove on, the battalion effectively passed through us, and was able to do the reconnaissance of Al'Kut. They found out that, it really seemed that it was a lot to do about nothing. That the enemy situation didn't appear to be nearly as severe as originally reported. The town appeared to be very much in control of the militia, and that there certainly wasn't any open hostile presence when we arrived. The remaining two weeks, or it might have been closer to three weeks, that we spent in Al'Kut, we, basically, spent conducting similar type company level armed reconnaissance or battalion minus level armed reconnaissance, through many of the surrounding villages. In each one of these circumstances, we met with minor, if any resistance. It began to become clear to everyone assigned to the task force that we probably would not be staying in Al'Kut for the remainder of our time in Iraq. We would probably be recalled up to Mosul, to reassume the mission that we had left prior to being deployed.

Accordingly, on or about 1 September, I think it was actually closer to the end of August, we received the word to redeploy from Al'Kut back to OBJ Agees, and we did that. OK, once we got back to OBJ Agees we literally, and I mean it in that way, found out that the company was now going to be removed from OBJ Agees, and relocated to FOB Marez on the western side of Mosul. The reason for this particular move, was that 1-23 Infantry received confirmation that they would be heading to the Baghdad area to serve, more or less, as a strategic reserve or operational reserve for the MNCI (Multi-National Corps-Iraq) commander. They were therefore, going to be pulling out of FOB Marez, and 1-14 was going to be assuming that mission. So, of course, once we moved to FOB Marez, we were going to be working for 1-14 Cavalry.

So, the company, more or less, did not even download its vehicles. We received the appropriate haul assets, and we uploaded all of the gear that we had left behind in OBJ Agees, and made our way north to FOB Marez in Mosul. Once we arrived at FOB Marez, we were given the initial mission set. We almost did not have time to unload our vehicles and put them into our living containers at FOB Marez, before we received word that 5-20th Infantry was beginning to experience significant enemy activity in Tal Afar.

Tal Afar

Obviously, one of those instances was the downing of an OH58 helicopter that ended up culminating in a very sustained, violent fire fight, where Bravo Company, Charlie Company, and elements of Headquarters Company, particularly the reconnaissance platoon, probably fought the most significant action in the three-month period in all of Iraq. Basically, they were requesting that our company now deploy from Mosul to Tal Afar, to participate in a more coordinated action against the insurgents, that were beginning to stand and fight in larger coordinated formations in that area.

Accordingly, on or about September 7th, the company moved from FOB Marez to FOB Sykes, out at Tal Afar. Once we arrived on the ground, we immediately received a hero's welcome from the battalion commander, and the other companies. We were immediately given suitable living accommodations, and began to receive the warning orders for the impending Operation Black Typhoon. In this particular operation, the company's role was going to be to establish, basically, an attack by fire position on the eastern, correction, on the western edge of town, and be prepared to overwatch designated quadrants, and destroy enemy elements as they presented themselves as targets. In order to achieve this, we were second in the order of march out for the battalion, the first being Charlie Company.

Once they seized their immediate objectives, we would pass to their rear, flow into position, and once we were established, we would pass Bravo Company to our front to establish themselves on the western side of Tal Afar, and to our north. That was basically a brigade level op. There was multiple types of air cover, the massive use of battalion 120-millimeter mortars in a preparatory mode, and was really a full-out combat operation. This was not any kind of a typical cordon and search, or any kind of a stability op, this was the real thing. So, in any event, we went through all the appropriate rehearsals, and we left on time. I remember before we left the gate along our route, listening to our friendly outgoing mortar elements, and listening to the preparatory fires of the gunships, and thinking that all of our time in Iraq, and all the time that I've spent in the military, has really been culminating towards this particular event. That if I ever really had to be on my game, that this was the one time, and that I hoped that the soldiers in my company were feeling the same way. I can be pretty certain that, to the man, they were.

So, in any event, we followed Charlie Company out. Charlie Company, I believe, took some sporadic contact, and we passed through their location with no issues. They were right on time, and in the right spot, and we followed the correct route. We did have one vehicle that attempted to pass through our element in a manner that was seen threatening, so we engaged and destroyed that vehicle and killed the driver, as we eventually pulled into our position.

We then gave the word back to the battalion that we were set, and Bravo Company began to pass to our front. Literally, as Bravo Company passed my northern trace, they immediately began to receive RPG and small arms fire from the western side of Tal Afar. They responded ferociously, with every single weapon that they had underneath their control at the time. Again, we were not receiving any fire, I think we were effective in getting into position with some relative stealth, and that the enemy was unaware that we were positioned immediately to Bravo Company's south.

Towards daybreak, enemy activity continued and increased to the northern most portion of my line, which was occupied by my first platoon. They began to receive some small arms contact, and more importantly, was able to clearly identify enemy elements that were attempting to maneuver on the Bravo Company. They were providing relatively accurate fire against them. In this capacity, I remember watching Sergeant First Class Jones, with Staff Sergeant Lopez, on the roof of a structure approximately fifty meters to my north. They began to engage with an M240 machine gun. They engaged with AT4s [84-millimeter anti-tank weapon], and also successfully employed a 60-millimeter mortar tube in hand-held mode, to destroy roughly a squad size element of enemy that were attempting to hide on the southern side of the building, and fire onto Bravo Company.

We also had the opportunity to call in an OH58, and have them fire some of their 2.57-inch rockets at some targets that we had identified. One of the things that I will never forget, is my fantastic MGS platoon sergeant, Sergeant First Class Howard, when he called over the company net and said that elements of second platoon were intermixed with him. They had been engaging some enemy on top of a rooftop approximately 400-500 meters to his front with limited success. Based off the range and based off the enemy's ability to just simply duck behind a concrete wall, and that he had very clear observation of those enemy through his sight, he was asking for permission to engage the target with the TOW missile. We hadn't used any TOW missiles, we had plenty with us, so I gave him permission to execute that target. I just remember watching that missile go off, hit the roof of that building with spectacular results, and just thinking how proud that I was to be leading men with that kind of initiative and that kind of skill. Really, it doesn't get any better than the situation that we were in that day as a company commander. No real enemy pressure, the opportunity to engage and destroy the enemy, no friendly casualties, and the operation, all in all, was very well conceived. It was extremely well executed, and I would say, was a stunning success.

So, in any event, as the morning wore on, the enemy contact became much and much less frequent. It eventually died down to nothing, and there was a huge exodus of civilians from Tal Afar that were leaving the area. I think that the final estimated numbers was, I think, it was over a hundred thousand folks, but anyways, just watching this parade of Iraqis stacked on top of each other in the back of pickup trucks and white flags flying, and all this kind of stuff, just really kind of brought home the stark reality of what we had done that morning. Which was, yeah, we may have killed some enemy, but we also displaced a lot of civilians that probably had a very limited role in the condition, the current terrible condition of their town. I mean, we literally kicked everyone out of a good size city! I felt kind of bad about that.

Once again, we had an operation that was supposed to last about 24-hours, that turned into an op that lasted close to two days. We eventually repositioned and began to execute a series of overwatch missions, for lack of a better way of putting it, on the north and the western sides of Tal Afar. These particular missions were boring to say the least, you had to contend with what seemed like an endless supply of flies, in and around the dumps surrounding Tal Afar, and they were pretty miserable. But they were important, as it kept the pressure on the enemy, and it's something that we had to do, so that's what we did to the best of our ability.

Mosul

Almost immediately following Operation Black Typhoon, its associated overwatch mission, and then second combat op, the company received word that we were going to be returning back to FOB Marez to reassume the mission that we had for approximately 24-hours before we received the word that we were going to be going to Tal Afar. So, the company packed itself back up, and we moved back to FOB Marez where we fell under the control of the 1-14 Cavalry squadron. Upon our arrival to this much larger FOB, I was kind of reminded of the mission that we performed down in Q-West, and it became apparent quickly that we were gonna be executing more or less a troop to task drill with respect to all of the things we had to accomplish.

Specifically, the company was more or less sub subdivided into a QRF platoon, which I really saw as our main effort, and then a counter mortar element, which was a platoon plus. Then, also I felt that, I had a requirement to kind of keep one platoon in a recovery mode, because the counter mortar requirement was, basically, sixteen hours a day that we would be have to be out on the streets of western Mosul. There was a lot of damage, and just wear and tear on the vehicle from conducting operations over very extended time frames. And then the QRF requirement necessitated that, obviously, all your equipment worked. So, I really saw that the recovery day was critical to the company being able to maintain that op tempo for our final few months in Iraq.

Now at roughly the time that we were returning to Mosul from Tal Afar, there was a shift, I would say, and a noticeable one, in the level of enemy activity on the western side of Mosul. I'm sure it was similar on the eastern side, although I can't speak with any kind of expertise about that. Specifically, what I mean is, whether or not this was insurgents that had fled Tal Afar and moved to Mosul, or whether or not this was just a spike in enemy activity at or about the time of our transition of authority, but 1-14 Cavalry had received some significant contact. A lot of soldiers had been wounded, several had been killed, and again coming into the final two months of the deployment, it really served as a wake-up call to many of the soldiers in my company who had seen, compared to many of their contemporaries, relatively limited direct fire contact. So, now, more than ever, we had to maintain our vigilance and do all the little things right in order to avoid a senseless causality before we left the country. So again, we stayed extremely busy.

The counter mortar operations that lasted for sixteen hours a day, really were a drill in trying not to establish patterns. We were given specific zones that we had to cover, and we had to cover those zones for specific amounts of time, and there really are only so many ways to drive a Stryker vehicle in and out of the relatively narrow streets of an Iraqi urban area. So, to the best of our ability, we tried to vary our patterns, and were successful, really, in deterring any kind of significant attack against our vehicles.

We did have several car bombs detonated on us, sporadic small arms contact, and some IED contacts, but we were able to survive those situations with extremely minor injuries. All told, at the end of the deployment, the company managed to escape Iraq with only seven purple hearts, and none of those injuries serious. All of the soldiers essentially fully recovered before we left the area. So, we're very lucky, and very blessed to have been in that particular situation. Anyways, so again, counter mortar operations consumed a majority of our effort.

When targets did come down for the squadron, because we were the infantry force that was available, we would typically get the lead on pursuing those targets. We executed several squadron level cordon and searches with limited results. It seemed to me that, when we conducted very large-scale operations, that were necessarily in response to a very prevalent, heavily armed enemy threat, that those types of operations typically had limited results. Asides, probably sending a very strong psychological message.

Whether that's just the inability of a huge organization to maintain secrecy, and I'm not talking about information necessarily being leaked, I'm just talking about with that many vehicles moving around, it becomes obvious. Or whether they were designed specifically for the purpose of sending a very clear psychological message. In either event, the operations that we conducted in Mosul above the company level, seemed to generate limited results in the eyes of the soldiers within the company.

As the remaining time in Mosul kind of came to a close, the company obviously began to shift some focus to preparing our equipment for sign over to Charlie Company from One Deuce Four, who was the company that eventually transitioned with us. They took over, not only our mission, but also our gear, and we spent a lot of time preparing the remaining equipment that we had for redeployment back to the United States. We stayed focused on the mission, and reminded our soldiers daily that they could die just as easily today, as they could die eleven months ago. So, they needed to continue to exercise the same amount of caution now, as they did back then.

So, I can remember at this point in time, that as a company commander, you begin to realize that the hard work that you've done for the past eleven months, the relationships that you've established with the soldiers in your company, the accomplishments of these men, all those things are about to come to a close. There's once again, it's the idea of something being kind of bittersweet. God, it's sweet to be able to go back to the United States and reestablish a relationship with your family, but it's bitter in some ways, because the way that it was back when we were in Iraq, you just understand that it's probably not going to be the same way when you return to the United States. So, as a commander, especially a commander with his time in command kind of drawing to a close, it was a time of tempered enthusiasm, that's probably the best way to put it.

I can remember when the initial elements of Charlie One Deuce Four arrived on the ground to begin the transition with us, it was their fire support officer, and I remember he was probably like the second coming of Jesus. I mean, just seeing this guy was clear proof that we were in fact, going to leave Iraq, and that someone else was going to pick up our job, and this was about to be the end. When the new company arrived, it was Captain Chris Hostel as company commander, and his first sergeant, First Sergeant Nutley, linked up with myself and First Sergeant Littenger, and we kind of gave him the one over world dump. Then we did everything that we possibly could under the specific guidance of our brigade and battalion commanders, but also under Matt's just doing what's right policy, to make sure that they had every single shred of information that we could possibly spit out of our mouths in a two-week period.

We made sure, that they had maps already laminated, and squads had made books for them, and we conducted classes on the use of the area specific equipment, and took their guys out on patrols, and then they eventually took us in the right seat ride mode, and we went out on their patrols. We continued to maintain at least two NCOs per patrol with them until we left the country. I think that kind of, like, the undeniable proof that the RIP TOA process is working, and working well, is that 3rd Brigade immediately left off where the 101st had stopped, and was able to achieve some fabulous results.

With 1st Brigade in country now, and 1-24 in particular, at least with from what I know, because I've been followin those guys since they've been there, has just done some amazing things from capturing the number one HVT, and some other really high-level insurgents, to defeating some significant enemy attacks. They've just done a fantastic job, and it's good to know that you at least played some small role in their success, by making sure that you equipped them with all of the tools and that knowledge that would be required to be successful, and make an impact immediately.

So, as we began to get ready to leave, I can remember Lieutenant Colonel Eric Kurilla, who was my battalion S3, and then brigade S3, when I was a lieutenant in Italy. He was the battalion commander of 1-24 at the time. I remember that he shook my hand, and he gave me a coin from One Deuce Four, and said, "Job well done." We were basically the last element of 3rd Brigade in Iraq. There was the 18th engineer company, and God bless Dean Mitchell and his men. We were the guys that were left on the ground, so it was very nice of him to extend that gesture of comradery to us, because the remainder of the brigade had headed south already to

Kuwait. I just remember feeling an immense sense of closure, and thankfulness to God, that all these men that I had led, were going to be coming back with ten fingers and ten toes, and I was really getting excited to see my family. It was really a great way to end a year in Iraq.

However, Attack Company would not be able to skirt out of Iraq without encountering some final resistance. Specifically, I remember we were waiten on the airfield in Mosul, preparing to board the aircraft that was going to take us back to Kuwait, and we did receive some mortar fires. So, that was a fitting end to a fun filled twelve months in Iraq. So, I guess that's more or less a chronology of things as they occurred for Attack Company during OIF [Operation Iraqi Freedom].

The first thing that I did when I got home was obviously, went, we did the little welcome home ceremony in the gym, Sheridan gym, and I remember following the ceremony, that I spent about the first five minutes in the gym searching for my wife and my children, who apparently were positioned on the wrong side of the mob of people. I just remember grabbing my sons, giving them a hug, and giving them a kiss, and grabbing my wife, and giving her a kiss, and saying a prayer, and giving thanks to God, that I had returned back from this life changing year, fully intact, and ready to assume my role as father and husband. So, what did I do when I came home? I spent time, every single waking moment of every day, that I possibly could, with my family, and just enjoying the pleasure of their company.

Final Thoughts

I think that for me, especially as a guy that arrived at Fort Lewis and spent twenty-two months on the battle staff before I took command, and before going to Iraq, is that for me, Iraq was kind of like the epitome event. It was coming full circle for the whole concept of the IBCT [Interim Brigade Combat Team]. There had been plenty of naysayers, there were plenty of pundits that said that the concept couldn't work, that it was ill conceived, that General Shinseki was putting his eggs in the wrong basket.

But I think that by Colonel Rounds and his brigade going to Iraq, and assuming the mission of an entire division, and executing that mission with violence and control by engaging the Iraqis and insurgents with direct fire, and the population with compassion. By demonstrating that the vehicle had the kind of capabilities that had been published, but had not been proven. Just in general, by showing the quality of the American soldier and his ability to adapt to and utilize the technology that's available to him. That we really, kind of, showed anybody that would have thought the concept not possible, that they were just, basically, well, they were clearly wrong. The fighting spirit, the ingenuity, and the perseverance, and the will of the American soldier can basically overcome any kind of challenges that are placed before him. And that the Stryker, is unmatched in Iraq.

The second thought that I kind of have on OIF, is that you hear often from leaders in the army, and from senior NCOs, that the NCOs are the backbone of the army. Being a soldier of only eight years you hear that enough, and you believe it. You see it in action on a range, or a CTC [combat training center] rotation, which are short lived, and less than life threatening, or life serious situations, and you gain an appreciation for it, but you really don't see it in a way that you can't forget.

Iraq, at least for me, was a clear indicator of that. I mean these guys, they trained brand new lieutenants, they were experts technically, they were moral rocks, they did the right thing all the time, they enforced standards, they would pat me on the back when I had a bad day, and lift my spirits. They would assist me with developing doctrine, they would critique my plan, they would ask the hard questions, they would take me aside when they thought that I was in error, or that I had made a mistake, or I needed some adjusting, or fine tuning, and let me know what their thoughts were. They were, in every way, critical to my development and growth as a company commander, and in every way, responsible for the company bringing back all of its soldiers alive and without injury.

First Sergeant Gregory Littenger, my platoon sergeants, Sergeant First Class Jones, Sergeant First Class, now First Sergeant Montgomery, Sergeant First Class Ward, Sergeant First Class

Howard, my mortar section sergeant, Staff Sergeant Johnson, my fire supporter, Staff Sergeant Warwood, I mean these guys were absolutely crucial in every aspect of the company's success. They were crucial in every aspect of preventing the company's failure, and they are heroes in my eyes, as are all the soldiers in the company. I won't forget the impact that they had on me, and the lives of everybody that worked with them.

Probably the third thing that I learned, is that one of the things that I struggled with as a new commander, and one of the things that I hopefully won't struggle with in the future, is that I found myself to be, maybe a micromanager before I went to Iraq, and I find myself often having trouble trusting junior and inexperienced subordinates. My platoon leaders, God bless them, every single one of them were fast learners, and they were all smart enough to know that they needed to listen to their platoon sergeant. And, in the absence of their platoon sergeant, when those guys went home on mid-tour leave, those guys absolutely stepped up with the assistance of junior squad leaders, and continued to perform their mission in a manner that the platoon sergeant could be happy with when he returned. In a manner that I was completely proud of during the time that they were leading in the absence of their right-hand man.

It's this kind of demonstration, of what can be achieved when you give your subordinates the initiative and the freedom to act within your intent, that first-hand evidence that this kind of stuff works. It works in an environment where the cost of doing business the wrong way, is potentially people's lives. It is, I think, probably what made me the kind of leader, that for the rest of my career, will feel certainly more comfortable powering down a lot of that responsibility, and understanding that by doing so, we can accomplish twice as much, if not more, than we could have accomplished, if I would have been very strictly micromanaging the organization, or holding and pulling on the reins.

Finally, with respect to the success or the failure of our mission in Iraq. All I can say for certain is, that every soldier that worked in any of the companies that I commanded, gave a hundred percent the whole time that they were there. They did nothing that brought discredit upon the country, they only had the best interest of the Iraqi people in mind, and we tried to conduct our operations when required with the appropriate amount of violence, and always with the appropriate amount of class. And, that the groundwork that we laid in training the ICDC or the police officers, with the insurgents that we took into custody, with the school children that we gave school supplies to, or the infrastructures that we helped protect or provide supplies for, all those things we did well. All those things I just mentioned, over the course of the long term, will have made a difference, and the successful self-governing and self-policing of the nation of Iraq. So, when specifically posed with the question, "Do I think that we were successful in our mission during our time between November of 2003, and November of 2004"? I would say, unequivocally, categorically, absolutely, yes.

As far as awards and decorations go, nothin Matt Dabkowski did in Iraq was especially heroic. I got the award that all company commanders and first sergeants in Iraq got when we were there, which was a Bronze Star Medal. It really was probably more than I deserved. Instead of preparing for another rotation to Iraq, I was blessed with the opportunity to attend graduate school at the University of Arizona, where I studied industrial engineering in preparation for a follow-on assignment to the West Point systems engineering department.

Eric Evans

Charlie Company Squad Leader

My name is Eric Evans, I was born in Washington D.C. I joined the army about two years after high school, my first duty station, my only duty station, has been Fort Lewis. I spent four years in 2nd Ranger Battalion before coming over to 5-20 Infantry. A lot of the training I did with my squad while we were in Kuwait was geared mainly towards a city fight. That was the impression I got going in, was that we were going to be spending a lot of time in the cities, so we trained mostly for an urban fight.

Samarra

Operation Precision Cut was when we first went in to Samarra after Saddam Hussein was captured. Operation Precision Sweep was all the night raids when we surrounded the city, and we did that whole big post thing you know. Going into FOB [forward operating base] Pacesetter I remember living conditions were pretty bad there, we had tents, but no electricity initially, no heat whatsoever, our we pretty much had to build indirect bunkers ourselves, the chow was less than stellar, although I guess it was better than MREs [meals ready to eat]. Let me tell you, the 4th Infantry Division didn't do us any favors when we arrived. I remember not sleeping a whole lot the month we were in Samarra; I don't remember sleeping very much at all.

As far as the feelings I had while we were in Samarra, I had probably one of the more exciting days of my life as the first actual night raid. We did a target house, and that was prior to the whole knock and search you know, that came over the battalion or brigade whichever side, they wanted us to do knock and searches. The first raid was pretty much like everything we had trained for you know, we went in hard, booted in the door, didn't ask for anything, just kind of did what we needed to do, and it was exciting to get to do what we'd been trained to do.

Tal Afar

The ground assault convoy into northern Iraq was pretty much as uneventful as the one into Samarra, although we were expecting contact being that we were a relatively new style of unit going into northern Iraq, but we received no contact. We figured that we'd be tested somewhere along the way, but we weren't. Once we arrived in Tal Afar, we immediately began transition of authority with the 101st Airborne Division. It was first thing in the morning when we started transitioning with the Rakkasans.

Once we got inside the city, we did some right seat rides with them in Tal Afar. We realized immediately the way that we were gonna be doing business was a lot different than the way they were doing business. They were real relaxed, I don't know, maybe it was cause they had been there a year, and they knew what to expect, but they seemed to be a lot more relaxed than us, so we knew the way we would be doing things would be a lot different.

I think we spent about ten months in Tal Afar, Charlie Company did, and a good four months of that was spent doing dismounted patrols two or three times a day, three- or four-hour patrols in the day, and another three- or four-hours on patrol through the city at night. We did a lot of patrols around the outskirts of the city in the surrounding villages and towns, never really did a whole lot of assaults during our stay there. Not a whole lot of combat operations there, mostly civil-military type stuff, but as a squad leader going up and gathering intel, and meeting with town leaders and village leaders, it was a little bit overwhelming. Everything I'd been trained to do was just lead a squad in a firefight pretty much, and to go in there and have to find out what these people needed to survive, what kinds of funds they needed, what type of infrastructure they needed rebuilt, it was a little overwhelming for a while. We eventually got the hang of it, but we were definitely working well above our level.

When I was wounded my feelings weren't really about me, as I was more worried about my soldiers at the time. We were on base security when the rounds were coming in, I was more worried about, you know, what were they hitting, were any of my guys hurt, and I knew I wasn't hit bad. I could still move my hands where I got hit somewhat, so it wasn't anything I was real worried about. A lot of my soldiers were a little irate about the fact that I was wounded, a lot of the religious ones decided that they weren't going to be religious until after they returned from Iraq. They felt that, I guess, that God in their eyes wasn't there that day, so they weren't gonna rely on him anymore. It was kind of an overwhelming experience for some of them.

As far as April 9th goes, the thing that sticks out most in my mind about that was after everything was said and done, first platoon was called on to go out and kind of hunt down, or see if we could hunt down, any insurgents left hanging out in the area. I think we found probably around five or six RPG [rocket propelled grenade] tubes, and I want to say three or four remaining RPG rounds that hadn't been expended, but we were unable to find any insurgents. We knew exactly where a lot of the ones that had been shot were, so we concentrated on those areas, but we were unable to find them. We pretty much did extensive searches of the surrounding buildings attempting to find the wounded or killed insurgents, but apparently, they had carried off their wounded or dead and we weren't able to find anything other than what munitions they had left behind.

One more thing I wanted to mention about Tal Afar, when we went in there to control that city, we went in with a company sized element roughly, 170 soldiers patrolling a city of about a quarter of a million people and outlying areas. Our company stepped into an area that a battalion plus had been controlling, so we as a company, controlled a quarter million-man sized city plus, what was the size of the area [pause], I don't remember the size of the area, but it was pretty much bigger than most counties in the U.S., and we as a 170-man fighting force were controlling all of that to ourselves. So, Tal Afar was an interesting, depressing, saddening, exciting, uh, pretty much every emotion you can imagine type place while we were there.

We were out in Tal Afar for a long time before we moved back to the FOB with the Cavalry. We did non-stop missions, but I don't have a whole lot to say about any particular mission, most were pretty uneventful for my squad. Little surges of excitement and, you know, a lot of work. After we were back on the FOB our battalion replaced the Cavalry and we did some battalion and brigade missions.

I recall the instance that led to the siege of Tal Afar was the particular day when the Kiowa was shot down. I remember about that day, we weren't a part of the mission that was out that day, I believe it was Bravo Company, the scouts, and some ING [Iraqi national guard]. I remember Charlie Company, we were down at our company hanger, we were having a reenlistment formation, or an award, or some type of formation. I remember hearing a lot of yelling and running around, the company commander Captain Beaty, and the platoon leaders at the time, we all went into the company war roo. My lieutenant, Jensen, comes runnin out and grabs up all the squad leaders, myself and my fellow squad leaders, and tells us that a Kiowa had just been shot down inside the city and that our platoon was going to spearhead the recovery of that particular downed helicopter.

So, at that point we ran back down to the containers, probably about a click, roughly about a click back down to where our Strykers and all our fighting kit was, and got geared up. Before we finally got out of the gate, we probably waited for about a half hour to forty-five minutes, before we were even given authorization to leave. But once we did leave, it took less than 30 minutes on an unimproved route that came up around the backside of the city.

Bravo Company had quartered off the down Kiowa and was in a pretty hellacious firefight, pretty much in all directions. RPGs were flying everywhere, Bravo Company was launching AT4s, once we got in there, we kinda centered ourselves around the downed Kiowa and proceeded to begin recovery operations. Right around the time we were startin to recover the helicopter, mortar rounds started coming in. The site I saw during that was probably one of the funniest things I've ever seen as Staff Sergeant Jones at the time, sitten up on top of the Kiowa with a quickie saw, sawing off the rotors with the biggest grin I've ever seen on a man's face, as mortar rounds were landing all around him.

Immediately following the mortar rounds, somebody, I'm not sure who called it in, called in a strike from an F16 or a gun run, I should say, on the suspected mortar position. They weren't allowed to put rounds where the mortars were firing from cause it was a historical landmark, so they did a gun run through one of the wadies and that pretty much ended the mortar fire for the day. Then shortly thereafter, I believe was when the JDAM [joint deployed aerial munition] was dropped, and that was a pretty amazing display of power.

Going into the siege of Tal Afar, other than the Kiowa being shot down, a couple of other things in my mind are what led to it. A lot of the media was reporting that the insurgents had control of the city of Tal Afar, pictures were being posted on the internet, and in newspapers, of insurgents inside the city, you know, posing blatantly inside the city with their RPGs, claiming they had control of the city. I think at that point everything kind of came to a head in the city of Tal Afar. They decided this is our city and we're takin it back, and they decided we were going to lay siege to the entire city.

I believe it was the whole brigade came up for that one as well, but 5-20 Infantry in particular was responsible for the northwestern corner of the city. I believe it was, if I'm not mistaken, and the thing I remember is sitting at the main gate to the FOB that night, sitten up on top of the Stryker waiting for the word to move, watching air strikes on the city, on suspected and known enemy positions, once the air strikes and mortar prep were complete, we got the word to go ahead and move into our cordon positions, which we did before daylight.

Charlie Company had a few small skirmishes with suspected insurgents. I remember Bravo Company was the next company over, they got into a pretty sustained firefight with their .50 cals and MK19s, but about the time day broke, one of the most amazing things I've ever seen was to watch a quarter of a million people pick up and leave a city. It was an amazing sight. I think we sat there for probably about 24-hours before we decided to start pushin a little bit deeper into the city, once everyone had cleared out.

I don't remember pushin real deep into the city, but just moved into key buildings and strategic areas. The big one for Charlie Company, at least for my platoon, was taking a feed granary that was in our sector. That was an interesting task, we got inside there and realized that there were tunnels, and hallways, and doors all over the place. I think it dropped probably about two or three stories below ground, not to mention they wanted us to clear up the grain elevators, up into the silos. So, we started clearing that granary out, we expected it to take an hour or so, but it ended up taking us probably about three or four hours to completely clear that granary out. It made for an interesting day.

After the siege of Tal Afar, that pretty much ended most major operations for us in Iraq. As a whole, we did a few route interdiction missions, just trying to make sure that things went well in the city until 1st Brigade came and relieved us. Once they showed up, things went pretty smooth. A few right seat rides and left seat rides with them to point out some of the areas that we had had problems with. We signed over most of our equipment to them, including our Strykers, which we were happy to be rid of at the time.

We were all ready to come home. We pretty much handed over the sector to them and flew on out to Kuwait for a few days before returning to Fort Lewis.

Shawn Fleming

Charlie Company Sniper Section Sergeant

My name is Sergeant Shawn C. Fleming. I was born in Linton Indiana. I didn't join the army immediately after school, I waited till I was about 24, it was 1994. Before this I was a stationed in Germany. When I first got to Kuwait, what we saw was pretty much pitch black. We got there kinda late I do believe, and we went straight into, uh, [pause] Udairi. It was a little different from what I thought for that time of year.

I had been to Kuwait prior to that for a short tour, but now all we saw was a bunch of tents and the desert. The good things that we did I think, or what we were thinking, was that we was going to go fight a war against terrorism. That's the way it was broken down to us, so basically, what we did in Kuwait was trained a lot. We did certain live fire exercises, and kicked in houses, and everything like that. Everyone just got acclimatized and waited for orders to move north.

When we left Kuwait, I remember crossing the border there with all the concertina wire and everything. We had a soldier that was hurt that night prior, he had a negligent discharge with a MK19, and a couple other soldiers were wounded. That kind of brought more reality to the guys as they thought maybe that could be them.

The day that we pulled out of Kuwait, I remember as soon as we crossed the border, the first town we went through was just the nastiest, dirtiest, stinkiest place I'd ever been through. The first thing I saw was a dude lifting his little man dress to utilize the street as a toilet, right there in front of us.

It was a long, cold ride; we were in truck seven which was a HMMWV gun truck. At the time, it had no up armor, not even doors, just a front windshield and a bunch of guns sticken out of it. Before all the IEDs [improvised explosive devices] in Iraq, that was how it was done. On our way up to FOB [forward operating base] Pacesetter we didn't know what to think, going through cities and everything like that, but we finally got there.

Samarra

We did a lot of good training before at Fort Lewis, Kuwait, and in Iraq I thought. If we weren't going on missions into Samarra, then you know, we continued training. Now there's Operations Precision Cut and Precision Sweep in Samarra, but just before that, our guys caught Saddam. OK, the capture of Saddam Hussein, I remember getting the word to stand down because the SOF [special operations forces] guys had grabbed Saddam. I talked to my girlfriend immediately after, and she thought that we were all comin home. She said a lot of people were happy that he had been captured, it let a lot of stress off of people, but little did she know that we weren't on our way home.

Jim Mapes, First Sergeant Jim Mapes, what an outstanding man, a true hero to the American people. I just can't say enough about him, just the ultimate example of a warrior leader in my opinion. I was on the sniper section for the company at the time, and he was always working with us. We had Staff Sergeant Shell and Sergeant Kelly with us also. We had my three-man team running that gun truck, and a lot of the time they would drop us off outside of the city, and they would watch our backs for us while we were moving in the city, in case we needed a little heavier volume of fire than a couple of M4's and an M24.

You always have some anxiety during infil. I'd say it's the adrenaline rush going in. I'd been to Kosovo a couple of times, Bosnia, I spent a year in Bosnia, another six months in Macedonia, and spent four and a half months in Kuwait. During all that time, you always knew that anything could happen, anything could happen, but this was a little different when you killed them. You know, it didn't seem like they wanted me there, didn't seem that they wanted us there at all. Most of the operations we did at night, and that was the first time that I had heard RPGs [rocket propelled grenades] being fired and that scared the crap out of me, my men were just as scared as I was, I think.

Tal Afar

We were detached from the battalion to 1-14 Cavalry after Samarra. The ground assault convoy into northern Iraq was to Tal Afar, and I don't really remember anything unusual about it. I worked on the transition with the 101st Rakkasans up there at the time. One of the things I remember about the Rakkasans was that not only were they cool, but they told us some of the events such as the 1,000-pound car bomb that hit them, and about some of their guys being killed in an RPG attack, and what not. They definitely gave us help with the whole right seat ride thing, which I thought was really good.

The only thing that I was sorry about was, I really didn't get to work with their sniper teams at all. We tried to hook it up, but it just didn't happen because they were busy, and then we were busy learning the ropes. We also knew that part of our job was going to be working with the squads and what not, so we were trying to get to know the city as well as just the local base. We took over operations from D Company, 1/187 Infantry in Tal Afar.

One of the first big events that I remember was our first RPG attack, Sergeant Evans was our first combat casualty. He took some shrapnel from a mortar round, and I think at that time is when it really hit, you know, hit everybody that they ain't messin around, they're trying to kill us! Now, and I think a lot of people turned their attitude towards killing them before they killed us. It wasn't the national or joint readiness training centers, or anything to that affect, and it just got worse from there.

Didn't seem like it was all that bad at first. Seemed like it was pretty quiet after the invasion, and started to heat up as we got to there. I don't know, maybe the people were tired of it, or maybe it took the foreign insurgents awhile to regroup and move to Iraq and fight, I don't know. But that place is dirty and poor, and they'll smile at you one minute and shoot mortars at you the next. Most of them just have nothing, and live in mud huts.

After that, every once in a while, we'd get hit by some mortars. As far as civil operations I worked guarding the CO [company commander] a lot, my team did. We got to go out and meet a lot of the mayors, the mukhtars, the sheiks, the police chiefs and I didn't think any of them were good people. Maybe I've just been, I don't know, prejudice that way or whatever, but I didn't want to let my guard slip either. I didn't want to die over there, and I didn't want my guys to become casualties either.

OK, just gettin back into the operations and everything, I think as far as the mortar attacks, we would have at the beginning probably more mortar attacks than actual gunfire. Jake Herring, who was later killed over there, I remember when he was hit the first time on a dismounted patrol with an IED [improvised explosive device]. Sergeant Glover was the team leader at the time, and Sergeant McLaughlin might have been with him also, I can't remember, once again that was one of those reality checks now.

They were starting to hit us when we walked out the gate, so we started thinkin a little bit more. We had more grenades being thrown at us, and we were taking shrapnel from those grenades, and that all led up to, Rock Base being attacked. Rock Base was a small compound inside of Tal Afar that C Company, Rock company, had to go ahead and secure and live in. That's where we conducted our operations, not so much FOB Fulda, I think that was the name of the Cavalry base at the time.

So, we conducted operations out of Rock Base then, I know that the commander had a meeting that morning up in, I think it was Barzan, and I had my two guys go ahead and escort him up there. I had to do a NCOER [non-commissioned officer evaluation report] on one of my NCOs at the time, cause he was gettin ready to go to another platoon. So, I was sitten in our little room, which wasn't bad at all, I thought we had a pretty decent room sitten there workin on my computer, and I was listenin to George Strait real low at the time. *I'm Gonna Miss Her*, by Brad Paisley, I think was playing.

I remember hearin some small arms gun fire, and then some loud booms, and I was like, "Oh shit, here we go," and I threw on my kit and the first thing I did was run out to ECP1. ECP1 was the entry control point on the southern side of Rock Base, and nothing was going on there, so I was like, "Well, what's going on"? So, I turned around, and I saw that ECP2, which was the northern ECP, was being hit. So, I started working my way up that way, and I remember seeing a translator on the ground behind one of the dragon teeth, and some grenades going off right near him. I also remember seeing Sergeant Rochelle pulling Sergeant Bell out of a guard house at the time, Sergeant Bell had been wounded and there were more RPGs coming in. I didn't know that there was anybody firing at me from the school, which was maybe 20 meters to our west on the, I guess second or third floor. I can't remember right now, but there they were firing on my position as I was watchin the northern gate.

Sergeant Rochelle and Sergeant Kelly both had 9 mils, at the time Lieutenant Eton was out there, also along with Sergeant Sagaven, I don't know if that was him or not, and they were taking some RPG rounds and everything. I worked my way up to the northern gate which was inside of our perimeter, but still you can be engaged as well from inside that gate from the outside, and you couldn't see as well from inside as you could from the outside.

I was outside at that time and I saw an insurgent, or anti-Iraqi forces (AIF), as we called them at that time, on a building across from us. He was shooting at, I think it was Lieutenant Eton at the time, and Lieutenant Eton was trying to get out of there, so I engaged the AIF member. At that time Sergeant Alexander, which was right around the door with his squad, was like, "Hey, what have you got," and I replied, "Hey, I got someone up there on the top of the building," and laid down a few more rounds. At the time, Lieutenant Eton was moving back along with Sergeant Rochelle and Sergeant Kelly, and Sergeant Bell cause he was wounded. I think Sergeant Sagaven stayed out on the ECP still returning fire.

We started moving back in, and started taking fire from somewhere, I didn't understand where it was from, and I can't remember who it was that was saying the schoolhouse, look at that second story or third story window. I can't remember, but I returned fire and got down to ECP1. I entered ECP1 and Sergeant Pallony was there along with, uh, Sergeant Jojo, I don't know how you pronounce Gingero, yeah something like that, and then I told them guys to stay there. Jim Mapes was once again in QRF1 [quick reaction force] with his flip-flops and body armor and everything, and they're engaging an RPG gunner at the southern end.

First Sergeant Mapes and chainsaw, which was Sergeant Jones, I think were arguing over who shot the guy as a matter of fact, cause they lit him up pretty good. After that whole thing, we went and got his RPG, and it was just full of bullet holes. Finally, we got everybody back inside and we stayed on the perimeter for a while those guys pulled out. I think they said ten was the number that actually attacked us from the north, the west, and the south. My guys sent word to Rock 6 at the time, which was Captain Beaty, that the base was under attack, and they ended up turning back. But they got back to us kinda late, and my guys were kinda pissed off, cause they didn't get none of that action. So that's April 9th, as far as I remember, except for the firefight at night and everything like that, yeah, we definitely destroyed that.

Later on in April, Sergeant Jake Herring was killed in action by an anti-armor grenade when it hit a Stryker. He was our only soldier in the battalion that was killed by enemy fire, we had two other deaths in B Company, but those were in a rollover accident. They were all because of Iraq though, and we feel sorry for their families just like we do about Jake. I tried to recruit Jake into my sniper section because I had one of my NCOs leaving, Sergeant Riner. Jake was gettin ready, he wanted to get out of the army and go to college, and I would talk to him day in and out about coming to my section. Just give me a couple more years, I could give you something else to go into the world with I would tell him, but he didn't come to the section. Everyone liked Jake, he was just a good dude.

OK, going on into September, they moved us back to the FOB, the cavalry changed out with our battalion over the summer. We had done a lot of operations the months prior to that, and we had gained a lot of intelligence prior to the siege on Tal Afar. We did a sweeping operation with the whole brigade, they brought the other battalions from the brigade down to Tal Afar, and we went in, we went in prior to daylight if I remember correctly, and my guys and I dismounted once again. We were working on overwatching the company at one point in time, as the company started pushing out. We were doing our usual chitter chatter with the commander and everything, telling him what we saw, and as the day went on, we were pulling nothing up.

We were taking fire every once in a while, returning the fire, and later on there was a group of kids, five kids and I say, they were all 13 and under. They ended up throwing a grenade or some sort of IED at our guys. Those kids threw this grenade, I saw them throw the grenade, I didn't know what it was at the time, and then I heard the boom. I couldn't believe that children were throwing grenades or the IED in the first place. Most people just don't get it; in combat anyone can be a combatant. Men, kids, women, everyone, whether they're fighting or supporting the insurgents, you just can't trust them.

So, I raised my rifle, and I fired a couple rounds in their direction. I didn't bead on them or anything, it was kinda hard to make the decision to go ahead, and you know, shoot a kid, but we fired at their feet. I remember that I called up to Rock 6 and he sent some dudes over. These kids went into a yard that was sectioned off, of course, and two older adults came out and it ended up that one of the platoons came down and helped us out.

They ended up arresting a bunch of people for that operation, but once again as the day wore on, we provided overwatch. At first, I didn't get to see how the ING [Iraqi national guard], or the ICDC [Iraqi civil defense corps] at the time, actually worked, cause I didn't get to go down with the 1st and 2nd platoons and work with those guys. But I had never seen a bigger group of incompetent people in my life. As far as accuracy and fire and everything like that, it's like they don't want to expose themselves to fire, so later on that day we were sitten on a house, on top of a roof, and the company was moving to a school, a schoolhouse I think it was, and the ING started lighting something up. We didn't know what it was, and, uh, I remember seeing a guy in a white man dress once again that had an AK47, and eventually saw him shooting at the ING, and that's who they were shooting at. So, we started looking if he was hit or not, I don't know, but that situation was over with and we just continued our sweeping operations.

Later on, I saw the Iraqis engage a dude that was maybe 30 meters in front of them, and I was two, maybe two hundred and fifty feet behind the Iraqis on overwatch position, as they were firing their rifles on full automatic standing in the open along with this other guy that was standing in the open firing his rifle full automatic. They were just firing and firing until they just got their rifles up in the air, not drawing a bead on anybody. So, I was trying to get my shooter on the target in time, and he couldn't find the target because he was down an ally way I guess, he just didn't have the angle or whatever, so I raised my rifle and shot the dude. I turned to my shooter, and I said, "Hey, I've never seen a bigger clusterfuck of soldiers, ever!" Just the way they were shootin, you know, we were just happy when that operation ended.

One of the good things about working with the commander was I always rode on his vehicle, the first sergeant, he was with us also, so I heard a lot about what was going on here and there. One of his [Captain Beaty's] famous sayings was, "giddy up." Before we started going out the gate, I remember seeing tracers just flying all over the place in Tal Afar. I do believe it was 1-23 Infantry that was movin in through their positions, their attack positions, and as we were moving closer to the gate and everything like that, you know, you could see everything that was going off. As we started moving out the gate, our battalion mortars were droppin 120s on planned targets, I mean it was an awesome sight they were just pounding them. Then we started lookin around and we could see a light just comin out of heaven, I mean you don't see with your NODs [night vision device] on, and we was like what's that? And all of a sudden, you just heard the roar of a Spectre gunship just tearin stuff up, droppin its 30-millimeter chain link cannons, then they had their 105s, and their mortars, and they were just laying waste to certain areas that the enemies were seen by UAV [unmanned aerial vehicles] and everything like that.

We moved closer into Tal Afar into our battle positions, blocking positions, and what not. A truck tried to run through a blocking position, not coming out of the city, but going into the city, and I remember them tryin to stop it and it wouldn't stop. I don't remember who sent up the call, but somebody said he's not stopping, and you know Captain Beaty, being Captain Beaty, said, "Burn him" and that's what they did. They stopped them, I don't know if that individual is dead or not, but he was doing the wrong thing, and who knows what he was going to do. But as the day wore on and daylight broke, we're sitten there and Battle Company's just lighten stuff up beside us. I see rounds just ricocheting off of stuff, and going through a water tower, there was an insurgent on top of the water tower and somebody was trying to engage him.

We were sitten there, and the first time that I had fired that day was when two vehicles were comin up, and they would not stop, and they were tryin to lay down suppressive, well not suppressive fire, but they were laying down rounds in front of the vehicle to get those vehicles to stop, but they still didn't. Every time a vehicle came down towards us, that's what they would do to push them back into the city because they didn't want to let them out just yet, because of the VBIED [vehicle born improvised explosive] threat. They warned all the good people to get out of Tal Afar before the operation, so anything moving was a threat. Every other vehicle had stopped, and I mean they'd put it in reverse, and they'd haul ass back in the city. But these two particular vehicles, they would not stop for anything, and we got it on tape cause Sergeant Shot was next to me at the time, I grabbed the XM107, the Barrett .50 cal, and that's the first time that I fired the Barrett .50 cal in a war time situation, cause we use the M24s, the M14s, or the M4s normally.

I was always carrying an M4, but I just thought it was a better weapon system for the situation we were in, and I shot the first car, and the second car, and they came rolling to a stop. I remember some people getting out, and they were upset you could tell, you know some people had ended up getting hurt and what not. I think we all felt bad, but it was just something that couldn't be helped because of the situation. I think they may have dropped that JDAM [joint deployed aerial munition] down at that time too, so it was a pretty interesting fireball.

Later on, we ended up settin up at a thing we called an ice cream factory, which was actually a flourmill, but everyone thought it was an ice cream factory. We set up in there, and I was overwatching the city. I was like three stories up, and I saw an RPG team moving towards the outside of the city to engage Battle Company. As I saw them, I engaged them, and they were, I want to say 1,400 meters out if I remember correctly, and I could not hit a damn one of them, it was making me mad! I was trying to get a spotter, but the guy that was usually shooting the M24 at the time couldn't find them, he couldn't spot the round. So, one of our MGS [mobile gun system] vehicles was tryin to spot for me, and they were tellin me where my splash was. So, you know, after five or six rounds where the dirt hit the cow at the side of the building, I didn't want to fire no more, so I just gave up on it. It's a loud weapons system, the .50 cal, it gives you a headache pretty quick, but yeah, I think that's about all.

After that we set up blocking positions. I think that was the last big thing that we were really involved in. There were small skirmishes before, and I think there were some afterwards, but before 1st Brigade came in, I think that was the last big operation there that happened. Yeah, we were very happy when 1st Brigade started landing on the FOB. I felt pretty safe at FOB Sykes at that time, which used to be FOB Fulda. As far as I was worried about an attack I mean, so I felt pretty safe on the post there. We did a few left seat, right seat rides, whatever, and we turned it over to the 25th Infantry Division. I think it was three days prior to that, that our battalion commander told us that none of us will leave FOB Sykes. I think that's when it all hit me, that we were gonna end up going home. I got on the bird and flew down to Kuwait, which I thought we should have flown straight home, but that was it as far as comin home, besides it bein hard gettin out of there.

Final Thoughts

As far as the war itself and my opinion or thoughts about it, I think, uh, I think we did the right thing. For something like twelve years this man [Saddam] had lied and cheated. At the time we thought there were weapons of mass destruction. In fact, there were weapons of mass destruction if you count the old chemical and biological type weapons, but I think most people think of weapons of mass destruction as nukes or something big like that. If you start counting all the people he killed over the years, I'd say that's mass destruction.

I think President Bush is a great president. I think there's a lot of people out there who don't realize they live on the blood of patriots and it's because of those patriots that they have the freedom to burn the flag and say what they say. We'll be going back sooner or later. I have no regrets. I don't think that I did anything over there that I thought was wrong. What I did well I thought, was gettin my men and myself back home alive. Those men around me, even if they weren't my men, we're all brothers in this company. We're all brothers and sisters in the army, but yeah, there's nothing wrong with what we're doing. We're doing what we're told to do, we're carrying out the orders of the President of the United States.

Christopher Galka

Battalion Sniper Section Sergeant

My name is Christopher Galka. I was born in Valparasio, Indiana on May 3, 1975. During high school I did a little bit of cross country, and a little bit of wrestling. After high school I went ahead and joined the Marine Corps. I went to a Marine security forces battalion as part of a FAST company, which is fleet, air and terrorism, security team. Did four years in the Corps as a sniper, got out, and did reserve time with the 84th training battalion for the Army for a little while. After 9/11, I went ahead and returned to active duty and came to 5-20th, 3rd brigade where I immediately went to the headquarters sniper section as a corporal.

I believe I arrived in Kuwait November 15th, 2004. Pretty much what I seen when I was in Kuwait was just a lot of getting ready to get on mission, ready to cross the border going to Iraq. Up-armoring our vehicles, testing all of our equipment and just pretty much training up a little bit on how we were going to dismount the vehicles and how we were going to roll with the scout element. At the time, I was thinking you know, we're hear to do a good thing, we're going to help the country of Iraq, you know, recover from this war, maybe help salvage the government, and find Hussein.

I guess you could say everyone was a little bit scared, a little bit nervous. We didn't know what to really expect when we crossed the border. When we crossed the border, the first thing we saw was a bombed-out town. It gave us a pretty good impression of what we'd be looking at, what kind of, uh [Takes a deep breath], what kind of situation that it was going to be. You know, how everything was standing at the time. How some of the towns would look, some of the people would react to us. Just, I guess, it wasn't a real good comfortable feeling when we came across there because we were getting the evil eye and scows from everybody.

Samarra

Once we got to FOB Pacesetter, it wasn't exactly what I was expecting. I was expecting a little bit worse conditions. Either worse or better, we were sleeping in some tents. It was pretty cold then, the average temperature was, I don't know, between 40 and 50 degrees. Sometimes dropped down to the thirties at night. We'd even get some rain, so riding in the Strykers and walking around in the mud, wet with the cold wasn't too fun.

[Takes a deep breath] Preparations we did in Pacesetter were to get ready to assault the town of Samarra. We were going to go in there and detain and eliminate or restrict any enemy that opposed us, and try to push the enemy out of the town. Capture or kill as many enemy as we can. During most of the operations there, I stood in an overwatch position with my sniper team and me.

One night we were out in the middle of a garbage pile, it was pretty stinky, and we sat out there for about five hours over-watching the town. Another time we were on top of a couple of buildings. We'd pick various buildings that had light and shadows, so we could overwatch the objective area, and just keep a good eye on our troops to make sure everything was going as planned. We were working as the eyes and ears for the commander.

My team was attached to Bravo Company a couple of times, and on one of our first missions the scouts found a weapons cache, so they called us out there. The Bravo Company sniper, Sergeant Davis, his partner was Wilson, set up behind one side of the cornfield, and we had about 100 meters between us as we set up on the other side of the cornfield. It wasn't too great in the cornfield, a lot of noise out there. We had some people that actually walked between our hide sites, but we couldn't effectively engage anybody because we'd end up firing on each other. Other than that, there wasn't a whole lot of activity for us. Being that it was our first mission out though, it was a little bit tense. We still didn't know exactly what to expect.

The operations after a while, to be honest, kinda got monotonous. In Samarra we would go out and stay at TAA [tactical assembly area] War Horse, which was a little tactical perimeter that we set up outside of Samarra. We would sleep on the ground out there, or in the vehicles. I would jot down some memories, and then we'd pull out and do missions. At that time, I was attached to Bravo Company with Sergeant Phipps. He was Specialist Phipps at the time, but I guess you could say we had a lot of bonding time out there, cause most of the time we worked together as a sniper team, and were attached to different companies.

In Bravo Company we didn't know a lot of people, there was a couple that we knew but, but most of the time it was just me and him. We relied on each other, promised to watch each other's back, promised to take care of any issues if we needed to for each other. If something happened to one of us, we would be the ones to talk to our families and let them know what happened, and what kind of situation it was, or whatever we could tell them.

One day towards the end of Samarra we took over a building and called it Fort Apache. We taunted the enemy to come out and fight us. We brought out the little Army bulldozers, built berms all around us, put up concertina wire, and we went on the roof with, uh, a .50 caliber sniper rifle and an M24, and some attachments from the scouts we had out there. This was my sniper team and the scouts, and pretty much we just over-watched Alpha Company all night.

We set up shifts, it was pretty cold, we had a fire going in a trashcan trying to keep warm. To make matters worse it started raining out there. Wasn't much activity, a few strange things, mainly people just checking us out, but no one really wanted to try us. We thought we would be there longer, with all the work we put into the place, but all of a sudden, they gave us the order to pull out. They had found Saddam right before we went into Samarra, and the town really quieted down after we stormed in, so I guess they wanted to get us up north to take over for the 101st.

Qayyarah

Our convoy to northern Iraq was a long trip. We stopped at a few places to fuel up, got to see a little bit more of the country, but not much really happened on that trip. Pretty much, we just stayed alert and pulled security. I rode outside of the hatch, watchin the area and just tryin to get a feel for the northern part, cause the country changes every region that you go to. How the people act, how they talk, how they look at you, just whatever. When we reached FOB Regulars, it was outside of, uh, Q-Town, Qayyarah, Iraq. That's where some of the 101st Airborne Division was.

I realized that we were placed in the 101st airborne division, with as much as a brigade, and we were covering the same area that they were, so with a much smaller unit. I was wondering how the people in Iraq would react to that, how the enemy would react? If they would know, cause they pretty much know everything that's going on cause of the people that work on the FOB, information leaks coming from these Iraqi civilians and politicians that are workin with us, it's proven fact. So, I just wondered if they would actually try to maybe overrun the FOB, or attack the FOB, being that the division was going to be replaced by a brigade, a much smaller number of people.

But I think being that we had Strykers, the people were pretty scared of those vehicles, they knew that they were armored well, they knew they carried a lot of fire power, and they knew that if they messed with them, there was 15 guys in the back that would come out and bust some heads. So, yeah, we had some concerns early on, but not really, I mean when I was on the FOB, I didn't really think about it, maybe it was an initial thought, but after we were there a little, I knew they weren't going to try anything big. The big difference between a battalion taking over for a brigade, is that you have to work three times as hard just to cover everything, because you only have about a third of the people, exhausting.

Uh, the reception, well I really didn't get to talk to anybody while I was there from the 101st. I didn't get any heads-up from them. Pretty much everything I got was stuff that I read, and just experience when we were out rollin through the town. They were just interested in telling stories about how experienced they were, about how they had been there for a year, and that they were goin home. We slept in some old buildings until the 101st left, and then we did some work to our scout area and lived in better buildings.

Hammam al Alil

We went forward to this little compound just outside of Mosul, called Objective Agees, to support the line companies. It was actually quite an interesting place. When we first got there, we were attached to Alpha Company. We brought the scouts up there, and they stayed for about a week. We put an OP [observation post] on the rooftop and we just scanned the area, cause they were getting rocketed pretty heavy, but when we got there, they actually quit rocketing the compound.

After that, the scouts went back to FOB Regulars, they left a couple of sniper teams: myself, Phipps, Staff Sergeant Horton and his partner Brown. We stayed and went on the rooftops at night and scanned the area, looking for anyone trying to come up to the compound to attack it, or recon it or whatnot. After Alpha Company was there, for, I believe it was a month-long tour, Bravo Company relieved them. Myself and Phipps went ahead and reattached to Bravo Company, and we were the solo team that stayed for awhile.

We were there for about a two-month period. During that time, we did a lot of operations. We were runnin about three missions a day. There were three platoons there, and we would support each platoon, so it was a lot of hours. It was very tiring, but we didn't really run into a whole lot of problems. One time we were out on a patrol and we got ambushed, I eliminated two enemy personnel there. It wasn't too exciting; it was about a hundred meters and on the run. I ended up taking out a guy that was sprintin away with an AK47 after he had already fired on us, and then we shot another guy through the laundry, he was hidin behind a sheet, so he wasn't very bright and probably deserved the bullet.

Myself and Phipps, we did a lot of operations out there, we actually got into ghillie suits and stalked at night. We worked by ourselves, we had probably about 2,000 meters between us and the compound. So, we were out there as an independent team. We would stalk out to different spots, hide out under railroad tracks and observe the town. We were watchin people put things in their wadies, and different sorts of stuff. We just basically went out and kept eyes out for the commander, gave him a heads up on what kind of activity was goin on. We would go over to the ruins, which were about 300 meters south of the town, and observe a different sector of the town. Try to see if any other activity was goin on out there.

One night we did have, actually a couple of nights, we had some excitement out there. People fired some rounds at us, we don't know if they actually knew we were there, but they were shooting. I think they were just reconning that site by fire, because the 101st put guys out there in that field, and made it known that they were there. I think the people were just doing recon by fire, to see if anybody was there, and if we'd fire back, which we didn't. We didn't engage because it wasn't a direct threat to us.

One night a rocket came over my and Phipp's heads, it sounded like a semi-truck flyin through the air. We thought a semi-truck or some kind of vehicle was rollin up on our position, but it hit about 300 meters from us. It was pretty pretty loud with a lot of force, it kinda knocked us silly for a second, shook the ground pretty hard. We went ahead and stayed out there, and just called it in, just observed the rest of the town. A couple of nights while we were out there, a fog rolled in, and fog is bad juju for us, because you know, we're just two guys in enemy territory, they know that terrain very well. We had to use a compass with azimuth to actually get back to the compound. Because we only had about 10-meter visibility, we went ahead after the fog rolled in and decided to do our E&E [escape and evade], our evasion plan. We went back to the compound and just went ahead and got rested up, and waited for the next mission.

Another night we were out there I had a machine gun team, M240B team, attached to myself and Phipps, and we were observin, I believe it was the eastern side of the town, when an RPG [rocket propelled grenade] attack took place. It was about 400 meters in front of us. They were attackin the ING [Iraqi national guard], and also another Stryker that was just a couple hundred meters past the ING checkpoint. We did not engage because we didn't have a clear shot, and also, we didn't want to be distinguished as unknown to the ING. We didn't want them firin on us because they didn't know who we were, plus the Stryker pretty much had it under control. They were returnin heavy fire towards the attackers, supporting the ING.

I'd have to say one of the scariest nights out there was when I was fearin a friendly attack from some Kiowa helicopters. They were circlin around us and they didn't know who we were, they thought we were Iraqis out there with weapons and flashlights and they lined up for a gun run on us. We we're tryin to yell over the radio to get them to stop, but we didn't have direct comms to them, we didn't even know where they came from. We were wearin ghillie suits, so we didn't have anything on us that identified us as Americans.

Well, it was myself, Phipps, Wilson and Sergeant Davis, the Bravo Company snipers, layin right next to a bridge. We were kinda dumbfounded, we didn't know what to really do, we were just tryin to stay as passive as we could, not look like we were any kind of threat. But we seen the choppers line up for a gun run, and they came in nose down tail up one behind the other. We thought this is it! But luckily, they didn't engage! Afterwards we found out that they were able to call those birds off at the last minute before they ended up lighten us up. After a while, we went back to FOB Regulars.

Qayyarah

Our guys really did a great job fixing up the FOB. A lot of the guys got Connex containers with heat and air, there was a big chow hall, and gym, and MWR [morale welfare and recreation] dome. The scouts and snipers had our own little CP [command post] and relaxation area. After the 101st left we had plenty of space. We didn't have a whole lot of combat going on in Qayyarah at that time, so there wasn't a whole lot to really talk about. Civil mode operations more so, we did do some civil affairs ops, where we went out and escorted a CA team to check on the towns and talk to the people, link up with the mayor, and stuff like that.

We took a few pictures of the Iraqis, got to play a little bit of soccer with some kids because most of the towns around that area seemed pretty friendly. We went out one day to hunt rocket man. We were getting mortared and rocketed, so myself, Phipps, Sergeant Daniels and Sergeant Foster rolled out to locate and neutralize rocket man. We ended up finding him one day, but due to the situation we weren't able to detain him. They finally got him, but he was so ineffective anyway, that nobody really worried about good old rocket man.

But things were about to change from our nice peaceful little Qayyarah area. All of a sudden, we were alerted to pack and move out in 24-hours for as much as 30 days. Moqtada al-Sadr and his militia were causing problems way down south in An Najaf, and we had to go down there with no notice, and help put down the uprising that was causing havoc in south and central Iraq. We got a 24-hour delay because northern Iraq started to heat up, but after the minor delay, we moved out for An Najaf. The entire country was now going crazy, they were blowing up bridges and causing problems everywhere. On our convoy going into southern Iraq, now that was our first ambush that the scouts were actually hit hard.

Task Force Arrow

The scouts always lead the entire battalion. We had been up for a long time, I think the entire trip took three straight days, but before dawn on day two, we were hit hard. My vehicle, scout vehicle 21 was caught in the kill zone. We were hit by a couple of

RPGs and it disabled our power in our vehicle, but the engine was still able to run. We didn't have any communications until we got an MBITR [multiband inter/intra team radio] hand-held radio up, and we're going off of hand mikes instead of CVCs [combat vehicle crewman helmets]. We basically were stopped cold in the kill zone, unable to move or communicate initially, but the Stryker is well armored and has a lot of firepower.

We just attacked back and gained fire superiority, we just started mowin these guys down. I had a thermal sight on my weapon at that time. So, when we were able to move, and started rollin down the road a little bit further, we had a blown-out tire from one of the RPGs. So, we're rollin kinda slow trying to get to a rally point where we could link up with the rest of the platoon, and get our vehicle fixed, and just get everything sorted out. On our way to the rally point, I saw two enemy ambush positions through my thermal and engaged. It looked like I initiated a firefight between them. They didn't really get too many rounds off, I probably hit a few of the guys that were out there as the machine guns were going off, but it was nothing compared to the initial ambush that hit us.

The initial ambush, it was a good ambush, they had it set up right, but their individual skills just are not very good. If they would have had better hits with their RPGs, and better aim with their rifles, they would've probably done some damage, because they did take us by surprise. One of our best defenses over there was the enemy's incompetence. Most times they would just shoot and run. Even when they tried to aim, they weren't very effective.

We also reacted very fast, and within seconds returned an overwhelming amount of firepower back at them. When you can place effective fire from a fortified Stryker, I guess it would be a little intimidating to some guy running around out there with a rusty AK or RPG. We got hit a few times on the way to An Najaf, but after about three days we finally made it to this little FOB with the 1st Infantry Division and a few contractors. They didn't have anything there. We did a quick refit and then started to recon An Najaf for an attack, but at that time, they weren't sure if they wanted us to assault because it was one of their Holy cities.

After a few days in An-Najaf they told us to pack up and get ready to move to central Iraq. We drove up and down that country, between the infil and then to An-Najaf, and now back up to the middle just north of Baghdad. They sent us to LSA Anaconda, a big supply post with an indoor swimming pool, PX and you name it, they had it. The biggest thing they were fighting was us trying to get out the gate that was run by the reserves and being in the right uniform for the chow hall. They sure did like to wear their helmets and body armor in the chow hall.

The uprising had brought everything to a halt. The insurgents had blown up most of the main bridges in the country, and no supplies were moving by ground. Hundreds of trucks were just sitting in secure areas afraid to move because convoys were gettin destroyed out there. That was interesting, we did a bunch of convoys between Anaconda and Scania. So, we went ahead and formed up as a company, normally the scouts and snipers work independently for the battalion or are attached to a line company, but for the escort missions we worked as a company with the scout, mortar, and engineer platoon with our company commander.

There was a huge backlog, but we went from Anaconda to Scania, stayed the night, and then brought another group north to Anaconda the next day. We went through Baghdad every day when we were doing the escort mission. The truck drivers didn't trust the MPs [military police] because they weren't very organized or prepared, and would leave the convoys if they were hit too hard. The MPs showed us a few routes in the beginning, but they were late, their radios never worked, and their weapons were dirty.

We ran into a few problems out there, not too much, but we got shot at a lot, and ambushed a few times. Once or twice, we had to disable a few vehicles because they were comin into our convoy and looked like they were possibly gettin ready to, you know, strike one of our vehicles. We would always try to use as much non-lethal force as we could. We had non-lethal rounds, used a lot of hand signals, and a lot of yellin. We used a lot of vehicles to block people off, but pretty much, we were safe on the road, we didn't really try to harm any Iraqis. We didn't want to hurt em, we just wanted to keep em out of our way, because we didn't want to take any chances with our own guys.

When we first started the convoys, it was kind of, I don't know, I guess I had some anticipation, and a little bit of excitement, because I'd seen some of the damage that was done on the side of convoys. They blew up all the bridges and you'd still see vehicles burnin on the side of the road. Burning military trucks, civilian trucks, everything from earlier ambushes, so I guess the anticipation was that we were just waiting to be attacked. But honestly, I never got what I expected, they never retaliated in a big way. We had small arms fire and IEDs [improvised explosive devices], but no major ambushes where they would stand and fight. We had cargo trucks hit by IEDs and explode, but we would return fire, secure the area, evacuate any wounded and continue on like it was just a normal day. The Stryker really worked great for the escort stuff, and like the other missions, the Iraqis are afraid of it.

We left Anaconda and convoyed back up to FOB Regulars. All our stuff was there, we had been living out of our vehicles or in a tent with a pack since we went to An-Najaf back in April. We were at Regulars for about a week as we packed our gear and turned in FOB equipment and buildings. They made us clear the property and buildings like we were back in the U.S.

Tal Afar

When we left FOB Regulars, we moved to FOB Sykes, which was in Tal Afar, Iraq. That was kinda scary. Before we went to Iraq, the snipers had HMMWVs for infil, but we didn't use them in Iraq. I actually had to drive a HMMWV up to Tal Afar two days before all the convoys that went up. Tal Afar had really gotten hot, so we were gong there to replace the cavalry, since we have a lot more soldiers than a cavalry scout squadron. All the convoys that went up before us were ambushed by RPGs, IEDs, and small arms fire. So needless to say, I was a little bit scared at the time, because a HMMWV is nothing like a Stryker.

I had taken over the section as the sniper section sergeant during operations in Anaconda, so I was in charge of having my sniper section drive two of these HMMWVs up there. Myself and Brown, which was my new partner, and then we had two other snipers in the HMMWV behind us. Luckily, we rolled through the town and there was no ambush that day. We didn't even receive a single threat at all. Rollin into Tal Afar was kind of a good experience. We looked around, seeing that most of the town was already shot up, and that there was a lot of activity. We had already heard that this place wanted to fight us like crazy, so we rolled up in there, you know, ready.

The FOB was smaller than Regulars, but we had our own containers and a gym. We had some pretty tough operations out of Tal Afar. On one special ops raid we did a six-hour road march to where we were going to assault an insurgent training camp. We assaulted, and got a few good intel articles, some cell phones, stuff like that, but we actually didn't fire a single shot during that operation.

Pretty much anytime we rolled out of the gate from Tal Afar to go anywhere, we were gettin shot at constantly. We rolled out on September 4th, 2004, to Objective Gilgamesh, we were going to detain some people. That day, I was up on a rooftop with my snipers, and an RPG had come down the alleyway and exploded by our ING. I saw the guy running away with the empty RPG tube, I was tracking him with my M14 and as soon as he came out on the corner to go inside the door, I shot him through the door way.

Seeing his body [Pause, deep breath] fall to the ground, that was actually the start of a very interesting day. After that, we had already heard gun fire all day, actually all morning, cause we got out to the objective at about 6:30, but a lot of the gunfire was now going towards Bravo Company's AO [area of operations] and towards the headquarters AO, and towards the Kiowas that were over us. They were really targeting the Kiowa helicopters that day.

We left Objective Gilgamesh and went down to support the attack. We were going down an alleyway, I had my snipers, and I heard a dinging noise, somethin bouncin down the road behind me. I looked back and about a hundred meters back an RPG had flown over one of our vehicles and was bouncin down the road.

So, I went ahead and grabbed my snipers, we put ourselves back on the vehicles so we could watch that alleyway, and take out anybody that was a threat with an RPG. When me and Brown got in the back of the Stryker, we looked up and seen a Kiowa, and we just watched an RPG fly up and hit the engine of the Kiowa, and watched it as it auto-rotated to the ground. Immediately afterward, when that happened, we got on the radio and we were tellin everybody to load the vehicles, we got a Kiowa down!

We had the location, so it took us about three minutes to actually get on site. We got over there, and as soon as I got off the vehicle, I could see the pilots, they had already exited the helicopter, they weren't too badly injured, but they were hidin behind a brick wall with their M4's. As soon as I got out of the vehicle though, I had to engage and kill an Iraqi at about 700 meters who had an RPG and was gettin ready to fire another one. He probably wouldn't have even come close because 700 meters is pretty good distance for an RPG. We ended up eliminatin him and [Pause, deep breath] the MEV [medical evacuation vehicle] pulled over to the down Kiowa pilots. I think it was Sergeant Williams that ended up helpin load the Kiowa pilots into the MEV.

Well, this was a start to a very long day. What happened after that, we had to recover this helicopter, so we were stuck. We were already takin pretty heavy enemy fire, we had, I would say at least 220 degrees of enemy fire, if not more coming at us. The only place that was actually open was to the east where we had come in from. So, what had happened was the scouts took up positions on the ground. I linked up with Lieutenant McChrystal, then took my six snipers, kicked down a door into a building, and headed for high ground.

We came into a courtyard with many doors. We had a couple of Iraqi's that were in there, so we put an ING guy on them, and we immediately got up to the rooftop, so we could gain some kind of a ground advantage. As soon as we got to the rooftop, we began to engage the enemy. We had an alley that was, I believe to the west, and people were comin out with RPGs. Myself and Phipps were coverin that alleyway. We dropped, probably at least seven between the two of us, I know it was seven enemy, and there were a few others wounded.

I positioned my snipers in various spots and ran all over the top of this roof tryin to engage enemy forces that were comin at us. We were takin 180 degrees fire from the roof, and the enemy was gettin as close as a hundred meters, probably some within fifty meters. We had a machine gun position that set up right behind us with an RPK [Ruchnoy Pulemyot Kalashnikova] and bullets started bouncin all over the walls and all around us. Sergeant Foster and Lumadue, Sergeant Lumadue went to fire rounds at this guy, then Sergeant Foster stepped out into enemy fire with a 203 and hit this guy square in the chest with a with a 40mm grenade. So pretty much, Foster turned him into spaghetti-o's and caused a lot of enemy to retreat from the east.

We had to get reinforcements up there fast, we were gettin pretty close to bein overran. There were a lot of enemy comin at us.

There were six of us and we're usin bolt-action weapons. We had a few M4s, an M14, some 203s, but we were also taken a lot of fire, a lot of fire from the alley way. We just couldn't kill them fast enough. We ended up callin down for reinforcements. The rest of the scout platoon couldn't really reinforce us at the time, because they were taken a lot of heavy enemy fire at that time too. Everyone was killin insurgents as fast as our weapons would fire. So, what I did was wait it out, we just kept on supressin the enemy, and killin the enemy, and finally they were able to send us reinforcements.

Now this was the hard part, we had to actually get the reinforcements into our building through heavy enemy fire. They didn't know exactly which building we were in, so we had to somehow mark the building during the day. We ended up findin a purple bra and Sergeant Head put it on a pole, and started wavin the bra in the air, and I sent Sergeant Foster down to the door to link up with the reinforcements. Sergeant Foster came immediately back up pretty much out of breath, and I asked him why he wasn't at the door guiding the troops in? He said as soon as he opened the door, he pretty much got all shot up, cause there were enemy Iraqi's outside the doorway.

We turned and engaged some of those Iraqi's almost straight down from the rooftop. Finally, we got reinforcements up there, we had Sergeant First Class Keyes and probably about ten reinforcements from the scout platoon at the time. We ended up gettin an M249 SAW [squad automatic weapon] up there and were able to suppress the enemy pretty hard.

That was a pretty tough day, it was a lot of thinkin that had to be done, and I had to do a lot of coordinating with all my guys to make sure sectors were covered, make sure no one was gettin tunnel vision, and just lookin at certain parts where they were lookin 360 degrees and were aware of everything. I think my biggest concern that day was just keepin the enemy away from these guys who were on the ground trying to rescue the helicopter.

We ended up killen over 26 confirmed enemy and wounding at least a couple dozen that I know of. I ended up killen 15 enemy that day and wounden probably a good handful more. The recorded count was 13 but whatever, it's not like you're worried about counting kills when you're about to be overrun.

We were taken fire all the way out of that town. We ended up gettin mortared while we were on the rooftop position. I was still on the rooftop, and probably 20 meters away, mortars were hitten. There's nothing we could do, I mean we had no cover to get away from them, so we just stood there and toughed it out. They ended up dropping a JDAM [joint deployed aerial munition] and kinda scared off a lot of the enemy when they saw how much firepower we could call in.

We pretty much removed a city block. They did some gun runs with an F18 but they didn't want to attack the castle, because it was a government complex, even though they believe that the mortar rounds were comin from there. As we were exiting the town, I was ridin on Sergeant William's vehicle with my snipers. We were rollin about 35 miles an hour, when an Iraqi appeared and tried to engage us with an AK47, that was the final shot I took that day. I hit him in the chest, actually I thought it was a pretty impressive shot cause of how fast we were rollin, but anyway, most people don't want to hear about that.

On September 7th, 2004, we decided to go ahead and assault the town of Tal Afar. I was pretty hyped up about it actually. We had got into some good fights out there with them now, and I was actually kind of excited. We got there with our mortars prepping our objective. We watched the mortars come in, I don't know how many mortars our guys fired, but it had to be in the hundreds. The 120-millimeter mortar can cause some damage. A Spectre Gunship was in the air, it was pretty impressive. Spectre was flying around eliminating where he thought possible IEDs and enemy positions were.

This was a pretty much a full-on attack, I mean we were going in to destroy the enemy. Well, we rolled out to our objective that night and I ended up engaging one personnel. He was at 950 meters, hit him with the Barrett .50 cal and eliminated him.

After that, a firefight kicked up between Bravo Company and the enemy. We had a little bit of activity in our area, but Bravo Company was mainly going full force at those guys. Kiowas were engaging, and there was a lot of fire goin on that day. It was pretty impressive because we emptied out that town. I mean that town made way, flags were comin out and we don't know if they were all bad guys or good guys, or what not, but everybody wanted out of that town. We killed a lot of enemy that day, maybe even more than September 4th.

We went ahead and seized the town for about five days. We set up a blocking position, I think it was to the south of the town, where we were at. After that big attack, really the only activity that happened to myself was a few scattered firefights here and there, and the day I got hit by an IED in my vehicle. I took some shrapnel to the helmet, it knocked me down outside the vehicle, and gave me a pretty good gouge in the leg. I had a piece of the seat actually stab into the bone a little bit. I received the Purple Heart for it, but it wasn't that bad.

What we were doin changed a lot from when we got there to when we left. When I got there, I was all for wanting to help the people, and when I left, it was about making sure, and it was solely about making sure, our guys just went home alive. I didn't really have a whole lot of concern for the people. I wasn't there to kill them, but I wasn't there to cuddle with them either. We changed what we called the enemy, but in Iraq the friendlies are Iraqi, and the enemy is Iraqi? We just wanted to do our job and what was handed down to us, and make sure everybody made it home.

When I came home from Iraq I went ahead and stayed in a hotel room the first night, just to be comfortable and not at the barracks. My parents came into town a couple days later, they helped me move into an apartment, spend some good time with us. They were really happy to have me home.

Final Thoughts

The way I feel about it now, I feel that it's their war. We took out their bad leader, we established the government, I think that they need to start fighting for their own country and weeding out the bad guys themselves, and we can give them some kind of technical support, and just back them a little bit. That's my two cents on that, it's a whole nother book there.

I received an ARCOM [Army commendation medal] and two ARCOMS for valor. One valor award was for eliminating two enemy snipers in the town of Afghani, one being about 400 meters away, the other about 700. They had us pinned down. The other award I received was a Purple Heart. I don't think we got as many awards as the 101st, or the support people at Anaconda, or on other FOBs. Our chain of command put us in for a bunch of awards. They put about 10 of us in for Bronze Stars after the Kiowa fight, but the higher command downgraded all of them except the Lieutenant's.

Matthew Goodine

Battalion Mad Max Section Leader

My name's Sergeant First Class Matthew Goodine. I was born in St. Peter Canada and moved to the U.S. when I was five. I graduated from Calus High School and joined the Army in July of 1990. I was in the 1st Armored Division in the early 90s, part of Desert Storm and Desert Shield. After that I went to Fort Campbell Kentucky, where I served with the Rakkasans for a few years, and then PCSed [permanent change of station] to Hawaii for four years. While I was there, I did Operation Uphold Democracy in Haiti in May of 1998.

Then I PCSed to Fort Lewis Washington, and later on in 1999-2000 helped set up the Stryker brigade. I've been involved with the brigade ever since. I got to Kuwait on 5 November, got there probably about ten days earlier than the main body of the battalion as I was assigned to the Torch Party. In my role as the pseudo-battalion master gunner, my main responsibility in Kuwait was to set up training for the rest of the battalion, sort of knock off the rust, since it'd been about a month and a-half since we done any type of tactical training. So, just let the boys knock the rust off before we went up into Iraq.

We were in a little FOB [forward operating base] in the middle of the desert in Kuwait, the tents wasn't bad living, had air conditioning, had heating, heating being more important that time of year. Basically, spent my whole time either setting up training or being an observer controller during training, or helping supervise the refits we were doing there. Once we got to Kuwait, we had to put the slat armor on the vehicles, and we received a lot of new equipment that the soldiers hadn't trained with yet, so we had to establish training to get them familiar with the equipment and sort of exercise the battalion TAC [tactical group] a little bit. One of my additional duties was battalion TAC NCO [non-commissioned officer], at that time sort of tactical action center or whatever it stands for. Just making sure the battalion commander and battalion S3 vehicles could talk to each other and able to communicate to the rest of the battalion when they went out, that's about it.

Once we left Kuwait, we did a ground assault convoy into Iraq. I remember a lot of the guys, myself included, didn't have a good understanding or weren't really able to wrap our hands on what we were going to be doing in country, whether it was peace keeping, peace enforcement, combat operations. I sort of did both in Desert Shield and Desert Storm high intensity mobile desert combat, and then Uphold Democracy, which was basically over armed policing in Haiti. Sort of having hit both ends of hazardous duty, I didn't really understand where this was going to fall, whether we were going to be in Iraq playing policemen or was it going to be combat? It ended up being a lot of both.

I remember going up, I'd sort of forgotten how miserable the weather can be in the winter in that area, the muddy roads, we actually had to do a big detour around the route we wanted to go to get into country. The guys were getting used to the slat armor on the Strykers, it was the first time we dealt with it, and it made the vehicles a lot bigger. I think a couple of donkeys paid the price for that driving experience.

Samarra

We eventually moved into Samarra where we were told we were going to be gaining control of a city that Saddam Hussein hadn't had any ownership of in a long time. I got up there, established in a FOB called Pacesetter, and probably spent about a week conducting more training and planning for the operation. We probably would have gone into Samarra earlier, but during that time period, Saddam Hussein was captured and I think the commanders thought to take a little time off, kind of back off, and see what the reactions would cause to the global population.

Eventually, rather than doing a full-blown operation like we planned, we sort of positioned forces outside of the city and would send smaller forces, 30-40 guys, into town, one patrol at a time, to sort of gauge the reaction, although it sounded like a battalion attack at the time. My friend, Lieutenant Beako, asked me to go along for the first platoon size patrol we put in the city. On the first day of patrolling we went into town, probably midmorning, I remember walking into town. None of us at that point, sort of had the familiarity with indicators like we would have later on, but teenage boys trailing us, groups of military age men, three of them on a motorcycle cruising through town, moving with a purpose from one position to another. Really, two months from then that would never have happened, but at that point, we didn't have the experience we gained later.

So, they ended up setting up an ambush for us. A couple sniper shots at first, I'd say one to two shots, no accuracy like a real sniper would have. I tried to run the people down, but these Iraqis, it's really easy for them to disappear and go from becoming a combatant to a bystander pretty easily. Just drop a weapon and get in a group of people, and that's it. The second time we got hit by one of the two rounds, the sniper was identified and some shooters made a couple of engagements, they put at least one guy down during that one. Sergeant Davis, he was in B Company at the time, took a guy off the sidecar of a motorcycle. We calmed down and started the patrol again. A little later we had a dud RPG [rocket propelled grenade] go by our heads. Again, RPGs used to be something that we became a little more used to as time went on, but at that point it was sort of a big bottle rocket going by your head and it probably took three to four seconds for everyone to gauge what it was before we reacted.

Sergeant Hale and Lieutenant McChrystal, the other platoon, I can't remember what number the platoon was, but they reacted pretty quickly. They positioned a machine gun, M240 Bravo, firing at the RPG position while the rest of the platoon flanked around a city block and came back up as we started to come back up the area, that was basically built up surrounding a large open field. There were soccer fields, and, I think it was trash covering an impromptu market they would have at times, but it wasn't happening at this point. So, it was pretty large, probably a 400- by 500-meter open area. As we came back up, we started to take more and more small arms fire from an assault vehicle.

I remember a couple thoughts as we were running around. One of the guys was doing just like they were trained to do, and it was sort of surprising. I expected some of the younger guys to be a little more hesitant in their reactions, but they reacted just like we trained them. They took cover, returned fire, they called out direction and distance, and the type of fire they were receiving, and just did everything by the book. They were exceptionally confident, no one, I mean no one really got that concerned.

I think the biggest thing that surprised me as we started returning fire, as we sort of strong pointed at an intersection, was that it was really the first time we really dealt with an insurgent fight in a built-up area. You know it was really hard to delineate who the bad guys were and who the good guys were. Yeah, the guys did a really good job holding back, not using force in a situation where it wasn't warranted, or against people who hadn't gotten themselves into the fight yet.

Part way through it I remember, don't know if it was planned or not, but they let out school, so you had a bunch of school kids walking between us and the insurgents. That slowed down our rate of fire, not necessarily our effective guys, they just bared down a little and used effective fire, but it didn't even faze the guys we were fighting. They just kept up the same rate of fire, but miraculously not one of those school kids were hit. But if I had to draw a conclusion, it would be that it wasn't intentional to release the school in order to sort of mask, or try to reduce our effectiveness in the fight, but it was like the insurgents didn't care if they hit one of those kids.

The other thing that, sort of, surprised me, it made me realize we were definitely in a different culture, is that people didn't stop work, even though there were 40 Americans shooting at about 15 bad guys over a 30–40-minute time period. The roofers kept roofing and the workers kept working, normally in a firefight you see someone on the roof that's a threat, but we took a little more careful consideration before we pulled the trigger to figure out who was a good guy, who was a bad guy, and who was just an idiot. Luckily, that ended up going pretty good. Official numbers, I think, were we killed 12 insurgents that day.

We left the city, gave it a chance to calm down. The rest of the time in Samarra there were a couple larger operations where we went in during the day and just methodically cleared from point-to-point, working with, I believe it was the 4th Infantry Division. Then, at night, the battalion actually got hold of a pretty good informant and cut some deals with him, to where he took us through the town at night a few times. I went in, I think it was Charlie Company that time, and did operations on 12 to 13 houses, counting both the daytime sweeps and the nighttime sweeps. We gathered a lot of enemy equipment, and gathered quite a few detainees, uh, I don't know the result of that, what the intel guys got out of them, but both were pretty successful operations.

A lot of the people we were looking for were suddenly out of town, they all had pressing vacations scheduled for somewhere other than Samarra. With the informant we used that night for the C Company, he actually approached our scout platoon leader, Lieutenant Hicks, an older prior, enlisted SEAL and Special Forces guy, and talked to him for a while. All he wanted to do was leave Samarra; he didn't have enough money and/or the means to get his family out of Samarra. He was probably not the best guy in the world, but he was willing to help us and we moved his family out of Samarra into a small farmers house that we requisitioned early on.

We found a huge cache of weapons there, and his family stayed there under U.S. guard, we got his family some medical attention, and that night he went into town with us while his family stayed there. He just took us from house-to-house of everyone he knew was a member of the insurgency, or not friendly to the Iraqi government. He would tell us before we went in, this is who lives here and he has two RPGs and three AK47s, and we'd go in and he would have two RPGs and three AK47s, which at that point was really enough to bring them in, at least to ask some questions.

The next morning our battalion commander, Lieutenant Colonel Reed had the mortar platoon move him out to an area, and gave him enough money out of our discretionary funds to get a taxi and go to Baghdad. He got what he wanted, and obviously, we got what we wanted. He helped us really clean up our zone of the city. At the end, it was probably four or five days of operations with that guy, and between him and our other operations, I think we broke the back of the insurgents in Samarra.

Qayyarah

After spending, I'm not sure exactly how much time in Samarra, but we were there during Christmas. After Samarra we moved up to northern Iraq to reinforce, and then replace the 101st Airborne Division and their sector. It was sort of challenging to replace a division with a brigade, but because of the mobility we had as a Stryker unit, it was doable. We replaced an airborne, or air assault, division with one medium brigade, so every place they had a battalion, we had a company or less. If they had a brigade there, we had a battalion there, and so on.

I worked with the 101st probably about 14 days, learning the sector, doing missions with them, getting an understanding of the area, briefings, obviously multiple times a day about intelligence or civil affairs, ongoing civil affairs operations and things like that. Eventually, after probably two weeks, the 101st started to leave and we picked up operations in the area. At that point the insurgency really hadn't started to pick up full speed yet, it was probably our honeymoon period if nothing else. After the initial ground war, the country was pretty quiet, but after the insurgents regrouped and the people realized their lives were worse, instead of better, it started to get real hot.

A lot of what helped us in the beginning was we still had some of the money that we captured in country, and other money, that foreign countries gave at the start of the war. Saddam's money that he squirreled away at different spots, and the other money gave us the ability to give people money to rebuild, whether it was medical clinics, schools, bridges, or roads. It kept a lot of people happy, kept a lot of people employed. Probably about a month into it though, the captured and donated money started to dry out and we were using U.S. taxpayer dollars at that point. It became a lot more restrictive on what you could and couldn't spend money on.

You had to have multiple bids to keep it legal. Take the best bid, and that may or may not have been good for what you were trying to accomplish in that area, as far as quality, employment, funding the right people and so on. If you found a guy that was a good guy, and you wanted him to build to provide employment to his people, but he couldn't do it because he was being undercut by someone in a different way, maybe even from out of town, it sort of created some complications.

At that point, the battalion was set up at what we called Q-West airfield outside of Qayyarah Iraq. We had one battalion in Q-West, the scout platoon headquarters and a lot of attachments, we had a company up at Hammam al Alil, which was within our battalion area of responsibility, but probably 40 road miles, no 20-30 miles away straight line, and this was all south of Mosul. One of our companies was detached out to Tal Afar Iraq. Charlie Company, they were assigned to 1-14 Cavalry, and we received a Cavalry Troop with less soldiers instead.

The cavalry troop didn't help out a lot because their mission is to look and to report, not so much to take direct-action. So, they just didn't have the number of dismounted soldiers really necessary to accompany us on a lot of the raids, and heavily man intensive operations that we were running. To show the flag and our presence, they didn't have the right amount of people there to take care of issues. They provided some great capabilities to our areas as far as overwatch and reporting, and other things like that, but just for direct-action not so helpful for us without any manpower.

The cavalry spent the most time out at, I think it was called Jaguar South. It was a huge Iraqi ammunitions and weapons storage facility that probably provided a lot of the IED [improvised explosive device] material in our sector. It was just too big, it probably was 20 kilometers by 30 kilometers, and we were asking 90 people with 14 Strykers to secure that 24-7, it just can't be done.

So, there were some problems there, but another intensive mission was training and standing up the Iraqi National Guard units within our area. One of the biggest things in our area was the Northern Iraqi Regional Training Center, which was an infantry officer academy up near Hammam al Alil. The company up there was responsible for securing that, and we had liaisons up there at all times, while the rest of the brigade was sort of securing Mosul just above them.

A little later I left the TAC. The battalion stood up what they called Mad Max Platoon, but just an up armored HMMWV section, to take the burden of some of the security on escort missions, like an AT [anti-tank] platoon does in the airborne or air assault. There wasn't a lot of risk at this point, but still, there were security requirements for units we were sending up to Mosul to pick up money, you know the battalion commander, battalion XO [executive officer] or anyone who was going to meet with the local mukhtar, mayor, or governor.

They needed security to go with them, and it just wasn't cost effective to send a whole Stryker platoon, so we stood up this up armored HMMWV section, and stayed pretty active for about two and a half to three months, before it started getting a little too warm for that. We really had a great time on convoy missions, meeting at seven in the morning, leave Qayyarah, go up to Mosul, stop at two or three FOBs, run out to Jaguar, and by the time you were done you've gone four or five hundred miles in a day, or maybe two or three hundred miles depending. We would get back at 1700 at night, so your whole day was done when you recovered the vehicles. It made time go exceptionally fast.

Task Force Arrow

At a certain point, I'm trying to remember whenever the uprising was, the battalion got the order to stand up Task Force Arrow, which was one of our line companies with elements of our headquarters company, and then a company from both 2-3 and 1-23 Infantry. Everyone met in Qayyarah in the course of two days, basically, at the time everybody was there, we came up with a plan and moved out. Initially, we were going down just north of Baghdad to link up with the unit that we were going to be assigned to for operations in An Najaf during the uprising.

I remember on the way down, just to the first link up point north of Baghdad, units were getten hit with IEDs, nothing super effective, but still a lot of contact. I saw my first lonely schoolboy with an IED that failed to go off, it was entertaining, you get to see a lot of stuff like that. We linked up in a FOB north of Baghdad with 3rd Infantry Division, maybe 4th Infantry Division, one of the two, no wait, 1st Infantry Division. We spent 12-13 hours getting there, and as soon as we got there, we had to reorganize and we rolled up a lot of their headquarters vehicles and HETTs [heavy equipment and truck transport] with their Bradleys on hand.

Part of the problem of the Bradleys, and the Abrams, is they just can't maneuver like a Stryker, being wheeled we could drive forever. It was just a matter of keeping fuel and oil in the Stryker, but the track vehicles didn't do as well with that many road miles, so they'd have to line em up and put them on low boys to transport them. So, you had a lot of that, and we secured them, reorganized them as best we could, but there were a lot of vehicles and half of them didn't have commo, or were National Guard or contractors, it was quite the convoy. I mean, our headquarters convoy alone was suddenly a mile or two long with all those extra vehicles.

We left the FOB, I can't remember the name of it now, and started trying to work our way basically west, southwest to get towards An Najaf. But we started to find that insurgents had blown a lot of bridges. Blown some of them up right in front of us when we were right there, or just a few klicks away. We thought we were going to get away with a crossing and they'd blow up the bridge. Had a couple significant contacts there with the scouts, as they moved towards one bridge, they got ambushed by I think 20-30 people, dug in trenches and bunkers, and well-armed. They had a pretty significant fire fight.

I remember one of my friends, then Staff Sergeant, now Sergeant First Class Horton of the scout platoon. His vehicle received somewhere between five and seven RPG strikes and no one was injured, at least not significantly. The worst damage the 20 to 30 guys dug in could cause was, I think, they knocked out power, jiggled the scouts inside quite a bit, and then we had to change a tire, but that was it. Imagine being in the center of a kill zone and rolling away with a few minor injuries and a blown tire, the Strykers really saved a lot of lives over there.

They kept forcing us to go further south so we got down actually south of SCANIA and came back up MSR [main supply route] Tampa and then cut west towards An Najaf. It ended up being probably a 48–72-hour drive and some of the guys were only looking at two or three hours of sleep before we started. With the long hours and constant contact, everyone was getting pretty tired.

Went to one town and got to see a lot of the al Sadr posters up, and colors displayed proudly, and people weren't looking at us that friendly. We got to the far side of this town, I don't remember the name, it was just a town along our long route. Fortunately, we were on a sunken road, and I don't think the insurgents understood how sunken it was when they initiated two large IEDs, and some small arms fire. Probably five to eight guys firing on our convoy, but because the road was sunken, they actually initiated the IED on a Bradley that was on a flatbed truck. I don't think they were aware or they could see it was on that truck.

The driver and TC [truck commander] of that truck, and the next one in formation were hit with shrapnel. One was in real bad shape, at the time we reported he was having a heart attack, a very small piece of shrapnel, couldn't really tell the injury, and I guess it had entered his heart, but no one knew it. We called for a MEDEVAC [medical evacuation] and proceeded to have probably our most frustrating night in Iraq. The convoy was huge, and we had terrible commo inside the convoy, let alone with battalion. Our guys ran from vehicle- to-vehicle to try to keep everyone informed, while the CO called in a MEDEVAC. I think they may have actually had to use TACSAT [tactical satellite], but eventually we got the MEDEVAC bird in.

When it came in, one of the civilian contractors we inherited, he wasn't assigned to us, he was assigned to the division we were working, decided he wanted to leave on the MEDEVAC. Unfortunately, MEDEVACs are for injured people, so they asked him what were his injuries and he didn't have any, so they sent him back to the convoy. Well apparently, remember it was pitch black and we're in the middle of a kill zone, but what he did was snuck around to the backside of the bird while no one was watching, and got on the MEDEVAC. That was great, we got the trucks fixed, and everybody ready to go, and no contractor! So, we spent about two, maybe two and a half hours in a kill zone searching the wood line, searching all the vehicles, and then searching buildings to try and find this guy. Eventually the MEDEVAC bird called us and confirmed that he was found sneaking off the bird.

The injured soldier ended up dying too, I didn't know him, the HETT guys were guard or reserve, and their platoon leader said they had lost somebody a few days or weeks earlier. They had no protection, no commo, and no training, out there in those big targets hoping they wouldn't get hit. I remember hooking up with the 1st Infantry Division while we were looking for the guy, they were searching buildings and we cleared with them, getting a better appreciation for how well our guys were trained. They were not the most impressive organization I've ever seen, as I watched them entering the buildings.

Got into An Najaf, sort of set up outside the city in a FOB, I think it was called Duke, with one of the brigades from the division we were working with and started doing some reconnaissance. We came up with one of the missions for my platoon; we were going to be the escort for injured, whether friendly or enemy, out of the city once we started the fight. We started doing some shaping operations outside of the city, and I actually went into it. A compound just on the outskirts of An Najaf, and talked to them with the battalion commander.

B Company I think, caught one of their Mahdi Militia guys. They were pretty aggressive until they actually saw Americans, and that guy they caught soon as he saw our vehicles, started chucking his uniform, so by the time we got a hold of him he was pretty much butt naked. We took him back and stopped at the local police station, found out where the police were in general. Iraqi police welcomed the military during that time period, since they weren't capable of conducting or doing their job. If nothing bad was happening it might be OK, but as soon as something bad was happening, they either stopped doing their job, or conformed to whatever or whoever was there at the time, and was telling them to do so. If Americans were there, they'd go with the Americans, if insurgents were there, they'd work with the insurgents, not exactly the bravest group on that playground. Hopefully next time we go back there, they'll be a little better trained, but I'm not sure if all the training in the world will help them.

We went in there, started getting the shape of the operation, figuring out what we wanted to do, but at that point the uprising had created a huge problem with supplies in country. All of a sudden, we were assigned to move to, uh, I wanna say LSA [logistical support area] Anaconda. We started escorting the supplies coming into there, and basically it was a combination of matching the mobility of wheeled vehicles with the armored Stryker. We are really the only force that can provide enough combat power, take enough of a beating, and move quickly enough over that long of a distance day in and day out.

So, we moved to Anaconda, and every day, at least one company would be moved down south, and either that day or the next day, moved back up north escorting a hundred or hundred and fifty semis at a time, with Strykers mixed in the formation. That went well, although I wasn't really impressed with what was going on with the rest of the Army at that point. A lot of it was just we were aggressively looking for bad guys, so I think it created some problems, and there were some concerns with use of force there with some of the units that just didn't jive with what we were doing.

At Anaconda, some of the guards could see bad guys launch mortars at the FOB and weren't allowed to respond to that, other than to call their superiors. They just had very restrictive rules of engagement, but they weren't combat units, so they were probably in a little bit over their heads. The infantry unit they did have there was out of the Washington National Guard, and was completely ineffective, other than handing out moon pies at SCANIA. The KBR truck drivers told us horror stories of being left in Baghdad as MP [military police] units broke contact and left them.

The stories go on and on, but we slept in our vehicles or in some old torn tents while the Anaconda units lived in air conditioned Connexus, shopped at the PX, watched movies, or swam in the indoor swimming pool. I'd like to hear some of their war stories someday. Once again though, I thought our guys and the Strykers did great. We had a lot of contact driving through Baghdad with those convoys, and the Strykers really performed well.

After a couple months down south on Task Force Arrow, either on or around June or July, we moved back up to Tal Afar. I know a lot of the convoys got hit going into town, but I flew up seven days earlier in a Black Hawk with Major O'Steen, the battalion S3 at that point, but he was quickly made the XO after that, to set up the infrastructure of the FOB to receive a battalion. An infantry battalion is a lot bigger than a squadron of cavalry, which is quite a bit smaller because they don't have all the dismounts.

Tal Afar

The battalion got in there, and other than Task Force Arrow, there was a lot of contact in Tal Afar. Whether it was two or three times a day, normally the first time we got into an area we were responsible for handing over operations, but in Tal Afar, we just started a lot of combat operations because there was a lot more contact right away. That's why they moved us up there; the cavalry just didn't have the manpower to handle such a hot area of operations. The sort of thing that's unique about Tal Afar, is that it's a city of about quarter of a million people and you're trying to control it with, once we got everyone there, with seven to eight hundred people.

But it's also the first major city coming off the Syrian border, so all the foreign fighters are coming in. The foreign fighters came in mainly through the Syrian border, that was sort of a first rest stop, and at least the perception I had was it was a good spot to do that. I thought of it as unit live fire training with us, a chance for them to get their feet wet and learn what they were doing, or if they were leaving the country, their last hoorah before they left. But again, it was the first major city coming off the Syrian border, and from Tal Afar it was Mosul, and then Mosul down MSR Tampa where they could hit Tikrit, Samarra, and Baghdad, or wherever they wanted to operate.

When we got to Tal Afar, the BC [battalion commander] pretty much decided at that point, with the kind of contact we were taking, that the armored HMMWVs weren't the way to go. So, my section actually got assigned to run the detention facility on our FOB. It didn't sound like a bad gig at first, the unit we were replacing said maybe once or twice a week it was actually stood up, but it ended up being from when we took over, till when we left, it was never empty. I think I got six hours off at one time for the guys, but it would be three or four guys working eight-hour shifts, three shifts a day, so one eight-hour shift a day.

Anywhere from two, to I think the biggest number we got to was maybe 40 detainees, and because we were making more contact, it was more difficult to get them out of Tal Afar to the brigade site in Mosul. So, we'd hold on to a guy for some time, two or three days, and obviously this was right after the Abu Ghraib nightmare, so there was a lot of emphasis placed on it, so it was just another time where a bunch of guys had to learn to do something they really hadn't been trained to do. Luckily, it went well since we took it real serious, we never had any problems with it.

At the same point, just because it was incredibly monotonous and boring duty. I'd get a group of guys together and when elements were going out, or needed more combat arms bodies -- cause we're going out, and we're doing all kinds of other things, so no one was really at full strength -- we'd take three or four guys at a time and still do missions in Tal Afar with whoever needed us just to keep the guys from gettin bored. A couple times we had to, it was too dangerous for the HMMWVs, but a couple times we did take unarmored or Hajji armored MTVs [medium tactical vehicles] into town and set up detention facilities when the battalion did its big sweeps. Nothing will make you feel more vulnerable than a three-foot by six-foot piece of glass in front of you as your only protection when moving through town. Obviously, Tal Afar got pretty exciting for a while, the battalion had a lot of operations in town, whether it was blacklists raids or when we went in when the Kiowa got shot down, it was busy.

Eventually the 1st Brigade came in and we did our hand over work. Time was short, so it wasn't as smooth as it could have been. I'm just pained we left them, obviously a lot of equipment that we had, that they didn't have, and then when we got back to Lewis we never got again. We were tired and they were fresh, and I don't think we communicated as best we could as a lower-level battalion, and brigade level, or even talking to them at squad level. Not as much cross talk as there probably could have been, but they didn't want to listen to our guys. Since they knew it all, and didn't want to listen, we didn't want to talk much at that point.

That's about it, we deployed back in I want to say, November 5th, 2004, and we'll go back to Iraq obviously. I had a section that didn't exist on paper, so when we got back, the first thing I had to do was find jobs for all my guys. A good 50% of them were getting out, and the rest of them got other jobs in the battalion, while I moved over to C Company and took over as first platoon sergeant.

Sean Sparks

Battalion Mortar Platoon Sergeant

My name is Sergeant Sparks. I was born in Denver, Colorado. My dad was in the Army, he was Special Forces and did three tours in Vietnam. Growing up it was kinda strange, cause it was like a military household, each of us performed tasks and made our beds with the hospital corners on them, and he was quite a character, but him and my mom got divorced after he retired from the Army. I grew up in West "by God" Virginia, and I graduated from Huntington East High School. After that, I joined the Army with an airborne infantry contract. I went to the 101st and did my first tour there, then I PCSed [permanent change of station] to Panama, where I met my wife and participated in Operation Just Cause as a PFC [private first class]. We had a son, Chris and then PCSed back to the United States, back to Fort Campbell.

As soon as I got there, I had to leave my wife and my new son with my dad, and I'm still paying for that today, because my wife had a pretty rough time livin with him, and adjusting to my dad and my stepmother in new country. But I went to desert storm with the 101st. Then we PCSed back to Panama and I spent a couple years there, became an NCO [non-commissioned officer] and we moved to Fort Bragg, North Carolina where I was at the 504th [parachute infantry regiment] and then the 73rd Armor. From Fort

Bragg I PCSed to Korea, did a tour there, came back and we PCSed to Fort Benning.

I thought I was going to be a jumpmaster instructor or a jump school instructor but my MOS [military occupational specialty] 11charlie, which was a mortarman, meant I went to 3rd Brigade, 3rd Infantry Division on Kelly Hill. I didn't like that too much, as a mech guy in a leg unit, so we did twenty months at Fort Benning and I PCSed to Alaska and got back to an airborne unit, the 501st. After three years in Alaska, we PCSed to Fort Lewis, bought a house and after I signed in off leave, we had thirty days till I deployed to Iraq.

Being the new guy in the company they sent me ADVON [advanced party], so I went eleven days early earlier than anybody had to. When we got to Kuwait, it was everything I remembered from Saudi Arabia. They put us in these big circus tents with cots and, uh, the good thing was the last time I was in Saudi Arabia and Iraq there was no air conditioners or heaters, so when it was cold out you were cold, uh, when it was hot out you were hot, but they had air conditioners and heaters in these tents.

We started getting the vehicles in, and then the main body arrived and the rest of the platoon got there. I was thinking that I didn't know anybody in this platoon, I was kinda missing Alaska. I knew they went to Afghanistan, and I felt kinda bad cause the boys I'd been training for three years there were in combat without me, and I was with a bunch of guys I didn't really know too well, except for Fred Delecruz. We were up in Alaska together, and me and him were battle buddies, so me and him did a lot of talkin and assessin of the unit.

I know the rest of the platoon, they were pretty scared of Sergeant Rakestraw, the other platoon sergeant, who I also knew very well, cause I served in Panama and at Fort Bragg with him. He had been in combat before, and I don't think he was really too thrilled about being back in a combat zone. The rest of the guys, they were pretty scared because they had never been to combat, so I mean, I was kinda nervous too, but on the other hand, you know I kinda like knew what to expect you know. How we're going to do things and stuff like that, yeah, so you know it was kinda like I was tryin to talk to the soldiers and reassure them and let them know everything was going to be OK, but it was kinda weird since I didn't know them.

It was also pretty exciting too, cause we knew we were getting ready to go into Iraq and do our jobs. We missed home a lot, and you know there was internet and phones, this was new to me as well, cause during Just Cause I got to call home one time with an enormous phone bill, cause we were guarding one of the houses and found out that the phones dialed out, so I spent about six hours callin home, an enormous phone bill! Desert Storm I think I got one phone call home the entire five months I was there, so having phones and internet readily available is pretty cool.

Once we figured out where we were going, we started getting ready to move. I guessed we received the order for the mission, which it turned out that we didn't execute that because as we were lining up vehicles and march order for the convoy out of Kuwait, they came back and told us we were going somewhere else, and doin something else. It was a pretty busy time, getting ammo ready and uploaded on the vehicles, and going to ranges.

We spent Thanksgiving out there on a range, because a sandstorm came in, so I ate a turkey with rice MRE [meal ready to eat] for Thanksgiving, nice [laughs]. But the MPRI [Military Professional Resources Inc.] guys, which is a private civilian contractor firm of ex-military guys, they did a good job of gettin everybody kinda ready to go into theater. We shot a lot of bullets, and they were good to go, they really knew what they were doing. The headquarters and line company support guys spent a few days training on convoys, to include live fires. The MPRI guys really helped us get ready for convoys and as it turned out we ended up putting a lot of miles on the Strykers convoying up and down Iraq.

I just couldn't believe how big the convoys were, just massive, hundreds and hundreds of vehicles, it was pretty incredible. We didn't go all at one time, but I think our headquarters company had like 150 pieces of rolling stock, that's trucks, Strykers and trailers, without any attachments. Uh, once we pulled out of Kuwait that morning, we drove up the highway and we got to, I think it was called Navstar, it was the last base prior to the Iraqi border. We parked the vehicles in march order that night, and racked down and got a good night sleep. Somebody in Charlie Company dropped a

40-millimeter AT [anti-tank] grenade or was loadin the MK19, which is a grenade launcher, and it injured a couple of guys, I think one had to MEDEVACed [medical evacuation] in fact.

That caused quite a stir that night, but the next morning we locked and loaded and moved into Iraq. My squad, which was first squad of the 5-20 Infantry mortar platoon, as we moved into Iraq, saw the squalid conditions people lived in there. I had soldiers really startin to feel bad for the children, cause they never seen anything like that before, but I guess that the slum in Iraq looks pretty much like a slum in any major city in the United States, or Korea, or Panama, or Egypt, or anywhere. Maybe there's just more of them in Iraq and other third world type countries. Same sights, sounds and smells you know, like rotting garbage and kids running around without shoes and dirty looking. It was probably the mentality that they were the enemy too.

So, for the soldiers, they were, yeah, they were pretty hyped. They were expecting to get attacked as soon as we went across the border. I knew the kids were just like all other kids, they wanted candy and food, MRE's, but it was against the published general order, saying that you couldn't give the kids any candy or food or anything, because they would run up to the vehicles, and then they could get run over you know. So, my soldiers wanted to give them something, but I wouldn't let them.

Our convoy, we were the headquarters company so we had a lot of the support vehicles with us, and some of the vehicles couldn't keep a speed over 25 or 30 miles an hour, so what should have been maybe a two-day, trip turned into a four-day ordeal of driving down the road, and just waiting to be attacked as we drove further into Iraq. The weather and roads didn't help matters either; I remember it being cold, rainy and muddy for a lot of the convoy. I was pretty surprised at how calm things were there originally, that first convoy drove through a couple major cities, people were just looking at us and it wasn't till about day three when we got to Baghdad. A child warned us he was moving his hands back and forth like an explosion, so the convoy stopped and there was an IED [improvised explosive device] under the overpass, an IED is an improvised explosive device, it's what they use to bomb the convoys coming up. So, that Iraqi child pretty much warned us, and then, yeah, well it probably saved somebody in that convoy.

So, then we moved through Baghdad, and we went to a place called Taji, which is north of Baghdad, and we stayed there for the night. The next morning, we got up and the fog was like really thick, so we went ahead and got the thermals pulled out and on, but you couldn't see anything with your eyes or with the thermals. I mean it was real thick, then the sun came up and that's another surprise, I didn't realize Iraq would be that green, I figured it would be all desert, but around the river valley there's a lot of vegetation, big palms and stuff like that. We drove north for a few hours and went to a town called Baqubah, and uh, Al Duloiya. The people in Duloiya were like really mean, they looked at us, and we could tell that they wished us harm, you know, but they didn't do anything.

After that we pulled into FOB [forward operating base] Pacesetter, which is around Samarra.

Samarra

When we got to FOB Pacesetter, it was pretty crappy. You know, before we left, we had this briefing where Command Sergeant Major Du showed us that we were going to be living in these Connexus with beds and wall lockers and heat and air conditioning, and I guess that's what I, and everybody else in my platoon was expectin. But when we got there, we ended up movin into a big tent. So, we got half the platoon on one side, and NCOs on the other side, and there was no electricity, no heat, no lights, nothing. It was pretty primitive conditions. We thought there wasn't a shower on the FOB, although later we found out that there were showers, uh I'll get to that part in a minute.

During the day it was pretty laid back at first, until we figured out, we were going to get into the theatre of operations. We ran a few patrols out, did some recons, stuff like that, and worked on our vehicles and equipment. We had porta-potties there, so that's what we had to use. The PX [post exchange] came once, and we were there in line at six o'clock in the morning, and they didn't open their doors till nine. Then the people who ran the PX knew some of the people in the camp that were there before us, so they let them all go to the front of the line, so by the time 11:30 rolled around we finally got in the PX and there was really nothing left. So, it was kinda disappointing, we were all pretty mad about that, and you know that I never figured anything like that would cause a riot, but you know, you bring enough I guess cigarettes and tobacco and stuff like that to keep you goin, and then the first opportunity to get a resupply, and nothing! We hadn't started getting care packages by that time, so you know, everybody was pretty upset about that mobile PX fiasco.

When we found out about the capture of Saddam, I thought that was going to be it, kinda like when we got Noriega in Just Cause. I figured there'd be a few months of operations after that, and then we'd be gone, so we were pretty happy when he got caught. We ended up going out in the tactical assembly area Warhorse, which was halfway between FOB Pacesetter and Samarra. The mortars were sent on a mission of providing security for the TOC, or the tactical operations center, and we didn't like that because we wanted to be shooting mortar rounds. But at the time, they had a restriction on indirect direct fire, so we couldn't shoot anyways. We did send out mortars for mortar support, and in case things got bad enough to where we could shoot into the town if we would be needed, but we didn't shoot anything. Things were, uh, pretty boring there for us, pretty Spartan. We had to dig straddle trenches or latrines [laughs] to take care of business.

We were supposed to be a week there and it ended up becoming 21 days. During that time frame the Alpha Company commander was replaced by Captain Dabkowski, which was the Headquarters Company commander, and that's when Captain Vogt came and became Headquarters Company commander. Turns out that's where we spent Christmas, I guess the battalion commander had a sensing session, where he wanted to find out how people were doing, morale and such, and somebody came up with that we wanted to call home. So, he had an issued satellite phone that he let everybody use for five minutes on Christmas day, to call home and tell everybody that they were OK, and that was pretty nice. I hope he didn't get in trouble for it, but that pretty much made everybody's Christmas. It's hard to be away during the holidays, especially if you're in combat and your family's really worried, but that short phone call, you know, really helped out.

While we were in the tactical assembly area in Samarra, there was an informant and he had given up the name of bomb makers and stuff. The battalion had promised him that they would get him out of that AO [area of operations] if he gave up the information, so he did, and the battalion secured his family and moved him to this little safe house about three or four clicks away from the tactical assembly area. When they were trying to figure out how they were gonna get him out of the AO, they tasked our platoon with doing that. Sergeant Rakestraw stayed back while we went out; I was the senior squad leader, so I was the acting platoon sergeant pretty much for that operation. We weren't allowed to talk about what we were doing, because to get him out of the AO we had to get him through our area of operations, and to another unit on the way to Baghdad where we weren't supposed to be operating. It was kinda like a hush-hush kinda thing, we didn't let anyone know we were going through their areas.

Anyways, so you know we were pretty happy cause we were helping this family out, and you know, we thought we were going to take them way out to another city. We didn't know if we were going as far south as Baghdad, or you know, rumor was we might even go to Basrah cause that's where the guy's wife's family was from. But it turns out, we drove them about thirty miles away and dropped them off on the middle of this highway with enough money to get a ride to Baghdad.

We felt like shit, but that was our orders, so that's what we did, and we thought that they might be killed, but we never did find out what happened to them, but we felt pretty bad about that. But anyways, you know we got them outta Samarra. They would have definitely been killed there, but the soldiers felt real bad about that, because we felt like we had screwed them over, you know, but it wasn't us, we didn't have any say in the matter. So anyways, that was that operation towards the end of Samarra operations.

Anyways, once we got done with our operations in Samarra, we moved back to FOB Pacesetter and got our showers. The bad thing about the showers is, there were these huge water blivets, and they had like generator heaters, and sometimes the thermostats would be broken, so your shower'd either be ice cold and or scalding hot! December in Iraq, it's raining and about 33 degrees out, so you don't want an ice-cold shower at that time, and nobody wants almost scalding hot. I mean when that water hits you, and you feel like your skin is going to melt off your bones, it was so hot. So, uh, that was the quality of the showers that we got while we were there in Pacesetter.

Qayyarah

A few days after we got out of the tactical assembly area, we got word that we were moving north again and we ended up goin up to Q-West, which was near the town of Qayyarah. It was the western airfield, so they called it QS, but everyone thought it was Q-West. We got ready to move into northern Iraq, we drove, it seemed like forever, but really it was only a day trip and we got up there to QS. It was rainy and muddy that day, and we came pullin in that evening. The buildings were like old Iraqi buildings, they told us how nice that FOB was gonna be, and I kept thinking to myself, man this place looks like shit [laugh]! I couldn't even imagine what it would look like. The first night we didn't really have any place. We were relievin the 101st and so they had occupied most of the buildings, and they weren't willing to move. So, they didn't know where they were going to put everybody the first night. We ended up spending it in a chapel, at least they had carpeting in it, and seats and, you know, the next morning we got up and the sun was out shinin.

The shower was two miles away, so we walked down there that day, and then went to eat. That was the first time we had KBR [Kellogg Brown and Root] chow, our cooks had been cookin for us up till that time in Iraq. The KBR food was really good, I know they got a lot of bad press, but KBR really did their job there, they are worth every penny we spend. You can't count on some of the other contractors, but KBR really gave us great support. Anyways, the sun was shinin, so everything started lookin up, but the mud there was really, it's not like mud, it's more like watery mud you know, it gets all over everything. You step down, and normal mud you'll sink slowly, but this stuff is like it wasn't even there, it had like the consistency of fresh snow or something, but it was way soupy. That stuff was everywhere in the winter! It also snowed on us in like February. That was pretty weird. I mean I'd come from Alaska, so I saw the snow and everybody else was like, "Oh man it's snowing," and I was like happy you know. I was walkin and I stopped and had to look again, I'd never seen snow on a palm tree before [laughs], so that was pretty odd I thought at the time you know.

After that we got word, they had found us a building, so we moved over to the building and they put all 27 of us in this one 15 by 20 room. We slept like that for about a week until the medics moved out of the other side, and we occupied another part of that building. We stayed there for about a month while the 101st was gettin out of their building. The scouts had the other side, and we used to build fires at night and Sergeant Inocentes, he was Matt Inocentes, he was the cook NCOIC [non-commissioned officer in charge], he used to bring his guitar out and we'd sit around singin and stuff.

We did a lot of area recon patrols around there, and knock and searches, and looked for weapons caches and stuff like that. Then one night there was a mission going on. I was out with my squad covering the movement, and the mission was supposed to end around 11:30, and, you know, we're sitten out there and gets to be 11:45, and sometimes missions take longer than you thought, and you don't want to call up and say "Hey, is the mission over yet"? You know, cause there's guys out there and they're helping the towns and stuff like that, and you know, they don't need somebody coming on the net saying, "Hey, when's the mission going to be over"? But by about 12:30, I figured, man, it's been an hour too late, so I said OK, if I don't hear anything by one, I'll call up battalion to find out what's going on. So, we're sitten out there, and then finally one o'clock rolls around and I called up battalion, and I said, "Hey, when's the mission over," and they said it's been over since 11:30.

So, I was like, "Man, why didn't anybody call me and let me know!" I was pretty upset about it, but I said, "That's fine," so we packed up our stuff and we moved back to the platoon area. When I got there, the platoon sergeant, Sergeant Rakestraw had a flashlight on and I said, "Man, why didn't anybody call us and let us know the mission was over"? That's kinda pretty messed up and he said, "You mad?" And I said, "Yeah," he goes, "Well me too," and I said, "Why"? And he goes, "Well you're the platoon sergeant now," and

I said what? He said, "Yeah, you're the platoon sergeant, they moved me to brigade." I was like, "So when's this supposed to happen, a couple weeks"? And he says, "Tomorrow morning I leave," so, I was like oh my God. Well, all right, I helped him pack his stuff up, and we chitchatted for a little while, and then we went to bed. I got up the next morning, helped him load his stuff up, and he said goodbye to the platoon, and then I was the platoon sergeant.

We ran a few more missions and then a helicopter crashed north of us. They wanted us to move up there and guard it till it could get picked up, so we moved out up there and secured the site. I don't remember what caused it to crash, it wasn't shot down or anything, it was flying and I guess it got an updraft or something, and it crashed. Both pilots were in the 101st and one of them was married to another lieutenant that was in Mosul. We were just at Mosul, and he was supposed to be going home like the next day or a few days later, and you know, it was pretty bad luck, I guess. Anyways we secured the crash site, and we were prepared to stay there for 24 hours till somebody else relieved us, or they got recovery assets out there, but about four hours after we got there, they got recovery assets out there. They put the helicopter on the back of a five ton and it looked like a crushed beer can, I mean, I was surprised it all fit on there, it looked really small when it was sitten on the back of that truck. We moved back to the FOB after it was loaded.

We kept running missions for a little while, you know recons and stuff like that, and then the battalion commander wanted his combat power out doing missions. He had a company running the front gate security, and so he put our platoon on it, and then the scouts would conduct surveillance with the LRAS [long range advanced scout surveillance system], which is high-speed optics you know. You can see like out a couple miles with them. When the 101st was there, they had a battalion on security, then we had a company, now we had two platoons with some attachments manning guard towers that weren't covered by the scouts and a line company MGS [mobile gun system] platoon running outer perimeter patrols for us. This was a pretty big FOB, when the 101st was there we had an infantry brigade, and aviation brigade, a Stryker battalion, an aviation squadron, a few hundred KBR and a bunch of other maintenance, money exchange, EOD [explosive ordnance disposal] and other contractors to include Iraqis. It was bigger than some towns at home, I bet, uh, we probably had 8,000 or more people there at one point.

So, we did front gate security. That was one long boring day. My soldiers didn't want to do that, they wanted to be out there running around, doing missions, but it was an important mission, and we did it. I think we did a pretty good job at it. So, we were only supposed to be doing it for about a month, and then they were gonna relieve us with somebody else, but it ended up dragging out to two and a-half months. During that time life was pretty routine. We spent a lot of time together, we got satellite TV, which was Arabic, but they had some English channels and a few movie channels. We got a VCR from the 101st when they had left, they sold us all their TV's and stereo's. We got a new building which the most guys that was in one side was probably only about ten. I shared a room with the lieutenant, and then headquarters section, which is the fire direction center and section sergeant, which was about five of them.

We had two electricians in the platoon, and they found some big, I guess they were probably 100-gallon drums, and they put three of them on the roof with tubing that would come out into another 100-gallon drum, and they installed a pump in there and a thermostat and heater. So, they made a gravity feed shower, with the pump we had pressure, and we cleaned out the showers real good, and so we had shower facilities right there with us. We got issued a set of weights and everybody started lifting weights and the guys didn't like it, but I mean, it was OK. We had phones, and what used to be a brigade sized AO, now became a battalion sized AO, so we didn't have to wait in line for the phones, except maybe five to ten minutes at the most. We had internet, life was good there, I mean they were even working on refurbishing an Olympic size swimming pool, but it never got finished.

This was around March or the beginning of April by then. We went to a talent show that they had there and there were some soldiers and contractors there that could actually sing pretty good, play instruments and stuff like that. Life was really good there, we enjoyed it. We got steak and lobster every Sunday night, and right at the end they just got our Connexus in place and reinforced. They were like what we'd seen in the pictures before we deployed, so we thought, wow this is going to be pretty cool. We settled down and we thought we were going to do the rest of our year there. I really enjoyed QS.

At some point in time, my lieutenant became the payroll officer, and I became the pay NCO for the Iraqi Army in our sector. So, we'd have to go up to Mosul and draw out $85,000 every time to pay them, and I was always nervous about having that kind of money on me. It fit in both my hands since it was $100 bills. I had to sign out for a safe and kept the money locked up in the safe. It was nice going up to Mosul for the runs because, you know, they had a PX up there, and we'd take some of the soldiers with us and they'd get stuff they needed. We also went up to the palace where the big headquarters was and saw how they lived. We thought we had it good, but they had it really good up there.

Everything was goin really well and then one day we get the word that we were gettin off the gate, so we were like all right. But we had 24 hours to get off the gate, pack up everything, everything we owned, we had to pack up and get ready to go south because the country was starting rebel. We got our mission brief and our convoy brief 24-hours after we got off gate guard. I think it was around Easter Sunday, I think that was about the day we took off. The day before we had a big prayer with the Chaplin and we started moving south the next day.

Task Force Arrow

I was the mortar platoon sergeant now, so I didn't ride in a Stryker anymore. We took two HMMWVs and an MTV [medium tactical vehicle], no wait, the MTV was used driving leave guys back to R&R leave in Mosul, so all we had was two HMMWVs. Yeah, it was quite an uncomfortable feeling transitioning from Stryker to a HMMWV, cause we didn't have the up armor at that time. Even with the up armor, a HMMWV is nowhere near as good a vehicle as the Stryker. I mean, I'm an airborne guy, but the Stryker is an outstanding combat vehicle. Check our casualty reports, and you'll see how much protection and firepower they have. So, we had pretty much a quarter inch steel welded Hajji doors and sandbags, you know, I wasn't naive enough to think that was going to stop anything. But I guess it was better than nothing.

I was drivin with the new lieutenant, Lieutenant Pcolka. He was ridin in the other seat because Lieutenant Holbrook was transitioning out, so he was in a Stryker. So, me and the new lieutenant were drivin and we drove all day long by the time we got down to, uh, Balad where the 1st Infantry Division was. That's where we stayed the first night, we had Easter dinner there at the chow hall, and by the time we got to bed it was about 10:30 or so, and at zero two in the morning we had to wake back up, and get everything in march order.

We left probably about four in the morning, and as we were driving, we heard that the scouts had gotten hit really hard by the

Iraqis with multiple RPG hits on each Stryker, that's rocket propelled grenades, they were soviet made anti-tank weapons and the scouts were returning fire and each of their vehicles took hits. I think one vehicle alone took probably about five or six direct hits from RPGs but they held up and they rolled right through it. Yeah, it was all a real confidence boost, cause that was the first time that the Strykers had been hit that hard.

We rolled on through, we drove all that day and got to a place called Scania, that's close to Hillah and the original ruins of Babylon. We stayed for three or four hours after we refueled. As the evening was setting in, we got back in the vehicles and rolled again, and it started raining and it was hard to see, and I was driving and I was trying to stay awake, but I didn't really sleep at the time. So, I asked the lieutenant to help me drive, so the next stop we traded out and I don't know the name of the town, but anyways, it was where you cross the Euphrates River. We rolled into that town and the people there were pretty brazen, they just stood on the street, and they just tried to stare us down, so I rotated in my seat, so I was facing out the window and just put my M4 out. I pointed it at them, you know, letting them know, "Hey, don't be tryin nothing."

We crossed the Euphrates and got on this road that was pretty straight, but we could see it was turnin to the left up ahead. About that time, I heard and big explosion, saw a flash. Well first we saw parachute flares, and heard some talk on the radio, and we knew that somethin was going to happen, and then there was an explosion, a flash and we heard and saw a few tracers comin back our way, but they weren't really close to us. Lieutenant Pcolka looked over at me and I said, "Well, let's get ready because we're about to roll into it." And about then some more tracers came our way. Then there was nothing, later I found out that one of my squad leaders, Sergeant Andy Turnbull returned fire, and, uh, I guess helped break up the attack.

    Anyways we came to a halt and everybody was at the ready. Well, the people that weren't combat arms MOS's were just hanging out in their vehicles, and I started getting mad cause I thought they should be pulling security, so I just started opening doors and whether they were sleeping or not, I just pulled them out of their vehicle on the ground and made them pull security. One of the civilian guys, he wasn't ours, so I don't know anything about him, but when the MEDEVAC came in to get the wounded that were in the truck that got hit by the IED, he jumped on the MEDEVAC, but didn't tell anybody where he was goin. So, nobody knew where he was at, and he was on an aircraft gettin out of there. So, we're ready to go and we discover we're missing one guy you know, the civilian guy, he was like a contract worker for the 1st Infantry Division. Well anyways, no one knew where he was at, so we had to start lookin for him in the middle of a kill zone. I guess that happened till about, I don't know, one o'clock in the morning or something like that, well four in the morning maybe.

They finally got word to us that he was on that MEDEVAC helicopter, so we piled back in our vehicles and this time it was my turn to drive. But now I've been up all night you know, so we're drivin and we were still in town, our convoy was enormous with all the 1st Infantry Division vehicles. But the next thing I know, I woke up and we were about twenty miles down the road. I didn't know how we got there cause I woke up, I was sleepin driving and lieutenant was asleep too, so he didn't know how we got there, and at that point I realized we were probably too tired to drive anymore, so we called up the last Stryker in my platoon and I knew there were some guys in the back sleeping, so I said, "Hey, send some of the guys out to drive the vehicle," and then me and the lieutenant got in the back of the Stryker.

That was it man, the next thing I know we woke up later at the new FOB which was close to An Najaf. That was probably the worst we lived the whole time we were in Iraq, cause that FOB didn't have anything on it. We didn't even have tents, we slept in the back of our vehicles. That was the sandy desert, no shower at that place and that's when it first started gettin hot too, it started getting up to like 105 or 110 degrees. That was more of a tactical assembly area, not a FOB.

So, we thought we were gonna go into An Najaf, to go after their town and Moqtada al-Sadr and his militia. So, for about four or five days we spent time doing pre-combat checks and inspections, and training and doing crew drills and stuff like that. We went out and shot some mortar rounds to practice and let them know we were there. But after about four or five days we went into get our operations order again and our jobs, and they told us the 1st Armor Division or somebody was coming up to relieve us, and that we that we were going back up to run convoy security. They were pretty happy about that.

Yeah, we left An Najaf and our platoon was normally tasked with getting the convoys together, so we had to give the convoy briefing and everything, so I wrote a standardized convoy briefing at that time, it was kinda like sustained airborne training except it was relating to convoy and combat operations. Captain Vogt liked it a lot and pushed it up the battalion and it became the standardized brief for the entire battalion. We moved past An Najaf and up north on highway one I think, ended up back in Scania again, so this is the third time we've been to Scania, but this time we stayed the night there.

The change of mission was the start of Operation Road Warrior. This was around the time that the trucks were getting blown up on the highways, the resupply trucks, the civilian KBR guys, and so they wanted those guys escorted by Strykers. So, our battalion was tasked with running convoy security with these guys. This began a two-month time where we just ran between Scania through Baghdad up to LSA Anaconda, which is Logistical Support Area Anaconda. We'd stay the night there and pick up the empties and take them back down to Scania, so we're driving through Baghdad every day for two months.

Scania was actually a small little refueling area, but they had some nice facilities there. They didn't want to let us use them because they considered us transients, even though we were runnin stuff, sleeping on vehicles, and they'd complain when we used their phones and stuff. Scania, it was nice though, cause we were away from the battalion headquarters [laughs], while we were down on those missions. We went out as companies; Headquarters Company had our platoon and the scout and engineer platoons escorting trucks the same as the other line companies. It was no frills definitely, by that time most people had personal DVD players and stuff, so we got to watch movies and stuff like that. I mean in Scania you dropped off your trucks, lined up, did PMCS [preventive maintenance checks and services] and got ready for the next day, and that was it, there was nothing else to do as far as work, so it was actually pretty nice. Too bad you had to get shot at rolling through Baghdad just to get a few hours off.

But anyway, Anaconda was a lot nicer, it was a really big base, I guess someone was telling me one time there was like 45,000 people stationed there. I could see that, I don't know if there was or not, but they had a PX, a movie theater, phones, internet, an indoor pool, everything. But they put us in tents again, and that's when we got introduced to sand flies, cause those things were all over the tents and stuff, and nobody would sleep in the tents because they got chewed up by them. A sand fly bite feels like a chigger bite, except it lasts a couple of weeks longer, sometimes a month, month and a half, so if you've ever had chiggers, you can imagine the itching that those things cause. They weren't any joke, so everybody was sleepin outside, until finally they fumigated the tents and we moved into the tents. Those LSA people were sorry. At first, we had to sleep on our vehicles and then when we'd get back from a Scania run, they'd assign us a different tent because we were transient. Some of the units over there were just ridiculous.

That was when First Sergeant Wabinga came back off of leave, and he moved down there with us. Up until that point, Sergeant Duff had been the acting first sergeant and he was kinda goin crazy [laugh], but we were runnin those convoys all the time. Anaconda didn't want us there either, like I said, they considered us transients, that's why they moved us in the tents, so it started feeling that no matter where we went, nobody wanted to see us. Here we are thinking you know, we're runnin convoys so all the forward operating bases from Baghdad north get food, water, fuel, everything, and plus we're all in the same Army, so we figured the people would be grateful, but they didn't like us too much.

So, at Anaconda we didn't feel welcome there either, we didn't feel like we had a home, we were livin out of our duffle bags and you know, no place to really say this is your home. The tempo was pretty bad too, because we were running through Baghdad almost every day, either going north or coming south, and had IEDs blowing up on nearly all our convoys, people shooting at us, so it was pretty stressful. I mean we had a couple close calls. One day this IED blew up a tractor-trailer, I mean this thing was huge. So, the IED goes off and then the gas tanks explode and this truck is just a big ball of flame. We thought that guy bought it, but somehow, he got out of the truck but was full of shrapnel. Our guys cleared the area quick while they got him in the S3's Stryker, and then the MEV [medical evacuation vehicle] and the CO [commanding officer], who was shaken up in the blast, called for an AXP [ambulance exchange point] at the nearest FOB, I forget the name of it. I don't know if that guy made it, but after we got back to Anaconda it was hard to find any of the contractors that cared. This guy was what they called a third-country national, so without his truck or paperwork it was hard to say who he worked for. There were just so many of those guys from other countries driving around Iraq.

    I guess by that time everybody was pretty much over their nerves and stuff, so it almost became routine. Then out of nowhere we got a mortar attack pretty close to our tents, and the colonel decided that he was going to build up the fortifications around the area, so he pulled us and the engineers, and maybe the scout platoon and we became the fillin up HESCO barrier platoons! HESCO barriers are big, uh, like huge cardboard bags probably about six feet high and four feet on the side, with steel wire around it, and you filled them up full of dirt. You can build a big wall around everything, but it took about two or three weeks to fill up. During that time, we got to get some PT, besides filling those things.

That's when myself and Fred DelaCruz learned a valuable lesson, you don't interrupt the CO or the first sergeant when they're getting ready to do PT cause you're going to be PTing with them if you do [laugh]. Yeah, we'd get up early and we'd be PTing, we'd come in and we'd have questions about the day, we'd ask them and grab some coffee and if you weren't careful then you'd end up doing PT again with them [laugh]. But it only took me once to figure that out, I think Fred did PT a few times before he figured that out, but I liked doing the HESCO barriers because we kinda settled into a routine where you'd do PT, and get to work, and then sometimes I'd end up going over to Captain Vogt and First Sergeant Wabinga's tent and watchin movies with them in the night when we had time, or sitting in this porch area our platoon made and telling stories.

I started telling "Crazy Bob" stories about my dad. It was just there were two stories that I told them, because at first, I was just tellin them about my dad and they didn't really believe my dad was like that, and then Captain Vogt started callin him "Crazy Bob," cause his name was Robert Sparks and he'd go by Bob. But yeah, my dad was quite the character. I guess I'll tell one "Crazy Bob" story, uh, let's see: One time my wife and kids were busy handing out fliers in the field at school or something, and my daughter Abbey was just a little baby then, and one of the cats scratched her and she started cryin and my dad, you know after a while, he got kinda upset about it, so he told my wife that if she didn't shut the baby up, he would throw the baby in the river [laugh]. My wife freaked out on him and you know my dad doesn't get too many people in his face, but my wife's a little feisty, and she got right up in his face and yelled at him. It was just stories like that, but it probably didn't come out right or won't have the same effect like when I'd tell them when you read it.

So, every night I had to tell a "Crazy Bob" story before went to bed, sometimes I'd tell three or four in a row. But after about a month I was runnin out of "Crazy Bob" stories, and then one day I called home and my dad said, "Your brother died," and I was like, "What"? I was like, "Oh my God," and so I was thinkin how did that happen, "When"? I need to get home, I can't believe it, "Oh my God!" All these thoughts shooting through my head, and then he said, "He died right in my arms tonight," and I was like, "Oh my gosh! How did Ian do it"? Ian's my brothers' name. He said, "Ian? I'm talking about your brother Michael!" Well, Michael was the cat. They called the cats my brothers you know, so I thought my brother was dead, but he's talking about the cat. He's all upset about it, so he's like, "Yeah, yeah it's OK, are you sitten down, how're you taking this," and I got really pissed off! I was telling him, dad you know, how could you do that to me? That's just the way my dad is.

Tal Afar

Finally, they said 1-14 Cavalry was going to come down and relieve us off those missions, so we packed up everything and we moved to QS. We thought we were going to be there, but two days later they said we were movin out to Tal Afar, and so we packed everything back up again, and we conducted inventories and cleared the property book, and then we drove out to Tal Afar. Uh, FOB, it was called FOB Fulda when 1-14 was there, and when we got there, we changed the name to FOB Sykes, but anyway we moved directly into Connexus, so that was nice.

The chow hall wasn't as good as the Q-West chow hall, but it was still pretty good and they had, uh, a big Hajji Mart, we called the Iraqis Hajjis because of the Haj, an annual Muslim pilgrimage. Anyways, they set up shops and a big caravan tent and they had pirated DVD movies that were burnt, like I saw Spider Man two weeks before it even came out in movie theaters. What they would do is, I guess they'd send somebody in with a video camera, and so you'd see people standin up in the movie theater and walkin across the screen while the movie was goin on, so it was pretty comical, but it's all we had.

The mortar platoon got put back on the front gate again and we settled into a routine. Tal Afar was pretty good, First Sergeant Wabinga found us a building right next to his building, the headquarters building, and we moved our weights in there and we got satellite TV and air conditioning set up. By this time, it was probably gettin up to about 125 every day, so the air conditioning was nice. That's when we all got hooked on Tour de France with Lance Armstrong. We had nightly meetings, about, let's see, at that time they were probably about 1700, but then the company meetings started getting pushed back till 1800 because we asked to watch the Tour de France, since it wasn't quite over yet, and all of us became cycling fans. The CO and first sergeant would go to the battalion meeting, and then we'd have a company meeting to put out the battalion and company info, but if there wasn't a mission going on, it didn't matter what time at night we had them, since nobody was going home or anything.

The phones and internet were really good there. Phones were dropped down to .7 cents a minute to back home, so I started calling home at least once a week, sometimes couple times a week. Fred DelaCruz, he called home every night, he was actually running his household from Iraq [laugh]. But Fred was an over-the-top kinda guy, he was kinda wacko sometimes, he was just one of those guys that his mouth kinda always hung over his butt, you know [laugh]. You never knew what he was going to say, or to who! But anyways, FOB Sykes was good, we had laundry service, it was really reliable, and nice shower facilities, and everything was going pretty good there. That's where I got promoted to sergeant first class, at FOB Sykes or FOB Fulda, no FOB Sykes.

I also went on midterm leave from there. Right before I went on midterm leave 1-14 came back, so headquarters platoon had to move. They moved closer to the buildings and to the big pyramid looking things. I guess it was an anti-aircraft bunker. They moved into there and we moved close to ASP [ammunition supply point] and then I went on leave. That was the fastest two weeks of my life.

I remember it seemed like the day I flew there, and then two weeks later, I was like, "Oh my gosh, where did it all go"? But it was nice, we went through Kuwait, it was a pain in the butt cause you had to turn in everything, and they don't really let you sleep, cause they just got you running to things or going through testing you can't sleep or eat or anything. Anyways, cause you're going home and then coming back was just reverse, you're just like, "Oh my God, what am I doing back here you know"?

But right after I got back off leave, we did Operation Black Typhoon, which was I guess a week after I got off leave. They did a big operation in Tal Afar with Bravo Company and the scouts when a helicopter got shot down by RPGs, and they got into a big fire fight there. Only a few Americans were wounded, but they recovered the helicopter and got it out of there. The QRF [quick reaction force] came in with our CRT [combat repair team] guys and recovered the helicopter and brought them all back. Nobody got killed, but the battalion commander had had enough of Tal Afar, so we started planning Operation Black Typhoon, which was I guess a brigade operation, cause 1-23 Infantry came down from Mosul, and that was when we did our big mortar attack on Tal Afar. We prepped all of the objectives, we shot three hundred and somethin rounds into the city. First Sergeant Wabinga was with us, and Captain Vogt was with us, but after that nobody ever messed with Americans in Tal Afar anymore while we were there. We cordoned off the city, went in after some HVTs [high-value targets] and kept everyone out of the city for a few days.

Then after that, we'd do missions and things were pretty good. Mortars got to get involved and do their job, and then we'd go back on the gate and stuff. So, Captain Vogt and First Sergeant Wabinga were out with the scouts and some line company platoons doing missions, they called that, uh, what did the call that, uh, Team Hound, yeah. Yeah so, they called that Team Hound, cause it was the first sergeant, the CO, the scout platoon, I think an MGS platoon and the line company mortar sections, and a MEV, they called that Team Hound, and they went out there and put eyes on things, surveillance, overwatch and stuff.

By that time, we knew we was gettin ready to leave. 1st Brigade started bringing their guys in slowly, and then we did the change of authority with them. The battalion commander said we still were needed to run missions, and that's when, well I know me and my platoon we were just like, man when is it going to stop. They had us scheduled to do missions till the day before we flew out of Iraq, but we didn't because once 1st Brigade got there, they were pretty much sayin, "Hey, we got it, we don't need any help," and we said, "Well, you might want to know a few things before you start running patrols and stuff," but they didn't want to listen to us.

So, we did one joint patrol with them to the Syrian Border and that was it, we signed our vehicles to them, and then they got a change of mission and moved to Mosul. After that we just did PT every day, we'd run around the FOB, and end up at the chow hall, go lift weights, call home, go to our meetings, and we just hung out for a while since we didn't have any vehicles or equipment. People were starting to look really tired by that time. We were just hanging out and watching movies, and you know it was kind of like a stress release, kind of time, you know, to decompress. Like when I went on leave, you run out of Iraq, and the next thing you're at home in the States. It's kind of weird you know, nobody shooting at you, nobody trying to kill you, it's just hard to adjust when you're home that fast.

The last day me and First Sergeant Wabinga were the last ones on the last aircraft out of there. The birds kept getting bumped back, and we were supposed to originally fly, I think at two o'clock or something, and then we didn't end up leaving there till like 5 o'clock that night. So, then we got to Kuwait, and once we got to Kuwait, we wore PT uniform and we could leave weapons guard, we didn't have to carry weapons around anymore, that's when we knew it was over and we were really happy. A few days later we got onboard the civilian aircraft and we flew back to Fort Lewis.

When we got back, we were supposed to have our ceremony, like an hour or two after we got back. Everybody's families were there, but it turns out that we're not leaving till 11 o'clock, cause we had to turn in and account for our equipment. Once we did the ceremony, we came back to the barracks and turned in our weapons. Lieutenant Eaton went on leave early from Iraq, and he did the right thing, he signed his weapon into the brigade or one of the other battalion arms rooms, but that armorer had taken off because all the battalions came in on different days.

So, we didn't have accountability of that weapon the first day back and nobody could leave until we physically had that weapon in our arms room. So, we stayed till like 1500, everybody was pretty upset, I was trying to calm wives and the platoon down, they were all snappy. Of course, I'm upset too, so my patience was startin to wear thin, but it all worked out. We went back home and the next day we had to be back to work. We had a bunch of ceremonies and stuff that month, but we finally got block leave in December. Not much rest since we knew we were going back in a year.

Final Thoughts

It was a long year, I learned a lot, but one thing that I found out though was that people that you didn't even know before you got there, were your really good friends, and you really knew all about them and their families and stuff by the time you left. I think it brought everybody kinda closer together. I mean, I know it did bring us a lot closer together. But at the same time, it was just very stressful. A lot of the time it was tight conditions, and you know, when we got back, I think it was probably a month before anybody gave anybody a call on the weekend, saying let's hang out or anything.

Yeah, you know it was all right, the Stryker brigade. I wouldn't want to be in anything else over there. All that time on jump status, but I was really impressed with the Stryker. All right, as I finish, I just want to say, of all my awards and decorations, I'm most proud of the combat star I received for my CIB [combat infantryman badge] second award in Iraq.

Laurence "Sonny" Wabinga

Headquarters Company First Sergeant

My name is Laurence Wabinga, but everybody calls me Sonny. I was born in Honolulu Hawaii, raised in Haleiwa Hawaii. You probably can't tell from reading this, but I've managed to retain a bit of my pigeon accent after all these years in the Army. I went to high school in Waialua Hawaii and I joined the Army in February 1982, went to basic training at Fort Benning Georgia before my first duty assignment with the 1st Ranger Battalion. Within the first year of the army, I went to Airborne and Ranger schools. Before coming to Headquarters and Headquarters Company 5-20 Infantry I was in the Sergeant Major Academy. When I got to 5-20, I became the First Sergeant for Headquarters and Headquarters Company.

In November 2003 our battalion arrived in Kuwait. We left McCord Air Force Base. Our battalion got on a 747, majority of the battalion that is, and flew for a very long time. We finally got to Kuwait International Airport and then the base where they initially in-process all the incoming units, I remember they were pretty close together. I think it was about a 20-minute bus ride. Once we got to that base we had to go through a series of in-processing requirements, we didn't get to sleep, it was in the middle of the night, dusty and everyone was tired and tired of traveling.

All I could see was lights, I remember seeing units that was either getting ready to leave or guys getting ready to go on R and R leave and I was thinking my gosh, we're just getting here and these guys are getting ready to leave for good after a year of combat in Iraq. Later on, the buses came, we loaded buses and went for a two-, three- or four-hour bus ride to another base where we would start our two-to-three-week training. We didn't know exactly how long we was going to be there. I think we were expecting to be there for a month but actually ended up only being about two weeks until we crossed the border into Iraq.

In Udairi we started training our convoys and our specialty platoons in Headquarters Company, we had RECON and mortar platoons, and had all the combat service and support elements for the battalion. We started doing weapons qualification and close quarter marksmanship. We also did a convoy live fire which was the highlight of our training there because most of our guys was combat service and support that would be running logistic and supply convoys out there to the line companies.

A lot of these guys probably never did really fire as much bullets as we did in Kuwait in their military career as we were preparing to go across the border into Iraq. There are just so many constraints on regular Army units back in the States, especially in a little post like Fort Lewis where there just aren't enough ranges. Most times you spend more time planning, preparing, briefing, and ensuring safety considerations are in place than you do training with limited ammo and ranges that you get. It was really good that these guys that are always supporting training got a chance to receive good training from retired MPRI professionals and able to shoot unlimited ammo in a realistic scenario.

While in a in Kuwait we went ahead and started all our planning, we got our operations orders and did our brigade rehearsal on how the brigade was going to go ahead and do our ground assault into Iraq. Basically, we were broken down into battalion elements and would go by serials into Iraq. Well one of the battalions I believe it was 1-23 Infantry started first, or maybe it was the 1-14 Cavalry, but anyway they started crossing the border and we get the radio call back from the base that they shot up a vehicle. Somebody shot up a vehicle with their .50 cal in their Stryker and they weren't even across the border yet, but anyway and they shot up some Kuwaitis so when it was our turn we didn't lock and load.

Our convoy element for Headquarters Company was mostly all the support vehicles so we had the mortar Strykers for security and we had MTVs and HMMWVs. We started and went to RON [remain overnight] at Navstar before crossing the border. We stayed overnight, I remember it rained, I was sleeping in the cab of the truck, and it was pretty miserable but yet still pretty exciting as we were about to go across the border the very next morning. During that night though at Navstar we were sitting down in our vehicles, Captain Dabkowski was the Headquarters Company commander at that time, we did our rehearsal with all the TCs [truck commanders] and drivers, our immediate action drills, what we would do incase we get ambushed or were hit by an IED [improvised explosive device] or anything like that, rehearsed everything with the TCs and drivers. During that evening on one of the serial lines we heard a big explosion, Boom! It was a Mark-19 that went off. It was in Charlie Company, something happened, and it went off and we had to MEDEVAC [medical evacuation] the guy. He was lucky he wasn't killed!

The next morning, we started rolling through the border and were in Iraq. There were a lot of soldiers on the other side of the border, that first town that we went through was really secure but as soon as we got on the highway our commo vehicle broke down. I mean it was just right there at the opening kickoff when our commo vehicle just went down. We had to secure the area and hook the commo vehicle up with one of our CRT [combat repair team] recovery vehicles and tow it with the ground assault convoy into Iraq.

As we were going along that day we seen a lot of British vehicles, I believe it was a British sector in southern Iraq. The highway was pretty much barren, some places where we would come to there were small villages next to the side of the road on the highway with a lot of children and people. They would, especially children, be standing on the side of the roadway wanting you to throw some food or whatever to them. They were pretty much begging for things all the time. I forget what the next stop was, but we had several layovers where we would refuel and then continue on or sleep and then continue on.

I remember at one place our mortar vehicle hit one of the civilian trucks and part of the slat armor, the birdcage looking armor, fell off. I was right behind that Stryker. I never knew how much that slat armor weighed but that small piece of armor fell off and I jumped out of the truck and went over there to try to lift it up. It was just about a three-by-three piece of slat armor but I couldn't even lift it. I had to call for somebody to help me come pick it up. We threw it back on top of the Stryker and continued to roll.

About all I can remember besides that is how nasty some of the places were, how much trash and litter there was around that country. But then there were some places where, probably because it was December time frame and as cold as it was, there wasn't any trash on the ground or in the area cause, I think I came to the conclusion that, the Iraqis would pick up any piece of trash or anything that they could find to burn to keep themselves warm. The one smell that we could guarantee was the smell of burning tires and plastic and burning trash all over the place. I saw them, they would actually burn tires to keep themselves warm next to their tents or their village or their house.

Back to the ground assault convoy into Iraq, yeah it was pretty much a long convoy into Iraq. We did a lot of movement; I think the longest one I can remember was when we started around five o'clock in the morning and I believe our serial was behind the time schedule because we had the slowest vehicles. When we started the five serials behind us, which were all comprised of

Strykers, pretty much passed us because we were going really slow and holding up the battalion. The next day we started out again at about five o'clock in the morning, we were behind schedule again that day, and they wanted to push on some more, so the scouts went ahead and pushed forward, but it was already ten o'clock that night. They reported that the road was a foot deep of mud and that the trucks hauling some of our equipment couldn't make it through. I believe they finally made it and went on to the next place, but our convoy turned around to go back to the refueling place and stay overnight.

It was too hard to get through all the villages and cities in deep mud with our vehicles that night. We had all the HMMWVs, the five-ton trucks and all the support vehicles. After a day or two we finally got into this one place in Baghdad, it was already nighttime, and we refueled and slept there overnight. That's what I remember for the ground assault convoy into Iraq, long hours, cold, lots of mud and trash.

Samarra

We got to FOB [forward operating base] Pacesetter and immediately linked up with the battalion operations sergeant major Sergeant Major Overbee. He went advanced party, so when we rolled in, he showed us where to go and pretty much our tents that we were staying in. That place was kind of sorry; there was an artillery unit from the 4th Infantry Division that was on that same FOB. They had the other half of the FOB where they were pretty much set up, but for us, they pointed out in these Hajji tents and said have at it.

Our command worked very hard to treat our replacements with respect and to set them of for success when they arrived. The 4th Infantry Division and 101st just pointed to empty space or burnt-out buildings, told us war stories and said have at it. Again, we briefed no smoking in or around the tents just like it was in Kuwait because I believe they soak the tents in kerosene to keep the bugs from getting into the material.

At Pacesetter the battalion headquarters was located across from where we were staying. The brigade was staying in other tents and hangers at so we had to drive there to do our rehearsals and receive orders. I think our first mission was when we started sending the scouts out to recon routes into Samarra. One night we heard that one of the Strykers from 1-23 Infantry had fell in the water and, I think three soldiers drowned. I think they were our first casualties that we had while we were in Iraq. The next day myself and a couple of the other first sergeants attended the memorial ceremony that they had out there, and I know Command Sergeant Major Leoto was the battalion command sergeant major for 1-23 Infantry at the time. It was pretty solemn, I kept thinking of the staff sergeant that had kids, that we just got there, and that these guys died in an accident, not even under fire.

FOB Pacesetter really didn't have very much. Our dining facility was one of big things. I mean for the first month, we pretty much got our food from the mobile field feeding team trailers and sat on the ground and ate in the cold and wet outdoors. The battalion commander and command sergeant major were all over us about the dining facility. We got tents and chairs eventually, but with one good storm we would find ourselves right back on the ground looking at the collapsed tents. FOB Pacesetter pretty much sucked. Our guys didn't go and get showers for, I think for the entire month and a half that we were there, because the shower facilities were on the other side of the FOB and never worked. The water was cold, the heaters never worked, and the 4th Infantry Division detail guys didn't care, so nobody went over there. Nobody wanted to take cold showers in the middle of December over there in Iraq. Most of the time it was rainy, muddy, cold. Our heaters didn't work in the tents and stuff like that, but we just tried to stay focused on work and prepared for our first order to go into Samarra.

They were gonna go head and cordon off the city. As Headquarters Company headquarters, I had to go ahead and run logistics packs, myself with the executive officer Captain Celver and my assistant Sergeant First Class James Green. Nobody liked Sergeant First Class Green, but I'll tell you he was a big help for Headquarters Company, although he was pretty abrasive, he did a lot for Headquarters Company and the battalion as far as logistical and admin support. Headquarters Company is spread everywhere, but our part of the mission was to do logistics runs into TAA [tactical assembly area] Warhorse.

Captain Dabkowski was our company commander at the time, a really smart guy. Anyway, Captain Dabkowski after going to the battalion orders still didn't have a job except to run things in the ALOC [Army logistics operation center] and push logistics out there, but I finally talked to Command Sergeant Major Mangosing and told him, "Hey you need to talk to Lieutenant Colonel Reed because Captain Dabkowski needs some missions, he needs to go out there instead of staying back on the FOB." So yeah, they decided later on to send him out there to TAA Warhorse. Myself, Sergeant First Class Green, and Captain Celver stayed back in the FOB to push logistics out to the tactical assembly area.

One night on the FOB we were in our tents after running a LOGPAC [logistics package] earlier that day out to the TAA. We came back to FOB Pacesetter and just as we were about to hit the rack, BOOM!, BOOM!, all of a sudden, I hear explosions on the FOB. Some of the explosions seemed like they were really close, like maybe only fifty or a hundred meters away. SSG Rodriguez, our reenlistment NCO [non-commissioned officer], got up and started screaming at everybody to get up! I saw a tracer round and BOOM!, a rocket just landed right over there and Rod was yelling, "Get up! Get up!" I was like, Shit!, so I got up, got everybody into the bunkers that we had built right next to our tent, and we pretty much watched for about the next 20 minutes.

We were too far inside the perimeter to do anything but watch. Machine gun fire, tracers, couple more explosions, and that was the night FOB Pacesetter. As rockets and small arms attacked us, I believe the return machine gun fire was fired from the guard towers that were stationed on the perimeter of the FOB. Later on, the next day I learned that one rocket hit about 150 meters from where our tent areas were, along with some machine gun fire.

We continued pushing LOGPACs out there into Samarra and I jumped in with our scout platoon and went on a couple of missions into Samarra. Captain Dabkowski grabbed me one day as we took the LOGPAC out and said, "Hey, First Sergeant Wabinga, I need you to stay out here, we have a big operation going into Samarra and I need you out here." I said, "Hey, great," and went out with the scouts again.

On that mission with the scout platoon, I believe it was to secure a building while the rest of the battalion was cordoning and searching one part of the city. I remember we stopped in the middle of this big open area, and I stayed with the section that was supposed to get off the Strykers, run to the building, and secure it. It was a high building where we could overwatch a large sector of the city. Well, we got off the Stryker and I believe I was with SSG Folkerson's section or team, and they started runnin. I believe it was about a 300-meter run with full kit, ammunition, and everything to a building and I swear I was talking to myself, "Why the hell are we runnin, we're not even getting shot at," because I was pretty much smoked at that point.

So, we got to that building, busted in the gate, searched the one house, went to the next house, busted in the gate and went in there and secured the target house. Fulkerson's team dispersed on the house and secured it for the scouts for the rest of the day. It had some Iraqis in there, seemed like the guy was pretty nice, but yet we went through the house, searched the entire house, pretty much held those guys until we withdrew from the house.

I remember in TAA Warhorse, that's where we pretty much spent our Christmas day meal, that's the day when Captain Dabkowski gave up command of Headquarters Company to take over Alpha Company, Attack Company, and where Captain Vogt, Toby Vogt, my Ranger buddy, took over Headquarters Company. It was a bit sudden, Captain Dabkowski had only been in command a few months, and all of a sudden, they were switching out two company commanders in the middle of combat operations. Both were great, so it didn't matter in the end, but Captain Vogt is a special ops guy that had just come to the battalion straight from a special operations deployment.

Cool, I don't know if he knew what he was getting into with Headquarters Company, but yeah that's when he took over. Ultimately it was the brigade commander that decided on the double switch since I guess he knew Captain Dabkowski. So, we did a change of command ceremony, if I'm not mistaken it was on

Christmas Eve, with a new company commander for Headquarters Company, and the old company commander for Headquarters Company going to Alpha Company in TAA Warhorse. We had a few operations out there before we got orders to return to the FOB and to prepare to move north to take over for the 101st Airborne Division.

We had been briefed that we were going to several places, but finally word came down that we were going into northern Iraq by ground assault convoy, up to Mosul. I remember we found out pretty much at the last minute. We were busy trying to account for all our equipment and ammunition because of the change in commanders and post mission inventories. It's kind of difficult when your still conducting combat patrols, planning for the next mission and looking through vehicles and tents for stuff that was in MILVANs [military container], back at Fort Lewis, lost or stolen.

So, Captain Vogt went up to northern Iraq with the recon party in a helicopter to the base we were going to outside Mosul. He went along with some of the battalion staff guys and I think the commander, to go recon that area. I remember when he got back, he got all us from the headquarters section and said OK, here's what we got. He showed us pictures of the FOB, some of the things that we would have to do, especially because we had mayor cell duties, or taking care of all the admin, logistics, infrastructure, and political stuff, and what goes on in and around the FOB.

He pretty much organized us into a couple teams where we had to brainstorm how to run a FOB or small city. Most people take everything for granted, but it was a real eye opener to provide everything to support a small city. We were responsible for two brigades, a Stryker battalion, Air Cavalry Squadron and probably about 1,000 civilians, to include U.S., third-country, and Iraqi contractors. It was better when the 101st left, but initially we probably had about 8,000 people we had to support inside the wire.

So, we brainstormed about the water, sewage, power, trash, dining facility, living and working areas, recreational facilities, cleaning services, and so on and so forth. Think about it, when you wake up at night and sip from a bottle of water we provided it, when you get up and turn on the light we generated the power, when you go to the shower Connex, we pumped the non-potable water, disposed of the sewage and had the facilities cleaned, you go to eat breakfast that we had shipped in and prepared, stop to call your wife on a phone or internet connection we established, and you get the idea.

Stuff you don't think about and take for granted we worked hard to provide day in and day out. So, we pretty much worked on that, how we were going to do it, then we talked about it and that was Toby's introduction to us on how to run mayor cell activities. You know, to get everybody involved and to get us thinking about what we needed to do, so that was real good preparation for us.

Rode up again in serials, we had the all the combat service support vehicles, but pretty much I think we had more Strykers in our group to go up to Mosul. The convoy assault to Mosul was pretty much uneventful; we didn't have anything really happen during our movement that I remember. I believe it took us a day to get there, so we left early in the morning and got there late that night.

Qayyarah

As far as our reception to FOB Q-West in Qayyarah, the 101st pretty much had that FOB all under control, we were just there in the beginning. We got there and they put us in temporary buildings until they left. The first sergeant that I linked up with for our building, at least I mean the Headquarters Company headquarters section was pretty good. He set us up and welcomed us there. It kinda felt weird because these guys had been there for about a year in combat, and we were just getting there, kinda like the cherries but we already had almost three months of our tour knocked out.

I tell you what, as a battalion we fell in on a brigade, but we were probably more powerful as far as firepower and everything than the 101st, with one Stryker brigade replacing an entire air assault division. Everyone was telling us what they had done and how we should do things, but our company fell in on a brigade Headquarters Company, a support battalion for mayor cell duties, the external responsibilities of an aviation brigade, and when we took over security of the FOB, another rifle battalion's worth of duties. We just didn't have the manpower to continue with all their good ideas, and keep the same amount of presence with the locals.

When we first got there to Qayyarah, you know our right seat and left seat rides with the 101st was pretty smooth, because I think the people wasn't as you know, as aggressive, at least the Iraqis wasn't as violent at that time. They didn't have that many operations against the U.S. forces, and there wasn't as much talk of insurgents during that time. I mean the minimum vehicle requirement to get off of the FOB and do missions was, I believe two HMMWVs and they didn't even have armor kits on their HMMWVs.

When I went out with Captain Vogt and the one captain from 101st that was in charge of pumping water from the Tigris River, to check out water pumping stations in Qayyarah, I mean we were riding around in two HMMWVs and no crew served weapons. So, it was pretty wild, you thought you were in like friendly territory, but yet you still had to beware of everything.

I mean the biggest thing we had to beware of was our own U.S. soldiers from the 101st on that mission. I mean we were out on this recon mission to the water place, and we were inside talking to the Iraqi engineers and workers that ran the water pump house, when all of a sudden, I heard a shot, BANG!!!! I looked at Captain Vogt and he nodded confirming my alarm, so I ran outside while Captain Vogt stayed inside with 101st captain and kept talking to the Iraqis.

When I got outside, I found out that one of the 101st soldiers, the driver that was doing security on the vehicle had an accidental discharge. I was like, "What the hell's going on!" I mean they pretty much brushed it off and covered that up. We drove on and they acted like it was nothing, but I was like my gosh, those guys are dangerous. Needless to say, Captain Vogt and I weren't too impressed with that crew.

So that was like the most exciting thing that happened that day besides the goat grab that is. While we were at the main pumping station, we ate lunch with the Iraqis. We all stood around big plates or pans that had rice, meat, banana, fruit, and vegetables with bread, and you just dug your hands right in. I just couldn't get used to that. They're great hosts and all, but if you're not eating enough, they'll pile stuff in front of your area to make sure you get enough. They always give the best they have, but we called it a goat grab because everyone is literally reaching into the big plate and grabbing what they want. Sometimes if it's a big enough deal, there'll be part of a goat in the center to tug on.

While we did our recon we really went out and about. Every time we went to a place the Iraqis were really nice and wanted to feed us or give us tea. So, we did that at first, but later on during the deployment all that stuff stopped because the insurgents got more aggressive, and you didn't go out with just two soft skinned vehicles.

So anyway, that was our reception and transition with the 101st in Qayyarah. When they started leaving, we pretty much got settled in and got things up and running the way we wanted.

Military operations over there were pretty much standard. We had a whole bunch of just going out and meeting with the mayors, having meetings with the Mukhtars and sheiks and stuff like that. At least for headquarters section, we had one of our missions was to go out there and meet with the local village leaders that they called mukhtars every week. It's confusing, but a mukhtar keeps track of births, deaths, population, etc. and is identified by the government. A sheik is a family title, so a Sheik can also be a mukhtar, but a mukhtar is not necessarily a sheik.

You might say, "So what," but when you remove a government, there's nobody to ask who's who. The Iraqis loved badges and identification cards, so in an effort to recognize the real mukhtars we went to this one big mukhtar meeting where I had to take pictures of all these Iraqi, so called mukhtars. But some of them weren't mukhtars, they just wanted their pictures taken because to be seen with us and the other mukhtars, and to have their picture taken gave them some sort of status you know. That was their deal, everybody wanted a picture taken and appear important. Then there were other real mukhtars that said, "Oh no, he's not a mukhtar!" Either way, we had our goat grab feast. Everyone got along, and we ate so on and so forth. It was pretty friendly going out there during that time of the deployment.

When we got back Captain Vogt went to the S2 [intelligence section] and got with his interpreter to identify a list of villages in the area. His interpreter had been to law school at the University of Mosul and was real sharp. Bashar, the interpreter, made the ID cards, and then they arranged them by the towns and villages they were supposed to be in charge of. When they finished with that, the real mayors came in and helped with the final who's who of the area. Either way, picture day was a success, and the lower officials liked to have an outlet and somebody to listen to them since there really wasn't an Iraqi government.

The mukhtars had some good info, but it was difficult to get their issues addressed. One time they complained about rumors of women being abused in Abu Ghraib. Captain Vogt filed an AAR [after-action report] at the TOC [tactical operations center] after each meeting, and talked to the applicable staff guys, so on this case the battalion XO [executive officer], Major Landis put in a request for information to brigade.

It came back and the brigade MP [military police] reassured us that everything at the prison was fine, and that female guards only had contact with female Iraqis, but it was hard to try and convince the mukhtars. Believe it or not, their human intelligence network was pretty good. They didn't necessarily tell us the whole story, or what was really going on, but they knew about the prison months before the story broke. That didn't help our credibility at all with those guys.

Another mission was Captain Celver, when he was told to improve the retrans site. Headquarters Company had guys everywhere, attached to each of the line companies, at the retrans site, in Mosul attached to the brigade and coalition provisional authority, you name it we were spread out. So, Captain Celver got this mission to go ahead and make the northern retrans a better place. The northern retrans consisted of an infantry squad, some of the signal guys from brigade, all their signal equipment, and some of our signal guys manned the northern retrans between Qayyarah and Mosul.

So, as usual, Captain Celver went all out. I mean he organized all these people, the entire headquarters section and Iraqis, took everyone to go up there in convoy with all this equipment, shower units, water tanks, refrigerators, satellite TVs. The Iraqi guys that loaded and rode a bus, go out there to the northern retrans and set this place up. Once we started, we stayed out there for a long time. Wheeled vehicle convoys without Strykers weren't supposed to be driving around at night, so we had to get back before nightfall, well we didn't. We didn't leave the retrans till it was dark.

I was in an MTV [medium tactical vehicle] when all of a sudden, I hear gunfire, Kar! Kar! Kar! I looked to the side at Wilkerson, Wilk was our driver and company armorer and Milan Daniels, our supply clerk, was on the gun. We were all in the same truck and I said, "Step on it!" Let's go ahead and gas the truck and get the hell outta here! I think when it was all said and done, it was probably just some Iraqi shooting off their weapons, they do that in celebration for weddings and stuff like that. You hear in the news about a lot of fratricide, not fratricide, but Iraqi's and Afghan's getting killed by soldiers, and come to find out they were just celebrating something, and American's thought they were shooting at them, so they all get lit up. But anyway, that was our northern retrans rebuild mission, and needless to say, I wasn't very happy with Captain Celver right about then.

Another mission was a big battalion mission, forgot the name of the town outside OBJ [objective] Agee, but Captain Vogt, Sergeant First Class James Green, and I had the mission to go out with the with the intel guys and set up a field expedient EPW [enemy prisoner of war] detainment and interrogation point. So, we went up there in the middle of the night and set up our point. There were some Navy SEALs with us, but they were supposed to be there, kind of observing or watching, and that's what they did, nothing.

The line guys brought in a lot of prisoners, a lot of captured weapons and stuff like that. It was pretty much a long task, because the battalion had cordoned and was searching the entire town. I forgot what you call these guys, but anyway the human intelligence source guy had to interview all these captured Iraqis. I swear it was cold at night, but it got pretty warm during the day, so they were out, we were out in the middle of a field with concertina wire around the EPW collection point.

These guys were blindfolded and restrained, and I swear they were like falling over, it's hot, handcuffed, can't move, nervous because they just got snatched in the middle of the night, praying, murmuring and complaining. We were trying to make them drink water, but they don't drink as much water as we do, and it was just hot everywhere. I was thinking, "My gosh, alright what are they going to do next?" But anyway, I think our task was to not hold them no more than 24 or 14 hours, or something like that, and then push any suspects up to brigade. I was pretty much thankful just to push them up to brigade and get them out of our hands, because I particularly didn't like dealing with the EPW stuff and guarding these guys.

OK, before you know it, the battalion got called up by brigade to do a mission down in An Najaf. Al Sadr and his militia had taken over the big mosque down there and the U.S. was building up troops in case we had to fight our way in. The Marines were in a fight, so the battalion got the mission to go down there. There was a lot of confusion in the beginning. This was a short notice order, and it wasn't the whole battalion going. They were sending our commander and staff, Battle Company, two other companies from different battalions, attachments and what amounted to a little over half of Headquarters Company, and oh by the way, we still had to man the FOB and continue operations as usual in Qayyarah.

Once again, Headquarters Company wasn't clearly tasked, we ran around getting everyone ready and trying to figure out exactly what the battalion wanted, and who would lead which element. I was picked to stay back as the rear detachment NCOIC [non-commissioned officer in charge] at Q-West and Captain Vogt went forward with the task force. It's not that easy to jump through hoops when you're tied into running a base. Thousands of people are counting on you, you have pay agents on orders, and are signed for a lot of property that won't be accounted for, or watched over when you're gone. You wouldn't believe the amount of looting that went on over there.

So, I stayed behind and made sure everything was straight as the battalion left to go down south. We were left there at Q-West with a small detachment, mostly all the combat service support guys, or some of the combat service support guys since some of the guys went down there with Task Force Arrow too. Anyway, Colonel Choppa came by and became the commander of the FOB. The aviation unit was still there, but someone needed to take charge of the FOB as far as you know, being infantry and stuff like that, so when Colonel Choppa came down, he immediately started pretty much taking charge.

He said that we needed to beef up the security of the FOB because he was sure that Q-West was gonna be attacked because the Iraqis knew that Task Force Arrow had left, or at least that a battalion sized element had Q-West. So, we went ahead and said OK, we're going to have to construct fighting positions around the FOB and get this place ready. We blocked off some of the roads in and out of the FOB, moved some barriers around and to make a little show of force we were also gonna have a live fire exercise.

So, we took a couple of days to do that, and Colonel Choppa and I went and checked out all the fighting positions there. We checked the aviation unit fighting positions, made sure everybody had their sector of fire and our signals, and that they understood they couldn't shoot across the airfield, especially because all the helicopters from that aviation unit was parked right on the airfield. We were going to protect the helicopters, since they were pretty much out in the open.

Also, on the FOB we had another civilian unit. I forget the name, I guess my memory's going bad, but anyway it was the Fijians! Those are the guys that initially were taking care of all the transition between the old Iraqi Saddam Hussein dinar and the new Bremer dinar. We also had the Special Forces guys there, and KBR [Kellogg Brown and Root], so finally the FOB defense culminated with a night rehearsal before the big live fire exercise. I mean when Colonel Choppa called the alert, then KBR would have to move from their sleeping areas and where they were working to a bunker and stay in that bunker. Everybody else would go ahead and man their defensive position and we'd go around and check everybody's position, we did that in the middle of the night.

The next exercise was a live fire where we did the same thing, but we called it early in the morning. By the time everybody got into position, it was daylight then we gave the command to go ahead and test fire, so we went ahead and test fired. One thing I remember, one funny thing that I remember was when Colonel Choppa's Strykers went to the blocking position next to the clock. His Stryker crew went ahead and started opening fire out there, outside of the FOB, and all of a sudden over the radio you heard Cease fire! Cease fire!

It was Colonel Choppa's voice on the radio. He called the aviation unit and told them to move their helicopters back away from the FOB, or opposite direction from the FOB, because he almost shot one down. He said, "Boy that would have been a hell of a 15-6 investigation if the cavalry shot down their own helicopter," so yeah that was pretty funny since it turned out all right.

Colonel Choppa also had us getting ready for direct-action missions, I mean he was determined to send somebody out there on a direct-action mission, but I'm so glad he didn't send us out. All we had left on the FOB to do direct-action missions was my headquarters guys. When Captain Vogt was back there, we made them practice CQM [close quarters marksmanship] and CQB [close quarters battle]. We did go ahead and practice for direct-action, and one thing that I did take Colonel Choppa through was the CQC [close quarters combat] assault course that Captain Vogt made up for our headquarters section, and he really was impressed about that, and some of the training that we had done in order to get ready for any type of direct-action mission.

Later on, the brigade anti-tank company, Charlie 52, came down and augmented the FOB security sometime during the end of May. I went on leave for two weeks back to the states, but before I came back from leave, I got an e-mail from Sergeant Major Mangosing that said as soon as I get off of leave, get myself ready and I'm going down there to Baghdad, to link up with them at LSA [logistics support area] Anaconda, to link up with Task Force Arrow.

So, the day that I got back to Mosul, I found out that Headquarters Company was returning back to Q-West to go ahead and secure their stuff, their equipment that they had, and some personal stuff that they had left at Q-West when they had to run south to An Najaf the month before. The day I got back it just so happens that Headquarters Company was there, so the very next day I was on the Strykers going down there to LSA Anaconda with them.

Task Force Arrow

During LSA Anaconda, all the companies from Task Force Arrow would rotate on escorting convoys to down south, I forgot what that place was too, the name of that place was, uh CSC [convoy support center] Scania, that's it! So normally, I'd stay back and to take care of admin stuff, but there, Headquarters Company would escort with the scout, mortar and engineer platoons as an additional line company, so I went out on convoy trips. Most of the convoys went through Baghdad and all I can remember was it was crowded, lotta cars but nothing significant ever happened when I was on convoy. I think I was fortunate, that whenever I went on a mission nothing happened, so that was a good thing. All the companies had been in some big firefights and IED explosions. Even Captain Vogt got shaken up on one of them, but I was lucky. If you were going through Baghdad, you could expect to get hit, but I was just lucky when I went out.

LSA Anaconda was a big supply place, they had a PX [post exchange], movie theater, indoor swimming pool, you name it, but we were treated like stepchildren sleeping in the parking lot and transitory tents with holes in them. A rocket or mortar would come in every now and then, but that's it, most of them never left the LSA. Somewhere, I think in July, but I'm not sure, we got the word to go to go back up to Q-West and pack all our stuff, then the very next day or two, I would be going to Tal Afar where we would be taking over operations in the Tal Afar area and FOB Regulars, it may have been FOB Sykes, I don't remember. But anyway, we changed the name of the FOB when we got there.

That, like many things over there, was ridiculous. Since we were Headquarters Company, we were signed for FOB Q-West through the property book office, just like being back in the states. Our guys were scrambling, looking for military and civilian equipment they hadn't seen in months, and trying to clear the property book. The Scouts and Mortars escorted the battalion's equipment back and forth until we got everything out of Q-West and over to Tal Afar. I don't remember how many times, but it was heating up and the convoys were taking fire.

Tal Afar, like the rest of the country, was heating up. We got the word to go convoy back up to Q-West and pick up our stuff. We got to Q-West and packed up all our stuff, then organized ourselves into serials to move from Q-West to Tal Afar. I was the convoy commander for the serial with the scouts and some of the mortars and some of the CRT and FFT [field feeding team] guys to go to Tal Afar. We did our rehearsals the one day, and then we slept in our vehicles that night, and the next morning we rolled out to Tal Afar. I don't remember how long it was, but it seemed like a pretty long trip from Q-West to Tal Afar. I guess about an hour or two for the convoy, it was really hot that day, and as soon as we got close to Tal Afar, I got the call on the radio that there was an IED that went off ahead and that we needed to hold up at actual Fort Tal Afar. It's an old Iraqi border fort, so we went in there held up in the fort until the QRF [quick reaction force] team cleared the improvised explosive device.

I would think it's safe to say that most of our casualties in Iraq were from IEDs. Sometimes we spot them and clear them, other times all you hear is BOOM! You don't really see anyone setting them off, but sometimes they'll shoot small arms fire with them, but the Strykers were pretty good. The QRF cleared the IED on our route, and then later on we were given the go ahead to move from Fort Tal Afar to the FOB. When we hit Tal Afar itself and turned onto the route, as we were going with the scouts we got shot at with an RPG [rocket propelled grenade].

I heard the explosion BOOM! Then off to the left-hand side of the convoy where the round exploded, I got the call from the scout platoon sergeant, Sergeant First Class Keyes, that they just got shot at by an RPG. There wasn't no small arms fire then, but the scout Strykers did the battle drill where they went ahead and stayed in place and started looking for whoever shot the RPG, but there was no sight of them. When they finished, we got all our wheeled vehicles, our HMMWVs and trucks, cause we had a lot of cargo trucks, HMMWVs, and MTV's, so we went ahead and passed through where the ambush was and kept rolling until we finally got onto [Pause] FOB Tal Afar, later known as FOB Regulars, wait maybe that one was Sykes?

The scouts had to turn around and go back to Q-West to pick up another convoy and escort them to Tal Afar that day. Later on, when they got back, they reported that they got into a big fire fight on the second convoy and basically the scouts, what they did was just opened up fire, so that pretty much became the TTP [tactic, technique, and procedure] of choice. When they did stand and fight, they were no match for the firepower we had. If you got shot at, you just opened fire with everything you had to gain fire superiority, and got outta the ambush site. Just like they teach at Fort Benning, when you're caught in an ambush, so as our time went on the scouts shot a lot of ammo using that TTP.

Tal Afar

While at Tal Afar, FOB Sykes or FOB Regulars whatever the name was over there, they had several operations. Headquarters Company took part in almost all of them between platoons, and medics, and CRT. At one time we were just under 300 soldiers in Headquarters Company, not including another 600 third-country nationals and Iraqi employees. Our company alone when we were at 300, was more than the BSB [brigade support battalion] from the 101st that we took over from at Q-West, but we didn't have the luxury of a staff as our people went everywhere. It's funny, a captain and first sergeant had a bigger command than a colonel and sergeant major, don't worry, they didn't pay us any extra.

The scouts took part in a lot of the operations, and our medics, and mortars. In most cases the company commander or myself would go with the scouts, mortars, or the medics on missions, but they did a lot of missions since the battalion commander wanted to keep the pressure on the enemy. So, we did one particular mission when a Kiowa warrior helicopter got shot down. Wouldn't you know it, that was supposed to be a short little morning mission, so we didn't go out with the scouts.

Captain Vogt and I pretty much monitored over the net about what happened and arranged an emergency ammo resupply, that I think Lieutenant Bennett led out with the QRF company and CRT for recovery as well. They got the helicopter out after a few hours, but the scouts were almost overrun that day when they got to the chopper. We put a bunch of them in for bronze stars, but I think Lieutenant McChrystal was the only one that got one. That was a tough day for the scouts and B Company. That was the day that the BC [battalion commander] had to call for a JDAM [joint deployed aerial munition], a 500-pound bomb to be dropped.

After that we planned another battalion, wait, no I think the brigade actually took part in this one, a mission to clean up Tal Afar from insurgents. It's funny, the 3rd ACR got all that coverage for Tal Afar, but we had done the same exact clear and enable the government type operations long before they moved into our old FOB. So that was the mission that the mortars got to go out and fire a bunch of ammo. Captain Vogt and I went with the mortars during that mission. The mortar platoon went out and set up our 120-millimeter mortars with Sergeant First Class Green as FDC [fire direction control] while the battalion was in assault positions, waiting right outside the city. I want to say we had AC130s and jets out as the mortars prepped Tal Afar with prep fire.

Our guys fired about 300 120-millimeter mortars that night, I don't know if you're familiar with 120s, but those things can do some damage. After the mortar prep the assault positions went in, I think the scouts went with C Company that night, to recover HVTs [high-value targets], military age males, equipment, and other insurgent related stuff. One thing that I remember was during the very early morning, there was still a lot of fighting going on in the city, we could hear fire fights going on with small arms fire, machine guns and fifty cal.

It was just going on for about ten to fifteen minutes when the mortars got the call on the radio for a fire mission. They called out instructions to one section to fire one round and then adjusted their 120-millimeter mortar and then fired seven rounds for effect. As soon as the seven rounds went off, we could hear the explosions in the city, that fire fight just stopped, nobody was firing at our guys and we got the word back from one of the company FO's [forward observers], that called for the fire, that there were like twelve insurgents killed.

Anyway, that was the end of the firefight thanks to the mortars, so the mortars were really effective on that mission. I think that was called Black Typhoon, yeah that was the name, Black Typhoon. The BC said about the importance of naming everything to include all the missions, but I can't even remember the FOB names let alone all the other stuff.

The first brigade 25th infantry division started arriving on our post, and actually we were all pretty happy that they were about to come here, and our battalion was about out of Iraq. So, my counterpart was First Sergeant Bobby Gilardo, we were both stationed in the 25th infantry division together, so I was pretty happy to see him. They were pretty excited, and we were happy to see them. There was a really quick hand over, for the first time in my military career a unit signed for all the equipment we had there within one week.

Part way through they changed the task org so they actually were pulled out. They got there, and initially was gonna be taking over our FOB and that area of operation around Tal Afar, but after a week passed it changed where their battalion was gonna go down to Mosul, and the cavalry squadron from first brigade 25th infantry division was going to go come over to Tal Afar and take over. So, it was a mad dash to sign for all the equipment and turn it over to them and then they just went ahead and took off for Mosul.

They were already doing combat operations before they even signed for our stuff. It was crazy, they were getting in firefights going to the outlying sites where our equipment was and then the commander had to go to Mosul to sign over the property book. On the way they killed a guy and got diverted to an Iraqi police station with a wounded guy, you don't kill people on your way to change out property back in the States.

The cavalry squadron from 25th infantry division, first brigade started coming in wanting to see what they had. Basically, a lot of things was taken already by the, I want to say they were the Deuce Four infantry battalion, but they already took that stuff over to Mosul, so the cavalry guys pretty much moaned, because they were getting left over equipment from what we had, but that wasn't because of us. So, everything pretty much went smooth with the cavalry, we were getting information that the airplanes leaving from

Mosul were getting shot at by small arms, I believe one airplane got shot at by an RPG, but our flights out of FOB Sykes, or FOB Regulars whichever one it was, went really smooth.

Headquarters Company was the last to leave that FOB, and when we got in the airplane it was really nice, and it was like oh, we're finally going home now. We rolled out on a C130 and one thing that I remember from that flight from Tal Afar to Kuwait was our C130 actually flew very low, I think it was flying about four hundred feet AGL [above ground level], for a few miles, then all of a sudden it just shot up. I was worried since they were flying kind of low here, but all of a sudden it just shot up, and got to altitude, and that's when I really was happy once it was up at altitude. Then we got to Kuwait, the wait was kind of long, I believe we was in Kuwait for about three or four days until we actually got on the 747 en route back to Fort Lewis.

When we got back home you know it was kind of a surreal feeling for me, because I was like gosh, we're finally home. But, you know, after a while it seemed like well, one year is more like we were just away for a little bit, since we knew we were going right back. I guess when it's all said and done, you go back to how it was, and it was pretty nice back home. But I can honestly say I really didn't do anything for the next couple months, I really didn't want to do anything, I just wanted to stay home and do nothing. I was already promotable to sergeant major, so I asked Sergeant Major Mangosing if the incoming first sergeant could take over right away, so that I can go ahead and transition to my new job as a brigade operations sergeant major.

Final Thoughts

I know we, Captain Vogt and I, talked a lot about OIF [Operation Iraqi Freedom] and our opinions, but I think overall the feeling is that as the military, as the Army, and as our unit, we did and will keep doing our job. I think we proved to the United States, and especially the Army, that being the first Stryker brigade combat team to deploy to combat, that we did an excellent job. The soldiers performed great in combat, and the vehicle performed above expectation, and without a doubt saved lots of lives and injuries.

There was a lot of mixed feeling about the Stryker vehicle, but it was exceptional in combat. Really, they did test to try and say the old 113s were better than the Strykers, that's just stupid, in today's operating environment, I'd like to see a brigade of 113s put the miles on that our Strykers did. There's a lot of stuff behind weapons sales, but all infantry units, to include the Rangers, could use Strykers, they're that good.

When we first got to Iraq, the weird thing is that, when we first got there the Iraqis were more willing to accept us, but I think as time went on and things got worse instead of better. The insurgents regrouped, in the beginning of the year with al-Sadr's uprising, and that just kinda opened it up for the insurgents to go ahead and start uprising all over the country because from that time on, the situation got worse. A lot of soldiers got killed or wounded during the time we were there, and no matter how many combat operations that we went on, it seemed like the situation never got any better.

In fact, just recently and this is September 2005, and our operation Black Typhoon was in I believe in August or September of 2004, but just recently in September 2005, the military unit in Mosul, northern Iraq, did another big operation on Tal Afar, so it's never changed. I guess the media just likes certain commanders better than others, because I saw a lot of their Tal Afar operation that probably didn't do anything different than ours. It's a weird thing, so I don't know if the situation is getting better, but that's my closing thought on Operation Iraqi Freedom.

Annexes

Annex A: Photos

C Co 1st Sergeant and Battalion Command Sergeant Major
Jim Mapes (L) and Andy Mangosing (R)
Rock Base, Tal Afar
(Baker)

Birthday Rug
Hakeem Lukeman

Q-West Snow Day
Bashar Shakar
(Vogt)

A Little Fun at Arie's Expense
Udairi Training Area, Kuwait
(Vogt)

Ghosts of Samarra | 329

B Co in Samarra
(Combat Camera)

B Co in Tactical Assembly Area Warhorse
(Combat Camera)

Ghosts of Samarra | 331

B Co in Samarra
(Combat Camera)

B Co in Samarra
Matthew Goodine facing camera on bottom picture
(Combat Camera)

Ghosts of Samarra | **333**

B Co in Samarra
(Combat Camera)

B Co in Samarra
(Combat Camera)

Gates of Mosul
A Co Mobile Gun System Platoon Leadership
(Bennett)

Q-West Barracks
A Co Mobile Gun System Platoon
(Bennett)

HHC Members of Task Force Sykes
Tim Bennett front row, far right
(Bennett)

HHC Executive Officer with Tigris River Pumping Station
Engineers
Ben Celver center
(Celver)

A Co Company Commander
Matt Dabkowski
(Dabkowski)

A Co Medics
(Scott)

Mosul Highway Marketplace
(Bennett)

Moving through Baghdad
(Wabinga)

Ghosts of Samarra | 339

Northern Iraqi Regional Training Center
Tom O'Steen second from right above
(Baker)

C Co On Patrol
(Baker)

Ghosts of Samarra | 341

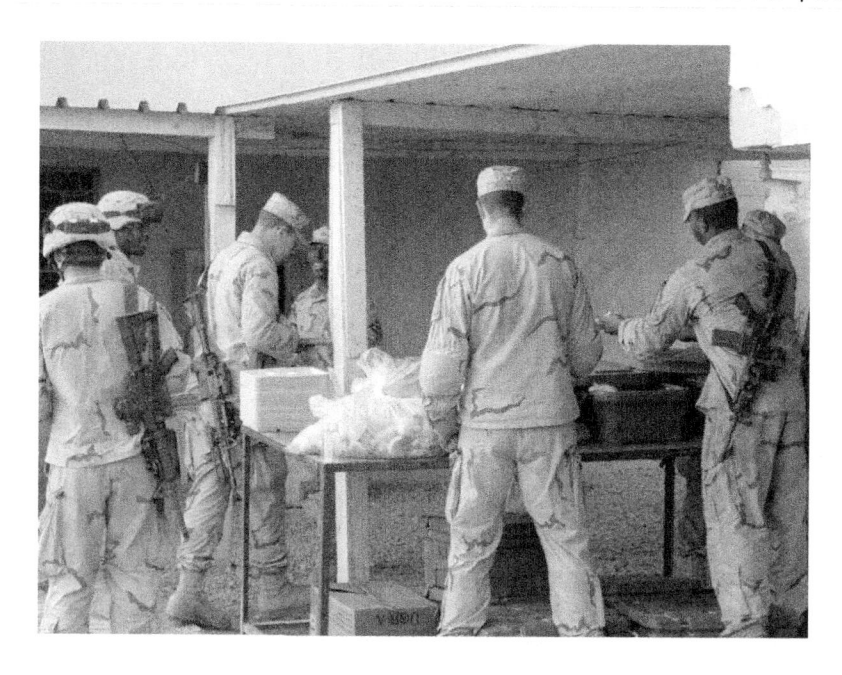

C Co Chow and Maintenance
(Baker)

Rock Base
(Baker)

Ghosts of Samarra | 343

Christopher Galka
(Galka)

HHC Snipers
(Galka)

Ghosts of Samarra | 345

HHC S3 Shop
(Leseman)

5-20 Infantry Battalion Commander Near Hatra
Karl Reed
(Baker)

Meetings
(Baker)

Ghosts of Samarra | 347

Q-West
City Hall and Mayor's Office
(Vogt)

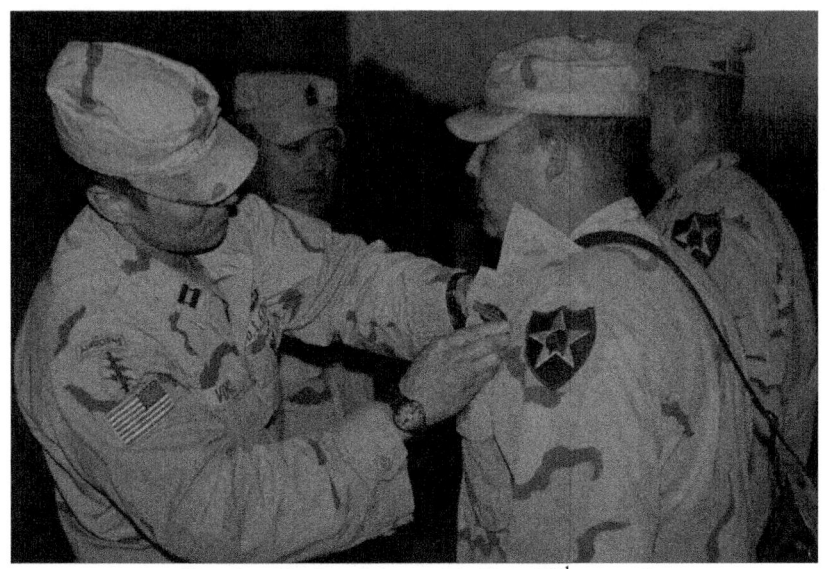

Combat Infantryman Badge 2nd award
Sean Sparks on right
(Sparks)

HHC Mortar Platoon on the Move
(Wabinga)

Ghosts of Samarra | 349

HHC Scouts on Patrol
(Hicks)

Sheik Force
(Hicks)

HHC Scouts On Patrol
(Hicks)

Ghosts of Samarra | 351

A Quick Bite of Goat and Rice before Heading back to Base
(Hicks)

HHC Scout Platoon Leadership
Mike Keyes (L) and John Hicks (R)
(Vogt)

A Few Iraqi Q-West Employees Enjoy a Snow Day
(Vogt)

Ghosts of Samarra | 353

Operation Road Warrior
(Wabinga)

HHC Command Post and Operations
(Vogt)

Ghosts of Samarra | 355

HHC Convoys Hit by IEDs
(Jorn)

Iraqi Forces Ready for Patrol
(Bennett)

OH58D Kiowa Warrior
(Sparks)

Ghosts of Samarra | 357

Ranger Buddies
Tobias Vogt (L) and Sonny Wabinga (R)
(Vogt)

Pulling Security
(Wabinga)

Vogt Brothers at Fortress Tal Afar (later Rock Base)
Tobias (L) and Zach (R) from a prior deployment
(Vogt)

Tal Afar Sunset
(Wabinga)

Annex B: 5-20th Killed and Wounded*

Killed in Action

Sergeant Jacob Herring (2nd Purple Heart Award)

Corporal Demetrius Rice

Private First Class Jesse Martinez

Wounded in Action

Staff Sergeant Eric Evans

Private Second Class Andrew Williams

Sergeant Anthony Glover

Specialist Seth Trible

Corporal Steven James

Specialist Jack Shaffer

First Lieutenant William Baynes

Specialist Leon Bell

Private First Class Josh Bressel

Sergeant Richars Rochelle

Specialist Enrique Murillo (2nd Purple Heart Award)

Staff Sergeant Kevin Pearson

Private First Class Enrique Rosano (2nd Purple Heart Award)

Staff Sergeant Brent Skinner

Sergeant Daniel Swanson

Private Second Class Rodney Robbins

Private First Class James Sene

Sergeant David Fitzgerald

Private Second Class Edgar Castro

Specialist Aaron Farely

Sergeant William Parker

Specialist Jay Thompson

Private Andrew Williams (2nd Purple Heart Award)

Private Second Class David Hardt

Staff Sergeant Daniel Allemani (2nd Purple Heart Award)

Corporal Myron Mikkelson

Staff Sergeant Joshua Newman

Private Oscar Ramos

Staff Sergeant Kurtis Wilkerson

Sergeant First Class Jimmy Thornton

Private Roberto Figueroa

Staff Sergeant Randy Garcia

Specialist Keith Maupin

Specialist Shea Hawkins

Sergeant Pili Masaniai Jr.

Staff Sergeant Nevin Gamble

First Lieutenant Christopher Sheehan

Specialist Jacob Orr Trindle

Captain Eric Beaty

Specialist Alberto Alcala Jr.

Sergeant First Class Michael Archey

Specialist Juan Barrera

Sergeant George Hudgeons

Specialist Thomas Lajudice

Sergeant Randal Davis

Staff Sergeant Erik Sandstrom

Specialist Matthew Benshawel

Sergeant Nakia Finney

Staff Sergeant Chrisopher Galka

Sergeant Jeremy Gonzales

Staff Sergeant Benjamin Hanner

Specialist Michael Hernandez

Staff Sergeant Benjamin Hollinder

Sergeant Felipe Tellez

Private First Class Michael Conniff

Specialist Benjamin Gardner

Staff Sergeant David Plush

*This list doesn't account for members of the battalion that received purple hearts for concussive events after U.S. Army regulations were revised in 2011. Or the great many servicemembers that were denied purple hearts years later because of missing medical records, battlefield records, or supporting statements. The Defense Department's failure to recognize internal wounds from explosive events until a decade after 9/11, and then establish standards that couldn't be met by most wounded servicemembers is a travesty. Hopefully, political leaders will revisit this topic in the future.

Annex C: Task Organization

The Arrowhead Brigade deployed to Iraq in 2003, with, three infantry battalions (1-23 Infantry, 2-3 Infantry, and 5-20 Infantry), a reconnaissance squadron (1-14 Cavalry), an artillery battalion (1-37 Field Artillery), and a brigade support battalion (296 Brigade Support Battalion). For Operation Iraqi Freedom I/II, the brigade had an aviation squadron (3-17 Cavalry) from the 10th Mountain Division attached throughout the deployment. Below the battalion/squadron level, the brigade also had a headquarters company, anti-tank company, engineer company, signal company, and military intelligence company.

The infantry battalions were organized with four companies each, Headquarters, Alpha, Bravo, and Charlie respectively. The Headquarters and Headquarters Company consisted of the battalion command group, staff sections, and a medical, mortar, and reconnaissance platoon. In Iraq, a headquarters company had approximately 300 soldiers and contractors with engineer, maintenance, and support assets attached. The 5-20 Infantry Headquarters and Headquarters Company also had responsibility for civilian base contractors and host nation employees, swelling the roles to peak strength of 900 personnel. Each line company consisted of a headquarters platoon with company mortars, a mobile gun system platoon, and three rifle platoons for a total of approximately 170 soldiers.

Acronyms

1SG	First Sergeant
ABCS	Army Battle Command System
ABCT	Arrowhead Brigade Combat Team
ACF	Anti-Coalition Forces
A Co	Alpha Company
AFATDS	Advanced Field Artillery Tactical Data System
AIF	Anti-Iraqi Forces
ALOC	Army Logistics Operations Center
ACE	Ammunition, Casualty, Equipment Report
AO	Area of Operations
AOR	Area of Responsibility
APOD	Aerial Port of Debarkation
ARFOR	Army Forces
ASAS	All Source Analysis System
AT	Anti-Tank
ATGM	Anti-Tank Guided Missile
ASP	Ammunition Supply Point
B Co	Bravo Company
BDA	Battle Damage Assessment
BDE	Brigade
BG	Brigadier General
BN	Battalion
BSB	Brigade Support Battalion
C2	Command and Control

C4ISR	Command, Control, Communications, Computers, and Intelligence Surveillance and Reconnaissance
CA	Civil Affairs
CAS	Close Air Support
CAV	Cavalry
CDR	Commander
CENTCOM	Central Command
C Co	Charlie Company
CI	Counter Intelligence
CIB	Combat Infantry Badge
CL	Combat Load
CO Officer	Company, Company Commander, or Commanding
COA	Course of Action
COL	Colonel
CONUS	Continental United States
CP	Command Post
CPA	Coalition Provisional Authority
CPL	Corporal
CPT	Captain
CRT	Combat Repair Team
CSM	Command Sergeant Major
CSS	Combat Service Support
CSSCS	Combat Service Support Control System
CV	Command Vehicle (Stryker)
CVC	Combat Vehicle Crewman helmet
DIV	Division
ECP	Entry Control Point

E&E	Escape and Evade
ENG	Engineer
EPLRS	Enhanced Position Location Reporting System
EPW	Enemy Prisoners of War
ESV	Engineer Squad Vehicle
EVAC	Evacuation
EW	Electronic Warfare
FA	Field Artillery
FBCB2	Force XXI Battle Command Brigade and Below
FFT	Field Feeding Team
FLIR	Forward looking infrared
FM	Frequency Modulation
FOB	Forward Operating Base
FORSCOM	Forces Command
FRAGO	Fragmentary Order
FRL	Former Regime Loyalist
FSO	Fire Support Officer
FSV	Fire Support Vehicle
GAC	Ground Assault Convoy
GEN	General
GPS	Global positioning system
GSR	Ground Surveillance Radar
GWOT	Global War on Terror
HEMTT	Heavy Expanded Mobility Tactical Truck
HETT	Heavy Equipment and Truck Transport
HHC	Headquarters and Headquarters Company
HLZ	Helicopter Landing Zone

HQ	Headquarters
HUMINT	Human Intelligence
IAV	Interim Armored Vehicle
IBCT	Interim Brigade Combat Team
ICLS	Interim Contractor Logistics Support
ICV	Infantry Carrier Vehicle (Stryker)
IN	Infantry
ING	Iraqi National Guard
INTSUM	Intelligence Summary
IO	Information Operations
IOT	In Order To
ISB	Intermediate Staging Base
ISR	Intelligence Surveillance and Reconnaissance
IT/IA	Information Technology/Intelligence Assessment
JAVELIN	Advanced Anti-Tank Weapons System – Medium
JDAM	Joint Deployed Aerial Munition
JSOTF	Joint Special Operations Task Force
JSTARS	Joint Surveillance Target Attack Radar System
JTF	Joint Task Force
KIA	Killed in Action
LAV	Light Armored Vehicle (Marine Corps)
LCC	Logistics Coordination Cell
LOGPAC	Logistics Package
LRAS	Long Range Advanced Scout Surveillance System
LST	Logistical Support Team
LT	Lieutenant (1st or 2nd)
LTC	Lieutenant Colonel

LTG	Lieutenant General
MAJ	Major
MBITR	Multiband Inter/Intra Team Radio
MC	Mortar Carrier (Stryker)
MCS	Maneuver Control System
MDMP	Military Decision-Making Process
MED	Medic
METT	Metrological Team
METT-TC	Mission, Enemy, Terrain, Time, Troops Available, Civilians
MEV	Medical Evacuation Vehicle (Stryker)
MG	Major General
MGS	Mobile Gun System
MI	Military Intelligence
MICLIC	Mine Clearing Line Charge
MLRS	Mobile Launch Rocket System
MRT	Mortar
MSR	Main Supply Route
MTV	Medium Tactical Vehicles (5-Ton)
MSG	Master Sergeant
NAI	Named Area of Interest
NBC	Nuclear Biological and Chemical
NCS-E	Net Control Station-EPLARS
NTDR	Near Term Digital Radio
NVG	Night Vision Goggles
OBJ	Objective
ODA	Operational Detachment-Alpha

OEF	Operation Enduring Freedom
OIF	Operation Iraqi Freedom
OP	Observation Post
OPCON	Operational Control
PFC	Private First Class
PLGR	Precision Lightweight Global Positioning System
PLT	Platoon
PMCS	Preventive Maintenance Checks and Services
PSYOP	Psychological Operations
PV2	Private Second Class
PVT	Private
RECCE	Reconnaissance
RECON	Reconnaissance
REMBASS	Remotely Monitored Battlefield Sensor System
RETRANS	Retransmission
RPG	Rocket Propelled Grenade
RPK	Ruchnoy Pulemyot Kalashnikova (Soviet era light machinegun)
RSTA Squadron	Reconnaissance Surveillance and Target Acquisition
RTO	Radio Teletype Operator
RV	Reconnaissance Vehicle (Stryker)
RWS	Remote Weapons Station
RWS	Rigid Wall Shelter
SASO	Support and Stability Operations
SATCOM	Satellite Communications
SBCT	Stryker Brigade Combat Team
SCT	Scout

SFC	Sergeant First Class
SGM	Sergeant Major
SGT	Sergeant
SINCGARS	Single Channel and Ground Airborne Radio System
SNP	Sniper
SOCCENT	Special Operations Command-Central
SOF	Special Operations Forces
SPC	Specialist
SPOD	Sea Port of Debarkation
SSE	Sensitive Sight Exploitation
SSG	Staff Sergeant
SQD	Squad
TAC	Tactical Group
TACON	Tactical Control
TACP	Tactical Air Control Party
TC	Truck, Track, or Tank Commander
TCP	Tactical or Traffic Control Point
TDA	Table of Distribution and Allowances
TF	Task Force
TM	Fire Team
TO	Task Organization
TOC	Tactical Operations Center
TOW Missile	Tube Launched Optically Tracked Wire Guided
TTP	Tactics, Techniques and Procedures
UAV	Unmanned Aerial Vehicle
UMR	Unit Manning Roster

WARNO	Warning Order
WIA	Wounded in Action

Selected Bibliography

5-20 Infantry Staff, *5th Battalion, 20th Infantry Regiment "Sykes Regulars" An Official History: Operation Iraqi Freedom November 2003-November 2004*, 2005.

5-20 Infantry Staff, *5-20 IN (SBCT) How We Fight SOP: Based on Lessons Learned During OIF I and II (November 2003-2004)*, 2005.

Armstrong, Karen, *History of God: The 4,000-Year Quest of Judaism, Christianity, and Islam*, 1994.

Boot, Max, *The Savage Wars of Peace: Small Wars and the Rise of American Power*, 2002.

Grossman, Dave, *On Killing: The Psychological Cost of Learning to Kill in War and Society*, 1995.

Gray, J. Glenn, *The Warriors: Reflections on Men in Battle*, 1959.

Hamid, Tawfik, *Inside Jihad: Understanding and Confronting Radical Islam*, 2007.

Hamza, Khidhir, with Jeff Stein, *Saddam's Bombmaker: The Daring Escape of the Man Who Built Iraq's Secret Weapon*, 2001.

Huchthausen, Peter, *America's Splendid Little Wars: A Short History of U.S. Engagements from the Fall of Saigon to Baghdad*, 2003.

Keegan, John, *The Face of Battle*, 1978.

Marshall, S.L.A., *Men Against Fire*, 1978.

Miller, Judith, Stephen Engelberg, and William Broad, *Germs: Biological Weapons and America's Secret War*, 2002.

Misra, Amalendu, *Afghanistan: The Labyrinth of Violence*, 2004.

Obeidi, Mahdi, and Kurt Pitzer, *The Bomb in my Garden: The Secrets of Saddam's Nuclear Mastermind*, 2004.

Rashid, Ahmid, *Taliban: Islam, Oil and Fundamentalism in Central Asia*, 2001.

----*Jihad: The Rise of Militant Islam in Central Asia*, 2002.

Reardon, Mark, and Jefferey Charlston, *From Transformation to Combat: The First Stryker Brigade at War*, 2007.

Richelson, Jeffrey, *Spying on the Bomb: American Nuclear Intelligence from Nazi Germany to Iran and North Korea*, 2007.

Snow, Donald and Dennis Drew, *From Lexington to Desert Storm: War and Politics in the American Experience*, 1994.

Task Force Olympia, *The Olympia Observer, Volume I: Issue 21*, August 16, 2004.

Tripp, Charles, *A History of Iraq (Second Edition)*, 2002.

Tucker, Jonathan, *War of Nerves: Chemical Warfare from World War I to Al-Qaeda*, 2006.

Yildiz, Kerim, *The Kurds in Iraq: The Past, Present and Future*, 2004.

Printed in Great Britain
by Amazon